# Educating FOR Justice

# Praise for *Educating for Justice*

"*Educating for Justice* is essential reading for educators dedicated to guiding their school communities on a transformative path toward anti-oppression. Offering a clear and insightful roadmap enriched with practical examples, this book is exactly what everyone needs in today's politically polarized environment. The authors persuasively demonstrate that justice-centered education is a fundamentally humanitarian effort, not a political agenda. This book shines as a beacon of hope, illuminating the path for the next generation of societal leaders."

—**Tracey A. Benson,** founder and CEO, Anti-Racism Leadership Institute

"I recommend *Educating for Justice* to every educator committed to fostering equity and empowering students. Through practical strategies, this book equips educators to cultivate critical thinkers who can recognize injustice and actively challenge it, paving the way for a more just society."

—**Almi Guajardo Abeyta,** superintendent, Chelsea (MA) Public Schools

"The authors are right to spotlight the need for deep collaboration between justice partners and schools. These partnerships are successful when there is shared investment over time to nurture the critical consciousness of both students and staff. This work is not for the faint of heart. As a former school system leader who now leads a justice partner organization, I appreciate the calling out of all parties having to work side by side, doing the difficult adaptive work to transform hearts and minds. It can be messy work, but it is what is needed to make a meaningful impact in communities."

—**Tommy Chang,** CEO, New Teacher Center

"This text recognizes a simple truth: that all educational institutions hold a precious power to communicate explicit or implicit beliefs about the world and our children's roles in it. In choosing (or denying) texts, in deciding what deserves public celebration or what world events require a schoolwide letter, we are all political agents—and denying it is irresponsible. These authors inspire us to claim that responsibility by providing concrete, usable examples that make a daunting task like social justice attainable and universally affirming to all students. Never naive about the polarized partisan climate we're in, this text inspires action through transparent strategy and successful preventative moves to address urgent issues in public. This case study reads like a field guide for educators needing a seasoned, successful companion."

—**Carolina Brito,** principal, Oyster Adams Bilingual School, Washington, DC

# Educating FOR Justice

Schoolwide Strategies to Prepare Students to Recognize, Analyze, and Challenge Inequity

Scott Seider
Aaliyah El-Amin
Julia Bott

Arlington, Virginia USA

2800 Shirlington Road, Suite 1001 • Arlington, VA 22206 USA
Phone: 800-933-2723 or 703-578-9600
Website: www.ascd.org • Email: member@ascd.org
Author guidelines: www.ascd.org/write

Richard Culatta, *Chief Executive Officer;* Anthony Rebora, *Chief Content Officer;* Genny Ostertag, *Managing Director, Book Acquisitions & Editing;* Stephanie Bize, *Acquisitions Editor;* Mary Beth Nielsen, *Director, Book Editing;* Jennifer L. Morgan, *Editor;* Georgia Park, *Senior Graphic Designer;* Cynthia Stock, *Typesetter;* Kelly Marshall, *Production Manager;* Shajuan Martin, *E-Publishing Specialist;* Kathryn Oliver, *Creative Project Manager*

Copyright © 2025 ASCD. All rights reserved. It is illegal to reproduce copies of this work in print or electronic format (including reproductions displayed on a secure intranet or stored in a retrieval system or other electronic storage device from which copies can be made or displayed) without the prior written permission of the publisher. By purchasing only authorized electronic or print editions and not participating in or encouraging piracy of copyrighted materials, you support the rights of authors and publishers. Readers who wish to reproduce or republish excerpts of this work in print or electronic format may do so for a small fee by contacting the Copyright Clearance Center (CCC), 222 Rosewood Dr., Danvers, MA 01923, USA (phone: 978-750-8400; fax: 978-646-8600; web: www.copyright.com). To inquire about site licensing options or any other reuse, contact ASCD Permissions at www.ascd.org/permissions or permissions@ascd.org. For a list of vendors authorized to license ASCD ebooks to institutions, see www.ascd.org/epubs. Send translation inquiries to translations@ascd.org.

ASCD® is a registered trademark of Association for Supervision and Curriculum Development. All other trademarks contained in this book are the property of, and reserved by, their respective owners, and are used for editorial and informational purposes only. No such use should be construed to imply sponsorship or endorsement of the book by the respective owners.

All web links in this book are correct as of the publication date below but may have become inactive or otherwise modified since that time. If you notice a deactivated or changed link, please email books@ascd.org with the words "Link Update" in the subject line. In your message, please specify the web link, the book title, and the page number on which the link appears.

PAPERBACK ISBN: 978-1-4166-3336-5    ASCD product #124009    n1/25
PDF EBOOK ISBN: 978-1-4166-3337-2; see Books in Print for other formats.
Quantity discounts are available: email programteam@ascd.org or call 800-933-2723, ext. 5773, or 703-575-5773. For desk copies, go to www.ascd.org/deskcopy.

**Library of Congress Cataloging-in-Publication Data**

Names: Seider, Scott, author. | El-Amin, Aaliyah, author. | Bott, Julia, author.
Title: Educating for justice : schoolwide strategies to prepare students to recognize, analyze, and challenge inequity / Scott Seider, Aaliyah El-Amin, and Julia Bott.
Description: Arlington, Virginia : ASCD, [2025] | Includes bibliographical references and index.
Identifiers: LCCN 2024036231 (print) | LCCN 2024036232 (ebook) | ISBN 9781416633365 (paperback) | ISBN 9781416633372 (adobe pdf) | ISBN 9781416633389 (epub)
Subjects: LCSH: Social justice and education—United States. | Social justice—Study and teaching—United States. | Social action—United States. | Students—Political activity—United States.
Classification: LCC LC192.2 .S45 2025  (print) | LCC LC192.2  (ebook) | DDC 303.3/72071073—dc23/eng/20241007
LC record available at https://lccn.loc.gov/2024036231
LC ebook record available at https://lccn.loc.gov/2024036232

34 33 32 31 30 29 28 27 26 25              1 2 3 4 5 6 7 8 9 10 11 12

# Educating for Justice

Introduction: Educating for Justice .................................................. 1

Center Justice in Curriculum and Pedagogy ........................... 25
    Chapter 1: Adopt a Justice Framework ........................................ 27

Foster Powerful Partnerships ............................................................ 63
    Chapter 2: Collaborate with Justice Partners ........................... 65
    Chapter 3: Elevate the Wisdom of Families and Caretakers .... 94

Engage Students in Social Action .................................................. 127
    Chapter 4: Empower Students to Take Action ........................ 129

Build Adult Capacity ........................................................................... 155
    Chapter 5: Let Teachers Be Learners ......................................... 157

Put It All Together ............................................................................... 189
    Chapter 6: Amplify the Impact of Heritage Months ............... 191
    Chapter 7: Respond to Local, National,
    and Global Tragedies ........................................................................ 215

Conclusion: Justice Is a Verb ............................................................ 234

Acknowledgments ............................................................................... 244

Appendix: Organizational Structures Referenced in
*Educating for Justice* ........................................................................... 249

References .............................................................................................. 256

Index .......................................................................................................... 272

About the Authors ............................................................................... 278

# Introduction: Educating for Justice

Schools can be powerful places for students to learn to challenge injustice. At Leadership Charter High School in New York City, seniors take a semester-long course called Sociology of Change that explores strategies and practices of social change movements ranging from the United Farm Workers grape strike in 1965 to the Black Lives Matter movement today. Drawing on what they learn, students design their own "Change the World" projects that they carry out in their final semester of high school. The projects offer hands-on social justice leadership experience. One student, Zoli, organized a community dialogue on gentrification in her neighborhood. She put up fliers to advertise the event, served refreshments, and moderated a vigorous discussion with 30 community members about the changes in their community and actions they could take in response.

Five hundred miles away in Ohio, 7th grade science students at Stone Middle School discuss how prevailing ideas about what a scientist looks like can lead some young people to believe that science is not for them. They read a blog post by Nabiha Saklayen

(2016) describing how often she hears, "You don't look like a physicist," then work to identify media counternarratives that push back against dominant messages about the stereotypical identities of scientists, including a website called "I Am a Scientist" (The Plenary, Co., n.d.), which features profiles of scientists with diverse backgrounds. At the end of their media exploration, students identify other narratives that privilege specific identities while marginalizing others. Their challenge throughout the semester, their teacher tells them, is to combat and resist the dominant narratives they uncover.

And at Sarah C. Roberts Elementary School—the school that inspired us to come together to write this book—4th grade students read a newspaper story about two Black teenagers in a nearby town who have been barred from attending senior prom because they wore their hair in braids. They also learn about the CROWN (Creating a Respectful and Open World for Natural Hair) Act, a bill being considered by their state legislature that would protect men, women, and children from race-based hair discrimination. After a class discussion, the 4th graders author letters to their elected representatives, sharing their own opinions and perspectives on the legislation. (Note: Subsequent to our visit, the CROWN Act was passed by the state, and similar legislation has been enacted in more than two dozen U.S. states as well as more than 40 municipalities; Legal Defense Fund, n.d.)

Leadership Charter High School, Stone Middle School, and Roberts Elementary School are three very different schools. They serve students in different grade levels, are located in different states, and have different student demographics. Teachers at one school have tremendous autonomy in designing their own curriculum, while teachers at another adhere to the curriculum mandated by their district. But each school is committed to nurturing students' ability to recognize, analyze, and challenge social injustice. At each of these schools, educators work to empower and prepare young people to build what we so desperately need—a more just world.

## Who We Are

The three of us—Scott, Aaliyah, and Julia—are educators with experience teaching in and leading schools across grades K–12. Collectively, we have witnessed powerful examples of schools offering students tools to champion and advance justice. We came together to share practices, structures, and curriculum ideas gathered over time in support of teacher leaders and school leaders invested in preparing their own students to challenge injustice and transform society.

Two of us—Scott and Aaliyah—are scholars and professors who have been researching youth and schools for the past decade. Scott is a developmental psychologist at Boston College whose research focuses on how youth develop the skill and will to challenge injustice. Aaliyah is a faculty member at Harvard Graduate School of Education who studies Black liberatory education models, social justice schooling, and critical pedagogy. Together, Scott and Aaliyah have written books, articles, and academic papers illustrating how schools nurture students' ability to recognize, analyze, and challenge injustice.

Scott and Aaliyah are also former K–12 educators. Scott was a high school English teacher and literacy coordinator in Massachusetts, and Aaliyah was an elementary school teacher and instructional coach in Georgia. Scott identifies as a White cisgender man, and Aaliyah identifies as a Black cisgender woman.[1]

---

[1] We capitalize race descriptors throughout this book because that is currently the style convention for the American Psychological Association (APA). We have read compelling explanations for and against capitalizing the term "White," but are influenced here by Eve Ewing's (2020) explanation that we must avoid actions that "contribute to its seeming neutrality and thereby grant it power to maintain its invisibility" (para. 10).

Julia, our third author, has worked as an early childhood teacher, principal, and district administrator in Boston Public Schools for the past 20 years. The 2021 Massachusetts Elementary School Principal of the Year and a National Distinguished Principal, Julia served as an elementary school principal for more than a decade and currently coaches principals and other instructional leaders on leading more equitable and inclusive schools. Julia is deeply invested in helping school leaders knit together their commitments to instructional leadership and social justice so that they can help teachers integrate their pedagogical content and social justice knowledge into curriculum and teaching. Julia led this work as a building principal and now coaches other principals to do the same. Julia identifies as a White cisgender woman.

All three of us believe—and have seen firsthand—that fostering students' capacity to recognize, analyze, and challenge injustice is essential for both young people's own well-being and a better world. We also believe that schools and educators have a key role to play in this work. Accordingly, this book is structured around three core convictions:

1. Injustice is pervasive in the United States, with direct impacts on education, schools, and every other facet of students' lives.
2. Schools are spaces where students can and should learn the knowledge, dispositions, and skills to work toward collective justice. This knowledge and skill building is part of the function of all schools.
3. Educators can learn to teach and support students to recognize, analyze, and challenge systemic injustice.

Each of these convictions has a rich history in education, and each is substantiated by decades of scholarly research (e.g.,

Duncan-Andrade & Morrell, 2008; Levinson, 2012; McGhee, 2021). However, not everyone agrees with these core beliefs. As we write, efforts are under way in various states and communities across the United States to prevent schools and teachers from helping students understand and act against injustice. New laws in several states prohibit educators from teaching students about oppressive systems, including racism, sexism, and homophobia (Maye & Sherer, 2023). Other laws ban books in both schools and public libraries with LGBTQ+ characters, characters of color, and stories about human rights and activism (Restrepo, 2023). In some states, new curricular standards instruct educators to teach students that violent historical periods (e.g., enslavement) were beneficial to people who were victimized (Planas, 2023). New legislation even seeks to regulate content by prohibiting educators from teaching controversial sociopolitical topics. For example, Florida's Individual Freedom Act (2022) restricts instruction material that can cause "guilt, anguish, or other forms of psychological distress" (Maye & Sherer, 2023). Against this backdrop, some teachers at this moment face genuine risk in teaching students about how structural and systemic injustice affects our lives.

Yet even in these challenging conditions, we firmly believe that educating students to recognize, analyze, and act against injustice is both possible and necessary. K–12 students themselves have advocated for their right to this knowledge and publicly resist these restrictive policies. Throughout the country, students have started banned book clubs to read books prohibited by their local district and libraries and anti-censorship clubs that distribute banned books for free (Alfonseca, 2023). Some students have even participated in sustained protests that led to the reversal of prohibitive policies and practices (Paz & Cramer, 2021).

If our students can fight for the opportunity to learn about the structures and systems of injustice all around them, so can we. As educators, we must ask ourselves, "Do we honestly want our students to inherit the world *as it is*?" If the answer is no, then we must take responsibility for leveraging the tools at our disposal to resist these pernicious laws, sanctions, and bans. We are not suggesting that this resistance is easy or magical, or that it will automatically lead to receptive communities, school districts, or states. We are, however, suggesting that, even if you teach in a state subject to book bans or restrictive policies, you can read this book with an eye toward creativity and subversiveness. To do this, you must think beyond the constraints of the status quo, challenge yourself to envision spaces of possibility, and ask yourself, "What *can* I do?" Although many of the examples in our book are from schools in states not facing restrictive legislative efforts, as you read, consider what you can adapt, take away, or modify for your context. What ideas could you try in the spaces where you *do* have latitude and agency? What local partners also pushing back against attempts to erase particular identities, histories, and content from students' education can you reach out to? In the following sections, we address the necessity for students to have knowledge and tools to recognize and analyze injustice and intervene in it. We then discuss how schools can work toward this outcome and outline how the rest of the book helps educators support young people to contribute to social change.

## Injustice Lives All Around Us

We live in a society plagued by pervasive injustice (e.g., discrimination, marginalization, bias, exclusion, exploitation) based on race, class, gender, sexual orientation, language, ability, and other identity markers. These injustices are evident in *all* our systems—law and justice, healthcare, housing and city planning, transportation, agriculture, and so on. Cumulatively, these injustices form systems of oppression (e.g., sexism, classism, ableism, racism) that marginalize, exclude, exploit, and perpetrate violence against distinct social groups in our country and confer power and privilege to other distinct groups.

Take our own field, education. On nearly every statistic you can think of, schools that are attended by more students of color contend with more structural challenges than schools serving predominantly White students (Shores et al., 2020). For example, U.S. school districts serving predominantly students of color are significantly more likely to be staffed by first-year teachers, uncertified teachers, and teachers who did not major in their subject area than those serving predominantly White students (Cardichon et al., 2020). These staffing issues limit the access of many students of color to advanced coursework such as Advanced Placement courses (Chatterji et al., 2021).

Disparities in educational opportunity are by no means limited to race. High-poverty school districts across the United States receive, on average, $800 less per student per year in state and local revenue than low-poverty school districts (Morgan, 2022). These funding differences contribute to inequitable access to higher education for students from different class backgrounds. A child born into a working-class family in the United States has a one in seven chance of earning a college degree, odds that are three times lower than for a child born into a wealthy family (Dynarski, 2015). Likewise, school districts serving the greatest number of English learners receive, on average, $2,200 less per student per year in state and local revenue than school districts with the lowest numbers of English learners (Morgan, 2022).

Our students recognize these systemic inequities in access to resources, roles, and realities, and many absorb these understandings into their own views about their power and potential. For example, when asked to draw a picture of a scientist, only a quarter of K–12 students in the United States draw a picture of a woman scientist, and girls become three times less likely to draw a woman scientist as they advance from kindergarten to high school (Miller et al., 2018). Sexist cultural stereotypes contribute to these patterns and are reinforced when teachers, parents, and other adult mentors underestimate girls' science, technology, engineering, and math (STEM) capabilities.

Even when educational opportunities and access exist, some groups are consistently more likely than others to have experiences in school that are harmful, marginalizing, or violent. For example, high school students who identify as lesbian, gay, bisexual, transgender, questioning, or queer (LGBTQ+) are almost twice as likely as their non-LGBTQ+ peers to be bullied, threatened or injured with a weapon, or in a physical fight in school. LGBTQ+ students are also more than three times as likely as their non-LGBTQ+ peers to have skipped school in the past year because they felt unsafe (Massachusetts Department of Elementary and Secondary Education & Department of Health, 2019). These negative and dangerous interactions contribute to the LGBTQ+ high school dropout rate being almost four times higher than the national average, constraining these young people's opportunities to thrive in adulthood (Wimberly, 2015).

Likewise, Black, Latine, and Native American youth are disproportionately suspended and expelled from K–12 schools, receive more punitive discipline than their White peers for the same misbehaviors, and are referred more often for infractions that are subjective in interpretation (Jones, 2018; Milner, 2013).

These more frequent disciplinary interactions contribute to students of color missing more school and learning opportunities and decrease their likelihood of attending or graduating from college (Davison et al., 2022; Rios, 2011). Such systemic injustices in our educational system have been extensively documented, and similar examples can be found in other societal systems.

What we have to remember about this vast marginalization is that it did not occur spontaneously. It has happened over time through intentional decisions and choices to privilege some groups over others in garnering resources, favor, and life possibilities. That is, the various injustices we see in education (and in all adjacent systems) were devised through human choice and are sustained through our individual actions and the systems, structures, and policies we have created and maintained over time. As you move through this text, it is important to remember that just as we have constructed this unjust society, we can dismantle it.

> **Just as we have constructed this unjust society, we can dismantle it.**

## What Schools Can Do

Given the injustices all around us and in our own field, educators are left to ask ourselves several questions: What can we do? What is our role in ensuring that all young people have the access, opportunity, and experiences they deserve? How can we work together with students and their families toward a more just and humane society?

Fortunately, as the late South African President Nelson Mandela reminded us, "Education is the most powerful weapon we can use to change the world" (The Nelson Mandela Foundation

Archive at the Centre of Memory, 2003, para. 15). Put differently, as educators, we have access to a game changer. Young people spend more time in schools than in any other institution in our society. Within our classrooms and schools, we have the power to take intentional steps to help students develop the knowledge, skills, and dispositions they need to transform society and create a more just world. This learning can help students push back against the barriers and hurdles constructed to limit their individual potential and equip them with the ability to protect the potential and possibility of others. Young people have a vital role to play in reshaping and rebuilding our society toward justice. But we must prepare them to fulfill that role by nurturing their ability to recognize, analyze, and challenge inequity—their critical consciousness.

The term *critical consciousness* originated with Brazilian philosopher-educator Paulo Freire. In the 1940s, when Freire was a literacy teacher working with migrant laborers in Brazil, he realized that many of the workers who joined his classes were motivated to learn to read by their desire to better understand their own social conditions and to participate in Brazil's political system (since literacy was a requirement for voting in national elections). In other words, their academic motivation was fueled by questions about their own life circumstances: Why were they working so hard for so little compensation? Why did they have so few rights and so little political power in comparison to the farm owners they worked for?

Freire (1970) invoked the phrase critical consciousness to explain the process by which these farm workers learned about

> Young people have a vital role to play in reshaping and rebuilding our society toward justice, but we must prepare them.

the oppressive social and political forces shaping their lives and developed the skills necessary to challenge these forces through social action. Freire proposed that developing students' critical consciousness should be a foundational goal of education so that people—particularly people from oppressed and marginalized groups—are equipped with the knowledge, skills, and motivation necessary to challenge injustice and transform society.

Over his long career as an educator and author, Freire continued to develop his ideas about the role that educators could play in nurturing students' critical consciousness. As he watched his students learn how to analyze injustice and act against it, he came to understand that people need access to two distinct skills to transform society: *critical reflection*, or the ability to recognize and analyze systemic injustice; and *critical action*, or the ability to engage in concrete social action to resist or challenge injustice.

Freire emphasized that people must access *both* critical reflection skills and critical action skills to engage in meaningful social change work. Just as a car needs both the gas pedal and the steering wheel to aim for a destination, students require deep analytical knowledge about the nature of injustice and how it is sustained by systems, structures, and power, alongside strategies for challenging it. Simply stepping on the gas or, in the case of critical consciousness work, implementing action strategies without a clear direction can result in misguided efforts. Similarly, solely focusing on determining the route for a car trip, or of a social movement, without pressing the gas pedal or taking action will not take you anywhere. Students need to both understand how injustice works and how to resist and challenge it, and they need to develop the skills to change the status quo.

Freire was not the first educator to document the knowledge and skills needed to advance justice. His concept of critical consciousness was greatly influenced by several other scholars and activists, including Afro-Caribbean psychiatrist Frantz Fanon, who wrote on the impact of colonization, and African American educators and scholars such as Septima Clark, Carter G. Woodson, and W. E. B. Dubois (Irwin, 2012). Contemporary scholars use critical consciousness alongside other terms to describe the constellation of knowledge and skills that position young people to act for justice. For example, literacy scholar Gholdy Muhammad defines *criticality* as "the capacity and ability of students to read, write, think, and speak in ways to understand power and equity to understand and promote anti-oppression" (2020, p. 12). Scholar Gloria Ladson-Billings's (2014) work focuses on *culturally relevant pedagogy*, teaching that nurtures students' academic skills, cultural competence, and critical consciousness.

## Is School the Right Place to Nurture Critical Consciousness?

When we travel across the country to engage with and support schools in this work, educators frequently express concern that there is not enough time in the school day to nurture young people's critical consciousness, especially given everything else that teachers are asked to do. Our response is that developing students' ability to recognize, analyze, and challenge injustice does not come at the expense of other learning objectives; instead, it can be integrated into all subjects and aligned with subject area requirements. As the opening vignettes show, and many following examples will demonstrate, nurturing students' critical reflection and critical action skills requires students to draw upon and hone the reading, writing, thinking, computation, discussion, and collaboration skills that are necessary for learning about any complex topic, and which are represented in state and district standards (Kirshner, 2015).

Consider our opening examples. Students in the Sociology of Change course read grade-level-appropriate texts to develop background knowledge for their social action work. In particular, they read, reflect on, and discuss Harvard professor Marshall Ganz's writings on strategies to successfully organize for change. For their individual projects, students draw on communication, writing, collaboration, and organization skills that can be found in state standards for multiple subjects. Likewise, 4th graders learning about the CROWN Act work collaboratively to decipher sophisticated legislative language and cultivate their argument writing skills in letters to legislators.

> Developing students' ability to recognize, analyze, and challenge injustice does not come at the expense of other learning objectives.

In both cases, learning about and responding to injustice are tied to content area academic standards. These projects enhance rather than impede students' academic skill development. Research demonstrates that not only can schools fully integrate this work with existing state standards, but that schools that do so can have a significant impact on student achievement (Dee & Penner, 2017).

## How Students Benefit

The effects of nurturing critical consciousness in students are well-documented. Armed with an understanding of how systems, institutions, and individuals perpetuate and sustain injustice and the skills to resist and challenge these forces, young people can leverage their voices and leadership, demand society do things differently, and push toward transformative change. Think of teens—including Malala Yousafzai, Greta Thunberg, Marley Dias, Autumn Peltier, the students of Parkland High School in Florida—who have harnessed their critical consciousness in the service of justice-based action. And even more young people whose names we do not know are at the forefront of action on issues such as police brutality, gun violence, Indigenous rights, educational justice, and climate change. Ultimately, the greatest and most important outcome of critical consciousness development is leadership and resistance in the service of an improved society.

A growing body of research suggests that attending to critical consciousness development contributes to students' overall well-being (Maker Castro et al., 2022). For example, young people with high levels of critical consciousness are more likely to demonstrate resilience and possess high levels of self-esteem (Ginwright, 2010; Godfrey et al., 2019). They also earn better grades in school, report more ambitious professional goals, and are more civically engaged (Hope & Jagers, 2014; Seider et al., 2020).

Why does learning to recognize, analyze, and challenge injustice have such a positive impact on students? First, opportunities to learn about injustice can be motivating and engaging for young people with systematically marginalized identities because it helps them recognize and interrogate the unjust forces shaping their lives and resist narratives that the structural conditions they are subject to are the result of individual choices or decisions. For example, students from low socioeconomic status (low-SES) families might internalize the belief that their SES peer group has lower college matriculation rates because they are less motivated, but critically conscious students can identify the interlocking systems of racism, classism, and xenophobia that shape current college-going rates.

Scholar Julio Cammarota (2007) interviewed high school students participating in a course called the Social Justice Education Project in Tucson, Arizona, which offered opportunities to analyze and address social issues in their own community. One participant explained that she benefited from "learning about real stuff, like seeing the realities, how you are blinded by society" (p. 91). She added that learning about injustices in her own community "makes you want to work harder. Because you understand. You realize what is going on and ... you go against it" (p. 91). In sum, nurturing critical consciousness in students who are members of marginalized and oppressed groups helps them recognize and analyze the obstacles that have been placed in their paths and engages them in actions to topple these obstacles in solidarity with others.

Learning about and challenging injustice is also essential to the well-being of young people who are members of privileged identity groups. In *Pedagogy of the Oppressed*, Freire (1970) argued that oppression strips away not only the humanity of those being oppressed but also the humanity of the groups doing or benefiting from the oppression. According to Freire, challenging injustice can combat the dehumanization that societies exact on members of both oppressed and oppressor groups. Along similar lines, psychologist Janet Helms (2019) found that, for White youth, developing a healthy racial identity entails learning to (1) abandon interpersonal forms of racism such as stereotyping and discrimination in which they might personally be engaging, (2) recognize and oppose systemic forms of racism, and (3) feel good about their White identity in the context of working toward a more just society. In other words, scholars argue that developing the ability to recognize and challenge oppressive forces is part of healthy development for young people from privileged groups. In short, nurturing young people's critical consciousness holds powerful benefits for *all* young people.

## How This Book Can Help

We wrote *Educating for Justice* because we believe that educators and schools have a vital role to play in helping youth develop the critical consciousness necessary for them to thrive in and transform the world. Even though many educators—including Paulo Freire, Carter G. Woodson, Septima Clark, Gloria Ladson-Billings, Jeffrey Duncan-Andrade, Bettina Love, and Gholdy Muhammad—have done groundbreaking work to make critical consciousness a primary goal of education, too often we visit schools and find this work taking place in just a few isolated classrooms, a particular department, or a single grade-level team. The teachers in these singular classrooms, departments, and grade-level teams are often engaging their students in powerful teaching and learning, but a few shining spots are not enough. School communities invested in positioning youth to transform the world need to take a more comprehensive approach.

Our goal with this book is to offer practical, specific, and actionable guidance to educators about how a school community can do powerful critical consciousness work schoolwide. While other texts are available to help unpack the *content* that students need to learn to be able to recognize, analyze, and challenge injustice effectively, this book focuses more on schoolwide structures, curricular processes, and adult partnerships that fuel this work. In sum, we want to help schools create conditions for educators to proactively nurture students' critical consciousness in every subject area, at every grade level, and in every classroom in collaboration with families, community partners, and the students themselves. We will draw on illustrations, artifacts, and resources from K–12 schools across the country that we have studied, taught in, and led. None of these schools carries out this work perfectly or flawlessly, because there is no perfect; however, they offer rich examples and materials to educators invested in doing this work. Throughout the book, we use the phrase *in action* to indicate when we are taking a close look at a school practice, offering a specific resource or tool, or zooming into a grade-level or community meeting.

> The phrase *in action* indicates a close look at a school practice, resource, tool, or grade-level or community meeting.

It is important to remember, as we illustrated earlier in this Introduction, that schools themselves are documented sites of injustice. Students experience the same types of marginalization inside schools that they do outside schools. Our intention in this book is not to ignore those realities. To allow us to focus on the strategies and practices that schools committed to this work have undertaken, we are going to trust that you are actively working to examine your own school culture, processes, and practices carefully, and we encourage you to read each chapter with careful attention to what has to be adjusted, eliminated, innovated, or changed for you and your colleagues to be authentic, honest, nonhypocritical ambassadors for critical consciousness development. It is also important to say that nurturing critical consciousness is complex. As a result, there are inevitably concepts and practices, as well as tensions, that we will not be able to cover in one book.

Over the next seven chapters, we describe and unpack the four strands of work that we believe are crucial to a school's efforts to nurture students' critical consciousness across elementary, middle, and high schools (see Figure I.1). Chapter 1 focuses on *centering justice in curriculum and pedagogy* by laying out an arc of professional learning that can support educators in developing and facilitating curriculum that engages students in recognizing, analyzing, and challenging injustice. Chapters

FIGURE I.1

**Four Principles for Nurturing Students' Critical Consciousness Schoolwide**

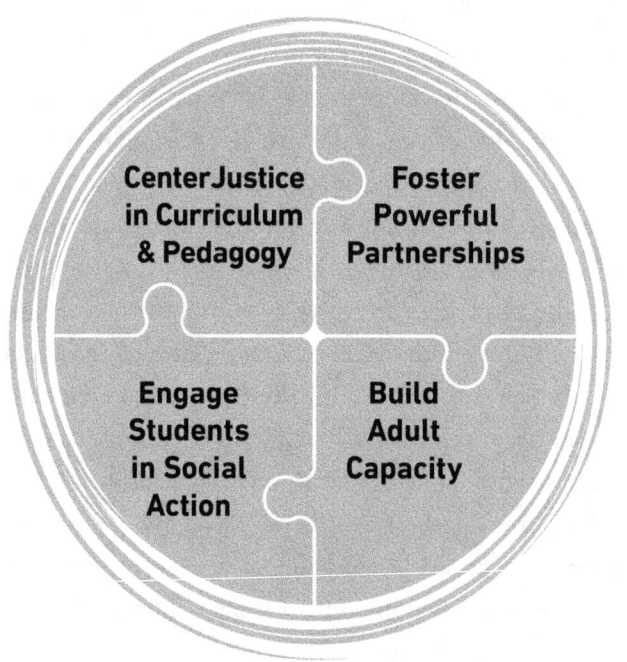

2 and 3 discuss *fostering powerful partnerships with community partners and families* to nurture students' critical consciousness and provide practical guidance for engaging resistant family members and caretakers. Chapter 4 describes how to structure authentic opportunities for *engaging students in social action* inside schools and, more broadly, in society. Chapter 5 addresses *building adult capacity*—strengthening the knowledge, skills, and motivation of adults in a school community to learn and reflect together about injustice and how to challenge injustice. Although building capacity is the final strand we unpack and describe, it is not a final step in this work. In fact, it is foundational to establishing the structures, practices, and professional learning laid out in Chapters 1 through 4.

Chapters 6 and 7 help synthesize the preceding five chapters by providing descriptions of how *putting these four principles together* equips a school community to harness many different types of events and experiences—from heritage months to national tragedies—to engage students in recognizing, analyzing, and challenging injustice. Finally, the Conclusion discusses what it means to courageously take up this work and outlines foundational understandings school leaders and school communities must embody to stay the course.

We know that a one-size-fits-all curriculum is a myth in education. You may need to adjust the way your school takes up the ideas, approaches, and strategies in this book. There may be some approaches and ideas in the pages to come that simply will not work in your community. To truly offer students critical knowledge and useful tools to advance justice, our approach needs to be contextual. The needs of one school will differ from those of another school right down the street, and what works in the first school may not work in the second. Our challenge in the ensuing pages is to recognize and honor the distinctiveness of every school community while still offering broad-enough structures, practices, and professional learning that can be customized for each unique school context.

To meet this challenge, we are drawing on what we have learned from our combined 60 years of studying, teaching, and leading in K–12 schools across the United States. However, the backbone of this book is the work taking place in a public elementary school that we refer to using the pseudonym Sarah C. Roberts Elementary School.[2] To a first-time visitor, Roberts Elementary School may seem unremarkable. It is a traditional public elementary school in a large northeastern city that serves 300 students in grades preK through 5. Black students, Latine students, and White students each represent about a third of the school's student body. Half of the students are eligible for free or reduced-price lunch, and about a quarter are English learners. Roberts Elementary's principal, Ms. Bethany Drake, is a White woman in her early 40s who has been principal of the school for more than a decade. The school building is over 100 years old and could use some work.

But what a visitor to the school quickly discovers is that its staff, families, and students have worked thoughtfully over the past decade to become a community that places recognizing, analyzing, and challenging injustice at the center of teaching and

---

[2] Sarah C. Roberts was a 5-year-old African American girl living in Boston in 1847. Her family challenged racial segregation in the Boston Public Schools by suing the city of Boston to allow her to attend her neighborhood school, which was only open to White students. Although the Massachusetts Supreme Court ruled against the Roberts family, Sarah is considered one of the youngest contributors to the U.S. civil rights movement. Third graders at the school we observed spend several weeks learning about the activism of Sarah C. Roberts and her family, so we chose her name for the school's pseudonym.

learning for every student, at every grade level, in every classroom. This is not a school with a few shining stars but rather a school that has developed a comprehensive approach to nurturing every student's critical consciousness every year.

This dedication to helping every student develop the knowledge, skills, and commitments to be a changemaker is particularly exciting to discover in an elementary school. Often, elementary and even middle school educators tell us that their children are too young to take up topics of justice and injustice; however, the teachers and leaders at Roberts Elementary School are emphatic that their students relish opportunities to learn about and challenge injustices in their lives and communities. Moreover, Roberts teachers explain that centering justice in their curriculum and intentionally nurturing students' critical consciousness has contributed to their school transitioning over the past decade from one of the very lowest ranked schools in the district to one that outperforms the majority of elementary schools in the state.

The three of us spent a year at Roberts Elementary School observing classes, attending meetings and events, shadowing the principal, interviewing teachers, collecting curriculum and student work, reading newsletters and correspondence, and speaking with students and their families. The leaders and staff at the school welcomed us fully into their community on the condition that we protect the confidentiality of the school, faculty, staff, and, most important, children and their families. Accordingly, we refer to Roberts Elementary School by a pseudonym throughout this book, and we do the same for every teacher, student, and family member that we spoke to or observed. Throughout the book, we share concrete examples from Roberts, including curriculum, planning meeting documents, and family communications. Although these artifacts come from an elementary school setting, the universal messages and pedagogical practices they illustrate are easily adapted to all grades.

We should also note that many of our examples of critical consciousness work center student exploration of racism and antiracist action. This is primarily because young people's critical consciousness about race is our collective area of specialization. That said, the strategies and approaches we offer are applicable beyond race-based work. They can be implemented and applied to multiple axes of identity and forms of injustice. As described earlier, interlocking, co-conspiring systems of injustice hold our country back, and nurturing young people's critical consciousness can help them recognize, analyze, and act against *any* form of injustice (e.g., classism, heteronormativity, patriarchy, ableism, linguism, xenophobia). Schools and educators have an essential role to play in this work. As educator Thabiti Brown, our colleague, explains, "We need to educate our children to go and change things in the world . . . so that when the world comes for them, they're ready to also come for the world" (Edutopia, 2019). We are honored and grateful for the chance to support you in this important work. Let's get started!

 ## Questions for Reflection

1. What opportunities do students in your classroom or school already have to recognize, analyze, and challenge injustice?
2. What ideas about engaging students in recognizing, analyzing, and challenging injustice did the three vignettes at the start of the Introduction spark for you?
3. What questions do you have about critical consciousness or the role of schools and educators in nurturing students' critical consciousness?

4. Which of the principles featured in Figure I.1—centering justice in curriculum and pedagogy, fostering powerful partnerships with community partners and families, providing opportunities to engage in social action, building adult capacity—feel like areas of strength for you? Which feel like opportunities for development?
5. To what extent are these principles intertwined or siloed in your school community, and why do you think this is?

## Additional Resources

Duncan-Andrade, J. (2009). Note to educators: Hope required when growing roses in concrete. *Harvard Educational Review, 79*(2), 181–194. https://doi.org/10.17763/haer.79.2.nu3436017730384w

El-Amin, A., Seider, S., Graves, D., Tamerat, J., Clark, S., Soutter, M., Johannsen, J., & Malhotra, S. (2017). Critical consciousness: A key to student achievement. *Phi Delta Kappan, 98*(5), 18–23. https://doi.org/10.1177/0031721717690360

Fanon, F. (1967). *Black skin, White masks* (C. L. Markmann, Trans.). Grove Press. (Original work published 1952).

Freire, P. (1970). *Pedagogy of the oppressed* (M. B. Ramos, Trans.). Herder and Herder.

Godfrey, E. B., & Rapa, L. J. (Eds.). (2023). *Developing critical consciousness in youth: Contexts and settings.* Cambridge University Press.

Ladson-Billings, G. (2014). Culturally relevant pedagogy 2.0: a.k.a. the remix. *Harvard Educational Review, 84*(1), 74–84. https://doi.org/10.17763/haer.84.1.p2rj131485484751

Seider, S., & Graves, D. (2020). *Schooling for critical consciousness: Engaging Black and Latinx youth in analyzing, navigating, and challenging racial injustice.* Harvard Education Press.

# Center Justice in Curriculum and Pedagogy

# 1

# Adopt a Justice Framework

Curriculum is a powerful—and underutilized—lever for nurturing students' critical consciousness schoolwide. Students and their teachers are working together on curriculum all day long, all year long, year after year. Unfortunately, many curricula, from preschool through high school and in every subject area, continue to center the experiences and perspectives of dominant groups within our society, failing to offer sufficient time, attention, respect, and care to the experiences and knowledge of minoritized and marginalized groups or to create space to explore the interconnected systems of oppression that shape life around us. These curricular decisions about what to focus on matter. They influence what our students do and do not learn—and do and do not internalize—about themselves, their communities, and the wider world. Further, they influence the worldviews that students will carry with them as they proceed through life.

The current curricular status quo *can* be shifted by individual teachers and schools. Over the past 20 years, we have observed many examples of teachers and students working together on subject-area curriculum and content that engage students in recognizing, analyzing, and challenging injustice. We've seen a history lesson on redlining at a middle school in Chicago. An advisory lesson on voting rights at an elementary school in Columbus, Ohio. A humanities project on activist leaders at a K–8 school outside Reno, Nevada. A science lesson on Henrietta Lacks at a K–12 school in Washington, D.C. A ratio math lesson in 6th grade on access to healthy food options across neighborhoods in Brooklyn, New York. A statistics lesson in 10th grade focused on comparing access to healthcare across the United States in Charlotte, North Carolina. The list could go on and on. Our arsenal of examples of schools with varied demographics in vastly different communities affirms just how feasible centering justice in the curriculum can be. In fact, a whole movement in education, ethnic studies, has sought to bring this work to the forefront of teaching and learning in school districts across the country (Sleeter & Zavala, 2020). Throughout this chapter, we will use the phrase *centering justice in the curriculum* to refer to a school's intentional efforts to bring to students' academic learning (1) the experiences, history, genius, and contributions of underrepresented, historically marginalized, and systematically excluded identity groups; and (2) topics of injustice and skills for challenging injustice.

In our experience, even powerful examples of centering justice in the curriculum are often restricted to certain teachers in the building, specific departments or grade-level teams, or times in the school year. Yet limiting opportunities for students to learn about injustice to social studies classes, one teacher's classroom, or heritage months sends an implicit (or explicit) message that this work is only relevant to particular fields of study, identity groups, or times of the year.

If we truly want our students to have the knowledge and skills to pursue a just life for themselves and their peers, we need them to understand that challenging injustice and transforming society is everyone's work, that every field of study can contribute, and that every day presents opportunities for even the smallest action. For that to happen, students need consistent opportunities in every content area and grade level to critically reflect on injustice and develop solutions for change. This does not mean that every lesson, text, or learning activity needs to focus on social injustice, but it does mean that every educator in a school community can be intentional about building opportunities for critical consciousness development into the curriculum units they teach.

> If we want our students to have the knowledge and skills to pursue justice, we need them to understand that challenging injustice and transforming society is the work of everyone, in every field, every day.

This chapter offers a process through which every educator—whether they author their own curriculum or use mandated curriculum—can learn to develop and deliver curriculum that nurtures students' critical consciousness. There are undoubtedly numerous approaches to establishing a schoolwide curricular commitment to students' critical consciousness development, but our approach calls for an arc of professional learning and practice for an entire school's staff that includes the following steps:

1. Identify a curricular justice framework.
2. Introduce and integrate the justice framework into curricular planning.
3. Create a common planning template.
4. Celebrate successes and failures.
5. Establish planning days.
6. Provide coaching to support justice-focused pedagogical shifts.

Importantly, this arc of professional learning must build on or dovetail with the adult capacity building processes described in Chapter 5. Teachers cannot integrate topics of injustice into their curriculum if they do not have basic familiarity with the topics themselves. In writing this book, we initially positioned guidance on building adult capacity as our opening chapter but subsequently decided, in the spirit of backward planning, to first describe justice-oriented curriculum, instructional practices, family engagement strategies, and social action work that school leaders, teacher leaders, and staff can implement to nurture students' critical consciousness.

It is also important to note that you will need to consistently revisit pieces of the professional development arc detailed in this chapter, such as introducing a justice framework, establishing planning days, and coaching, because almost all schools see an influx of new teachers each year. Schools committed to this work need mechanisms for bringing new teachers into the fold and providing ongoing development for returning and new teachers alike, including but not limited to new teacher orientation, intentional and ongoing teacher-to-teacher mentoring, and differentiated professional development.

To help illustrate and unpack what each step of the professional learning arc could look like, throughout the chapter we consider the practices followed by Roberts Elementary School. In the following sections, we will explore excerpts from teacher lessons, teacher meetings, and other resources and tools. Afterward, we will offer suggestions and strategies for modifying this arc for teachers and school leaders who feel constrained by district or state mandates about the content or pacing of their curriculum or who follow scripted curricula. We will also share a brief overview of common approaches to ensuring that both new and returning teachers have continual access to this learning.

## Step 1: Identify a Curricular Justice Framework

Many educators rely on a powerful approach to lesson and unit planning called *backward design,* which calls for unit design to begin with identifying what students "should know or be able to do by the end of the unit" (Wiggins & McTighe, 2005, p. 14). Backward design has helped teachers at every level of education to develop rigorous, engaging, and effective curriculum units (e.g., Bullard, 2019; Popa, 2009), but it doesn't ensure that those curriculum units will give students opportunities to engage with topics of justice. To plan curriculum that engages students in recognizing, analyzing, and challenging injustice, teachers need access to another tool to help guide them and hold them accountable for interrogating power and centering topics of identity, injustice, and social action as they plan. We refer to this planning tool as a *curricular justice framework.*

A curricular justice framework is a guide for curriculum planning that positions engaging students in learning about and challenging injustice as integral to skill building and knowledge acquisition rather than a tangential goal. In other words, a curricular justice framework makes nurturing students' critical consciousness central to student learning.

> A curricular justice framework positions learning about and challenging injustice as integral to skill building and knowledge acquisition rather than a tangential goal.

There are numerous such frameworks a school or school leader can choose to implement. One of the most widely known is Gloria Ladson-Billings's (1995) culturally relevant pedagogy framework, which calls for teachers to build curriculum with three key goals in mind: academic success, cultural competence, and critical consciousness. For Ladson-Billings, academic success refers to supporting students' intellectual growth, and nurturing students' cultural competence entails helping students celebrate and take pride in their own cultures while also developing understandings of other cultures. Finally, her conception of critical consciousness draws on work by Paulo Freire, Septima Clark, bell hooks, and others on helping students learn to recognize and challenge injustice. Other influential frameworks include Django Paris's (2012) culturally sustaining pedagogy framework, Gholdy Muhammad's (2020) culturally and historically responsive literacy framework, and Zaretta Hammond's (2015) ready for rigor framework.

As a school leader embarking on the process of choosing a curricular justice framework, it is important to prioritize shared leadership by leveraging diverse, representative voices from your community to make an informed choice. Consider including community members who typically influence instructional practices, such as instructional coaches and leadership teams, as well as representatives from committees that shape school policy or culture (parent–teacher associations, equity teams, governing bodies, and even student councils). Educators, families, and students all bring unique perspectives and funds of knowledge to teaching and learning that can illuminate invaluable connections or anticipate misconceptions. Authentic feedback or endorsements from these groups will help garner essential support for the complex work ahead.

## *Identify a Curricular Justice Framework in Action*

Roberts Elementary School chose Muhammad's (2018) culturally and historically responsive literacy framework as its curricular justice framework. This framework emerged from Muhammad's (2012) historical research on African American literary societies—including reading rooms, lyceums, and debating societies—in 19th-century America. She believed that the present-day narrow focus on skill building and knowledge development in K–12 schools is doing a disservice to all youth and to youth of color, in particular. She wondered if and how literary societies founded by African Americans in the 1800s had offered their members a richer set of goals, practices, and motivations for the learning they were pursuing that could inform the work of educators today.

From this historical research emerged Muhammad's (2018) culturally and historically responsive literacy (CHRL) framework, which calls for educators to build opportunities into every curriculum unit to nurture students in five areas:

- *Skills*—mastering the competencies that students will need in their lives to pursue rich educational and occupational opportunities.
- *Intellect*—developing meaningful knowledge and understandings about a topic or concept.
- *Identity*—working to answer the question "Who am I?"
- *Critical consciousness* (which Muhammad terms "criticality")—learning about and challenging oppressive forces shaping students' lives and communities.
- *Joy*—finding opportunities for joy in learning.

Roberts educators chose this justice framework because it pulled together two strands of professional learning that they were already focused on: developing skills and intellect to lay the groundwork for rigorous, content-rich instructional units and tasks. Building on work that was already in progress helped teachers see the justice framework as an extension of their previous professional development and goals. Further, the connections between the justice framework and identified school goals helped scaffold teachers' learning and readiness for change.

Importantly, the CHRL framework also introduced two components—identity and criticality—that the school had not yet intentionally woven into its curriculum and pedagogy, pushing the community toward deeper comprehensive critical consciousness building. One of the key ideas of the CHRL framework—that schools, as places that center genius and thinking, need to nurture students' identities and critical consciousness—really resonated with Roberts teachers, families, and leaders.

If your school requires adhering to prescribed curriculum units, you might be asking yourself what value there is in identifying a justice framework. Because a justice framework offers an analytic lens to examine all curricula, chosen or prescribed, the steps for integrating a justice framework into planning and teaching can benefit both educators who have substantial freedom to develop their own curriculum units and teachers with less curricular autonomy. Teachers with limited autonomy may need to use justice frameworks differently and may contend with additional challenges, so we will offer guidance about how to take on these challenges.

## Step 2: Introduce and Integrate the Curricular Justice Framework

The next step after choosing a justice framework is to train and support teachers to use it. To plan, roll out, and execute an arc of professional learning that introduces a justice framework to an entire staff requires partnership and collaboration among school leaders and teacher leaders. For some schools, these collaborating educators may be members of an instructional leadership team (ILT).

An ILT typically includes the principal, instructional coaches, grade-level team leaders, and content-area department heads. The group works collaboratively to strengthen teaching and learning across the school. Ideally, a school's ILT also comprises a diverse group of educators in terms of race/ethnicity, years of experience, years teaching in the particular school community, and grade-level team. This diversity of experience enables ILT members to anticipate a wide range of questions and concerns from their colleagues about the adoption of a particular justice framework, design professional learning activities to address these concerns, and increase buy-in from their colleagues. Even when teachers respect, admire, and like their administrators, they want to hear from respected classroom teacher colleagues that a shift in classroom practice will be worthwhile and feasible.

Your ILT might or might not be the appropriate partner for identifying the curricular justice framework for your school, introducing the framework to your school's staff, and designing a professional learning arc to help teachers integrate the framework into their planning and teaching. For each school, the *who* might be different. The important piece to take away is that this work needs to happen in collaboration with multiple members of the school community rather than issuing from a single administrator or teacher-leader. Take a moment to consider who might be powerful partners for curriculum development in your school. Who is best positioned to help invest teachers in incorporating a justice framework in their planning? Who can best anticipate teachers' needs, questions, and concerns?

Let's turn our attention to what the collaborative work related to training educators on a curricular justice framework might look like. This professional learning sequence comprises three steps: lead model unit discussions, participate in unit interrogations, and hold teaching simulations. The sequence resonates with approaches that emphasize content learning, deconstructing an exemplar, co-constructing an example, and transferring the new skills to practice (Brisk, 2015).

## Lead Model Unit Discussions

A *model unit* is a curriculum unit for a particular grade level and content area that exemplifies a particular approach to unit design and development. Discussing and reflecting on a model unit can be a valuable way to introduce educators to specific unit planning processes or new elements to incorporate into their work. Educators working to familiarize themselves with a particular justice framework can benefit from reading, deconstructing, and discussing model units that integrate the selected justice framework developed by others.

### *Model Unit Discussions in Action*

At Roberts Elementary School, Principal Bethany Drake and her ILT started by reading *Cultivating Genius* (Muhammad, 2020), which describes Muhammad's justice framework in detail, and began using their meeting time to discuss and deconstruct model curriculum units included in the book. They also found sample curriculum units online that incorporated the framework and in the book *Unearthing Joy* (Muhammad, 2023). For each of these model units, Principal Drake and the ILT worked together to identify and discuss how the unit cultivated students' skills, intellect, identity, critical consciousness, and joy and how these different pursuits combined to support students' growth and learning. They also raised questions or concerns they had about leading students in learning about and discussion of specific topics such as racism, injustice, and identity and discussed the implications of those concerns. They wondered together about supports and practices that the ILT could implement to mitigate any discomfort teachers might have addressing these topics with students. They also evaluated units in their own curriculum for suitability for this work.

Figuring out how to roll out schoolwide professional learning is important. One possible approach, after an ILT or school leadership team has analyzed several model units and deepened their own understanding, is for team members to go back to their grade-level teams and lead similar model unit conversations, thereby introducing the justice framework to the entire staff and kicking off discussions among each grade-level team about the strengths and limitations of the chosen justice framework as well as individual teachers' questions and concerns about it. Following these grade-level discussions, members of the ILT can bring questions and concerns back to their next meeting.

## Participate in Unit Interrogations

A *unit interrogation* refers to educators working together to improve and adapt a previously taught curriculum unit. Unit interrogations provide a valuable opportunity to collaboratively practice alternative approaches to unit planning using familiar content.

This work can start with an ILT dissecting a curriculum unit currently taught with the school's new justice framework in mind. They use the framework to evaluate the unit's essential questions, its methods for increasing students' content knowledge and skill development, and its culminating assessment task. They then gauge the presence (or absence) of each of the key components of the school's justice framework. For example, with the CHRL framework, a team might ask if the unit features built-in opportunities to nurture students' skills, intellect, identity, critical consciousness, and joy. Does the unit contain problematic narratives that might be harmful to students' identity and critical consciousness? Does it miss opportunities to help students analyze existing injustices? To address components of the justice framework that are absent from or weakly represented in a particular unit, team members can brainstorm ways to amplify or add them.

### *Unit Interrogations in Action*

The Roberts ILT conducted a unit interrogation of a district-mandated 2nd grade unit on immigration that did not include any stories featuring Asian immigrants. Given the increasing numbers of Roberts students of East Asian and South Asian descent, the team felt the omission meant the unit failed to provide an opportunity to explore social topics relevant to students' identities—one of the key pursuits in their justice framework.

The ILT brainstormed children's books to add to the unit that offered Asian American students pathways to reflect on their own identities and give all 2nd graders the means to learn more about groups of immigrants whose role in U.S. history often goes untold. They also discussed how placing greater emphasis on the experiences of Asian American immigrants would deepen students' critical consciousness about the ways in which Asian Americans experience racism through portrayal as "perpetual foreigners," as well as the amplification of these stereotypes during the COVID-19 pandemic, which contributed to a rise in hate crimes against the community.

Following the cycle of adult learning, ILT members then facilitated similar interrogations with their grade-level teams, using previously taught curriculum units that were planned for later in the year. The kindergarten team interrogated their upcoming unit on construction, and the 5th grade team analyzed an upcoming unit on the rainforest. Through these discussions, each grade-level team had the opportunity to reflect on whether the unit's texts and learning activities were nurturing not just students' skills and intellect but also their identity development, critical consciousness, and joy. Through such collaborative unit interrogations, teachers at every grade level can practice incorporating the school's justice framework into their planning and teaching.

This two-step cycle of professional development—leading model unit discussions and participating in unit interrogations—helps teachers solidify a vision for curriculum that thoughtfully embeds the key components of the school's justice framework. When looking at model units from outside their curriculum, they can ask questions, push back on ideas, and explore concepts freely. Afterward, they can turn to their own curriculum armed with a new vision of what is possible. A school's ILT or another group of school leaders and teacher leaders is essential for facilitating both steps for the rest of the staff because these leaders can bring questions, concerns, and stumbling blocks that they and their colleagues encounter back to the ILT to develop further professional learning activities to address them.

## Hold Teaching Simulations

After teachers examine model units and practice revising their own curriculum, they need practice teaching lessons incorporating their school's justice framework. A *teaching simulation* involves an educator teaching a lesson—or a portion of a lesson—in an artificial or simulated environment so that they can develop or hone a specific teaching skill. Teaching simulations are a staple of preservice teacher education programs, but they can also be useful professional learning experiences for veteran teachers seeking to bring a new pedagogical approach or skill into their teaching practice.

For a school community working to incorporate a justice framework into their curriculum, teaching simulations complement model unit discussions and unit interrogations. Model unit discussions and interrogations inform *curriculum planning*; teaching simulations allow teachers to *practice delivering lessons* that incorporate a justice framework, making space for them to hone language to describe concepts, anticipate and practice responding to student questions, and note where they feel challenged or stuck.

Teaching simulations can take place during whole-school professional learning or with smaller grade-level teams. To build trust, break the ice, and model the practice, members of the school's leadership team can initially take on the teacher role, with the rest of the staff acting as students. Importantly, these simulated lessons need not be perfectly designed or flawlessly executed; their purpose is not to showcase perfect pedagogy but to model for staff how to design and communicate lessons that pursue the goals of a justice framework and to create space for staff to learn about pedagogical approaches to teaching justice-oriented topics. Inevitably, some simulated lessons will pursue justice-oriented goals more effectively than others, and there will be triumphs and fails along the way. Often, teachers learn just as much from a lesson that does not go as intended as one that does. To ensure each simulation is an honest and open place for learning for both the practicing teacher and participants, always schedule time for debriefing afterward. Participants can discuss strengths, weaknesses, and opportunities observed during the lesson as well as questions and concerns the lesson raised.

## *Teaching Simulations in Action*

Members of the Roberts 2nd grade team led a simulated lesson for colleagues from their unit on immigration. The unit included an autobiographical children's book by Areli Morales titled *Areli Is a Dreamer* (2021), in which Morales describes her experience as a young girl immigrating to the United States without documentation. In the debrief of the simulation, teachers applauded the 2nd grade team for engaging students in learning and discussing the challenges facing immigrants to the United States but expressed concern that the lesson ignored the richness and joy that are also part of immigrant communities and families. This feedback engaged the entire staff in thinking deeply about how to design lessons and units that pursued each of the elements in Muhammad's justice framework. Thus, simulations also contribute to building collective educator efficacy.

When teachers see that their school community is encouraging them to engage in rich, intellectual, and important work—and they feel supported to learn, grow, and take risks in carrying out this work—they are far more likely to lean into it. Model unit discussions, unit interrogations, and teaching simulations represent a significant investment in time and capacity building, but they turn teacher professional learning into a collective effort, normalize both critique and growth, contribute to a culture of trust and positive risk-taking, and give teachers opportunities to deepen their understanding of the school's curricular justice framework.

## Step 3: Create a Common Planning Template

After teachers have learned more about their school's justice framework through model unit discussions and interrogations and participated in teaching simulations, they can begin incorporating the framework into their own planning and teaching. One valuable support for this work is a common planning template that prompts teachers to build the key goals of the justice framework into their curriculum units throughout the school year.

Developing a common unit planning template that includes the justice framework also reinforces the idea that developing and delivering justice-centered curriculum is relevant to teachers at every grade level and in every subject area. Figure 1.1 depicts a sample template based on the one used by Roberts Elementary School. With a planning template in hand, teachers can ensure that they are building opportunities for nurturing their students' critical consciousness into every curriculum unit.

Of course, different school communities will make different decisions about the use of a common unit planning template. Some will establish an expectation that every teacher follow the template in their planning processes, while others will treat the template more like a resource for teachers to make use of as they see fit. School communities will need to agree on what approach works best for them.

FIGURE 1.1
## Sample Unit Planning Template

| Grade: | Unit Title: |
|---|---|
| **Unit Overview** ||
| Unit description from curriculum document:<br><br>Paraphrased unit description and how it relates to students: ||
| Essential questions: ||
| What will students *know* after completing this unit? ||
| What will students *understand* (skills) after completing this unit? ||
| Grade-level standards (copy from curriculum): ||
| **Culturally and Historically Responsive Literacy Framework** ||
| *Identity:* How will students learn something about themselves and/or others? ||
| *Skills:* What skills and content will students learn? ||
| *Intellect:* What knowledge will students gain? ||
| *Critical consciousness:* How will students think about power, equity, and anti-oppression in the text(s), society, and the world? ||
| *Joy:* How will students derive joy from the unit? ||

*(continued)*

## FIGURE 1.1
## Sample Unit Planning Template *(continued)*

| Texts/Resources |||
|---|---|---|
| • What are the key ideas of each text, and how do they connect to the unit's essential questions? <br> • What knowledge is built by the texts, and what forms of bias may be present? <br> • Describe the complexity of the texts. |||
| **Curriculum Text(s)** |||
| Title | How is this text complex/enabling? | How will you provide access/supports so that all students (e.g., multilingual learners, students with disabilities) can access this text? |
|  | Meaning/purpose: <br> Structure: <br> Language: <br> Knowledge demands: |  |
|  | (Add more rows if needed.) |  |
| **Supplemental Texts** |||
|  | Meaning/purpose: <br> Structure: <br> Language: <br> Knowledge demands: |  |
|  | (Add more rows if needed.) |  |
| **Assessment Evidence** |||
| • Is the final performance task specifically meaningful and relevant to your students? What could be added or enhanced to ensure relevance? <br> • Is bias present in any of the assessments? How will you address bias? What will you supplement or replace? <br> • What standards/skills/concepts from previous units might need to be fed into instruction to set students up for success with culminating assessments? |||

| Assessment | Aligned standard(s) | Skills/knowledge demands | Access/supports needed | Link to exemplar |
|---|---|---|---|---|
|  |  |  |  |  |
|  |  |  |  |  |

*Sources:* Unit Overview framework adapted from Wiggins & McTighe, 2005; CHRL framework adapted from Muhammad, 2023, and Jones, 2023, p. 132; Curriculum Text framework adapted from Shanahan, 2013.

# Step 4: Celebrate Successes and Failures

An important way to encourage educators to try out a new practice or approach to teaching is to publicly celebrate both successes *and* failures. Many teachers are hesitant to share their teaching successes with their colleagues because they fear coming across as self-important. But it's incredibly helpful for a community of teachers to hear about what their colleagues are trying in their respective classrooms so they know what students in their community can achieve. Sharing earnest efforts that fell flat is also important because it reinforces the message that we can't wait for perfection or total confidence before trying out a new approach or practice and reminds adults that you can learn from falling short. Scott's first teaching job was at a high school in Massachusetts where the principal instituted a practice of giving out a "golden plunger award" (literally a toilet plunger painted gold) at monthly faculty meetings to a faculty member who had tried to do something innovative and important in their classroom but couldn't quite pull it off. Each month the award was presented with much fanfare and laughter—which conveyed the unequivocal message that it is praiseworthy to try something new in your classroom, even when your effort doesn't pan out.

## *Celebrating Success and Failures in Action*

As Roberts teachers began to incorporate the CHRL justice framework into their planning and teaching, Principal Drake created space during staff meetings and whole-school professional learning sessions for them to share their successes and failures with colleagues. At one staff meeting, the 3rd grade team reported how blown away they were by their students' understanding of how excluding groups from history books constitutes a form of systemic racism. In another meeting, the 5th grade team described the strengths of their unit on Jackie Robinson, while acknowledging that they had failed at the outset of the unit to help students understand the time period in which Robinson had lived, played baseball, and fought for civil rights. As a result, students had asked earnest questions throughout the unit about whether Robinson had been an enslaved person and why he'd been allowed to play baseball during slavery. The 5th grade team had several ideas for addressing this issue in the future, including being more intentional about building students' knowledge of the Jim Crow era prior to reading about Robinson and constructing timelines on the walls of their classrooms to help students visualize the timeframes of the historical events they were learning about.

Opportunities to share successes and missteps with colleagues play a powerful role in conveying to the entire faculty that it is OK—and even expected—to experience both triumphs and challenges as they build the key components of their school's justice framework into planning and teaching.

## Step 5: Establish Planning Days

In this chapter, we have laid out a series of steps that school leaders and teacher leaders can take to support colleagues in developing and delivering justice-centered curriculum. But when do educators have the time for such curriculum development? With all the responsibilities on teachers' plates, how can they carve out the time to either plan a unit from scratch or adapt an existing unit? One answer is for school leaders to establish protected planning time for teacher teams.

Many school systems give teachers 60–90 minutes of common planning time each week, often by contract, but developing curriculum units centering justice and resistance to injustice benefits greatly from more concentrated time and attention. We encourage school leaders to strategically and creatively arrange for teacher teams to have additional planning days away from their classes to work with each other and an instructional coach (if available) to prepare upcoming curriculum units. We have seen schools successfully use student teachers, specialists, and substitute teachers to cover teachers' classes during such designated planning days.

This planning time allows educators to engage deeply with the content they want to share with their students. They can discuss potential readings, conduct research, or plan a new culminating task. The goal is for these planning sessions to function as both a collaborative and an intellectual process for teachers.

## *Planning Days in Action*

At Roberts, Principal Drake works hard to establish four yearly planning days for grade-level teams. The 2nd grade team used one of their planning days to address the lack of representation of Asians in their district-mandated immigration unit by adding a new children's book, *Paper Son: The Inspiring Story of Tyrus Wong, Immigrant and Artist* (Leung, 2019). The story references the Chinese Exclusion Act of 1882, so the team used their planning time to read up on this law—the only legislation in American history to close the United States to a particular ethnic group—and discuss the most effective way to introduce this content to their students. Their collaborative work strengthened their ability to use the unit to nurture students' critical consciousness.

That same fall, the 5th grade team used a planning day to work on replacing the original culminating task for their unit on Jackie Robinson with one that better nurtured students' critical consciousness about social change. The original task asked students to write an opinion essay in response to the prompt "What factors were most important to Jackie Robinson in leading social change?" During their planning meeting, the school's instructional coach pushed teachers to lean harder into the action component of critical consciousness by asking them, "How can we have the students take what they learned and *do something* in the world?"

One teacher suggested asking, "Given what you have learned about Jackie Robinson, what is an effective recipe for a social change leader?" The rest of the team liked the way this culminating task was more personal and meaningful for students but maintained the task's standards and skills focused on essay writing and textual evidence. Just as the principal envisioned when she established planning days for grade-level teams, the protected time and space allowed teachers to focus on developing justice-centered curriculum that nurtured not only students' skills and intellect but also their identity, critical consciousness, and joy.

A visitor to Roberts Elementary School listening in on these planning days might attribute these educators' impressive work solely to the four hours of collaboration. But it took following all the steps outlined in this chapter to pave the way for grade-level teams to use that time in the service of developing students' capacity to recognize, analyze, and challenge injustice.

## Step 6: Provide Coaching to Support Justice-Focused Pedagogical Shifts

The first five steps we have outlined in this chapter build educators' capacity to develop and enhance curriculum to center justice. These efforts center around the "what" of teaching—the content students engage with throughout each unit of study. However, of equal importance is the "how"—the instructional moves and practices for implementing the curriculum with integrity. Just because educators have developed curriculum with a justice lens does not mean they have the pedagogical skills to implement it in a culturally and linguistically affirming way. Educators need and deserve coaching and feedback on their teaching pedagogy with a deliberate focus on justice.

> Educators need and deserve coaching and feedback on their teaching pedagogy with a deliberate focus on justice.

### *Coaching and Feedback in Action*

At Roberts, Principal Drake and the ILT worked collaboratively with a community partner—the Lynch Leadership Academy at Boston College—to develop an observation tool for coaching teachers on instructional practice (see Figure 1.2). Although the tool was developed before the school implemented the CHRL framework, the two resonate with one another in their emphasis on the intersection between the quality and rigor of the instructional task, how students are engaged in the task, evidence of student learning, and equity. The observation tool intentionally features equity at the top of the document to indicate that issues of equity and justice live in all the other components of the observation tool.

## FIGURE 1.2
## Classroom Observation Tool

| Standard of Excellence |||
|---|---|---|
| **Equity** <br> • Trust and belief in students as intellectuals and people of strong character are communicated explicitly and implicitly <br> • Culturally competent and responsive pedagogy <br> • Curriculum and tasks do not explicitly or implicitly subscribe to or advance bias <br> • All students are able to access learning because of intentional design and execution of instruction that takes into account disability, language barriers, and other factors that may prevent access |||
| **Student Product** <br> • Demonstrates high degree of mastery and nuance <br> • Students are able to accurately assess and reflect on the quality of their product | **Clear and Rigorous Expectations** <br> • Internalized routines <br> • Scaffolds support learning, not limit it <br> • Standards-aligned, appropriate objectives <br> • Communication of how the lesson is situated in a larger context (of the unit, of the year, of the world, etc.) is evident | **Rigorous Tasks** <br> • Align with rigorous objectives <br> • Require nuanced critical thinking <br> • Require content knowledge <br> • Require students to make contextual and transferable meaning |
| **Precision of Language and Idea** <br> • Nuanced, precise, and specific language used by teachers and students to express nuance and sophistication of idea <br> • Content-specific vocabulary used by teacher and student <br> • Students are introduced to new terms and concepts with the correct vocabulary, rather than cute names or modified language <br> • Students are accountable for precision of language orally and in writing | **Student Accountability and Feedback** <br> • Students do the vast majority of the work, with teachers "shining the light" <br> • Teacher pushes students to correct or deepen their thinking <br> • Teacher provides students with specific, accurate, academic feedback that follows the "Excellence/Steps/Support/Belief" frame <br> • Teacher crafts exemplar answers and uses them to guide in-class feedback | **Academic Discourse** <br> • Students are engaged in discourse with peers and adults, asking high level, open-ended questions, probing for deeper understanding, and articulating their understanding <br> • Discourse requires evidence, reasoning, and analysis/synthesis/evaluation <br> • Students build on each other's thinking <br> • Teacher "shines the light" to push students to dig deeper for most salient ideas |

*Source:* Lynch Leadership Academy, Professional Learning Innovations. Adapted with permission.

After ILT members watched videos of instruction to agree on "look-fors" and best practices, they used the observation tool to support observation and feedback cycles, instructional coaching, peer observations, and schoolwide instructional rounds. This helped teachers understand the relationship between planning at the unit and task level and teaching with a justice lens. It also provided common language and aligned expectations for planning, teaching, observing, and reflecting on instructional practice.

Many schools and school districts use observation tools for coaching and supervision, and some are included in the negotiated contract between the district and the local teachers' association. We are not suggesting that you throw out your existing observation tool. However, it is important that observation tools emphasize centering justice in the curriculum, using justice-based pedagogy, and supporting students to advance justice in the tasks they are engaging in and the thinking they are doing. As schools identify justice frameworks to support their commitment to critical consciousness development, they should consider adapting their existing observation tools to ensure alignment.

## Working with Mandated Curriculum

This chapter's guidance on identifying and integrating a justice framework into curriculum planning may feel more applicable to educators and school leaders who have some flexibility and autonomy to develop their own curriculum. But what about educators teaching in schools and districts that feature more prescribed curriculum? Are these educators less able to develop and deliver justice-centered curriculum?

Fortunately, the answer is no. Yes, having a prescribed curriculum makes the process of integrating a justice framework more complicated, but from our experiences as educators, teacher educators, and education researchers, we can attest that teachers working in schools and districts with more prescribed curriculum can absolutely develop and deliver justice-centered curriculum, primarily by *critically consuming* their prescribed curriculum.

Critically consuming curriculum involves evaluating which texts, learning, and essential questions from an existing curriculum unit will contribute to the goal of engaging students in learning about topics of injustice, power, and resistance to injustice, and which will need to be supplemented with (or subbed out for) different texts, learning activities, and lessons. Excellent teachers—whether they work in a school with mandated curriculum or not—are critical consumers of curriculum. This is because there is no such thing as a curriculum that perfectly reflects every student's identity, strengths, and needs; moreover, every packaged curriculum features more material than a teacher can teach. Accordingly, teachers make decisions about what materials to use exactly as they are presented, what to supplement with, what to enhance, what to adapt, what to prioritize, and so on.

This doesn't mean throwing out mandated curriculum. Sometimes critical consumers keep prescribed texts but adapt discussion prompts or use questioning to help students be critical of the texts themselves. Sometimes critical consumers augment a lesson by providing students with time and space to make connections to events in their community or the wider world. Critical consumers are also careful to balance adjustments with the rigor demanded by standards.

## *Critically Consuming Curriculum in Action*

As educators at a public elementary school, Roberts teachers are expected to use curriculum units developed or purchased by their district. However, these expectations do not prevent them from using their chosen justice framework to adapt and revise units to meet their goals for nurturing students' skills, intellect, identity, critical consciousness, and joy. As we have noted, a district-mandated English/language arts unit for 5th graders focuses on baseball player and civil rights activist Jackie Robinson. The 5th grade team appreciates numerous aspects of this unit and engages in many of its lesson and learning activities every year. But they also use their justice framework as an analytic lens and make additions and adaptations to the unit.

For example, one of the prescribed lessons introduces students to the concept of bias by having them compare accounts of Jackie Robinson's first game in the major leagues from different newspapers. The 5th grade teachers decided that this task, while useful in helping students explore bias, misses the opportunity to make connections between historical accounts and present-day similarities—an important concept in critical consciousness development. They decided to extend the lesson by asking students to apply the same skills to two different newspaper accounts of the protests in Minneapolis, Minnesota, following the 2020 murder of George Floyd by a police officer.

> Making connections between historical accounts and present-day similarities is an important concept in critical consciousness development.

*Teacher:* Take a look at this image. It's a protest from right after George Floyd was murdered. What do you see in this image?

*Student 1:* I see a bunch of people protesting. Someone has a sign that says, "End police brutality."

*Student 2:* They're protesting for their rights because this can happen another time. Just because someone is a different color doesn't mean you have to kill him.

*Student 3:* I see people of different races protesting together.

The teacher shows students a photo from a different newspaper reporting on the same protest. The centerpiece of this photo is a burning building.

*Student 4:* I see trees and a building collapsing because of the fire.

*Student 5:* I see a building that caught on fire and a bunch of people protesting.

The teacher hands out the first two paragraphs of the newspaper articles that accompanied the photographs in the two newspapers. She asks students to seek out words in the articles that emphasize either the peacefulness or the violence of the protest.

*Teacher:* Editors choose pictures and words on purpose.

This extension of the original lesson reinforced for students that media bias is not limited to Robinson's time and that it is important to stay vigilant about whose perspective is present and whose is missing in the news we read. By adding on to the original district-mandated material, teachers enhanced their students' ability to recognize and analyze injustice in their everyday lives.

Teachers working in schools and districts adhering to a prescribed curriculum can follow the lead of the teachers at Roberts Elementary School. You don't have to ignore or reject your responsibility to teach the curriculum selected by the district, but you can seek out opportunities to adjust the curriculum to support the growth and critical consciousness development of your students.

## Critical Consciousness + Math

Teachers can often envision bringing justice content into English, history, science, and even art curriculum, but we are frequently asked how to do so in math class. Two of Aaliyah's former students, math teachers Jason Hirschhorn and Kathryn Norcross Pegram, developed a unit for 6th graders that simultaneously nurtures students' math knowledge, math skills, *and* critical consciousness. The mathematical goals for the unit are for students to be able to calculate the area of irregular figures using composition and decomposition and estimate areas of curved, irregular figures using coordinate grids. A critical consciousness goal for this unit is for students to learn how choices made around visual representation can perpetuate and/or shape bias.

One of the learning activities in this unit asks students to calculate the areas of local parks in different neighborhoods. Students then overlay the demographic data of each neighborhood onto their calculations and discuss their observations. Why are parks in some neighborhoods consistently larger than the parks in other neighborhoods? What might be the underlying root causes of this observable difference in space?

Building on students' developing mathematical and critical reflection skills, a subsequent lesson entails calculating and comparing the areas of North America and Africa in square miles. Through these calculations, students learn that Africa is two million square miles larger than North America, though this difference in size is not immediately apparent from many world maps found in U.S. K–12 schools. The lesson poses specific discussion questions for students about *why* world maps are often skewed in this way and *how* this skewed visual representation influences our beliefs about and understanding of the two continents. Building on students' critical analysis skills, the unit ends by asking students to decide on a critical action plan that can challenge or change the inaccurate visual representations of the world that we consume in the United States. Students are also asked to leverage their mathematical calculations as evidence in their critical action plan.

Units like this make it clear that mathematics curriculum *can* be constructed to nurture students' critical consciousness in concert with their mathematical knowledge and skills. It's also easy to see how this math unit could be aligned with social studies or humanities content.

A second way to bridge teaching mathematics skills with meeting critical consciousness goals is to approach curriculum design with an interdisciplinary lens. A grade-level team integrating justice content into a humanities unit can incorporate authentic opportunities for students to use their mathematics skills to help them recognize, analyze, and challenge injustice in the topics they are learning about. At Roberts Elementary School, for example, the 3rd grade team engages students in a mandated language arts unit on equitable access to books. As part of this unit, students learn about the importance of children reading books that offer "mirrors" to reflect their own identities and "windows" into identities they do not hold (Bishop, 1990a, 1990b).

The 3rd grade team adapted the unit by adding a final project in which each student develops a list of books that resonate with them personally as powerful "mirror books" and/or "window books" to share with their local librarian. Students critically analyze their "book bundles" through both writing assignments and math tasks. For example, the students tally the racial identities of the authors and characters included in their book bundles and graph representational data points. They then seek out demographic information about the community served by their local library, compare the demographics of the characters in their book bundles to those of the surrounding community, and consider making adjustments to their book bundles to ensure that children taking up their book recommendations have access to numerous window books *and* mirror books. Students also identify the price of each of the books included in their bundle, tabulate the cost of acquiring multiple bundles to distribute to Little Free Libraries across the city, and work together to raise funds to carry out this plan. In these ways, Roberts 3rd grade teachers have found authentic and meaningful ways to combine a language arts unit with grade-level mathematics tasks to simultaneously nurture students' academic skills and critical consciousness.

Although we understand why math (and science) teachers often feel a little more challenged to center justice in their curriculum, we have found that the challenge is typically more related to imagination and training than feasibility. Centering justice in curriculum can be a process of integrating topics of justice and resistance to injustice into the existing curriculum, and it can also involve positioning content areas as lenses for analyzing and challenging injustice. Consider, for example, guiding questions such as the following:

- When and how has math been used to challenge injustice?
- In what ways has mathematical reasoning perpetuated harm and bias in our community?
- Is science value-free and neutral?

These questions can serve as powerful frameworks for students to explore a range of mathematical and scientific concepts. We encourage school leaders and teacher leaders to consider how topical professional learning communities (described in Chapter 5) could serve as a transformative learning space for STEM teachers to work together to debunk the myth that critical consciousness work is harder to implement in these domains and to begin their journey as critical consumers of curriculum together.

## This Work Is Not One-and-Done

As educators, we know that young people need more than one opportunity to digest new content. Adult learners are no different. The arc of adult professional development we've outlined cannot be a one-time event. Both new and returning teachers need repeated exposure to each aspect of the arc and multiple ways to engage and practice. Schools can and should provide ongoing support in the following ways:

- **New teacher orientation.** During new teacher orientation, teachers should have the opportunity to learn more about your school's commitment to nurturing students' critical consciousness, be exposed to the school-adopted justice framework, and see (live or recorded) model lessons that integrate the framework.
- **Intentional mentorship and coaching.** Throughout the year, both new and returning educators should have multiple opportunities to receive coaching, feedback, and guidance on their use of the justice framework in their classrooms. Mentors can be classroom teachers who excel

in this work. Coaching can take place in grade-level meetings, one-on-one meetings, or small groups and can be conducted by school-based staff or justice partners (see Chapter 2).
- **Differentiated professional development.** Just like students, teachers have unique learning needs and may need to be separated for more contextualized learning. A one-size-fits-all approach for professional development does not model best practices for teaching and learning. Differentiated professional learning can include instructional rounds for teachers, professional learning communities, or external professional development opportunities focused on topics related to critical consciousness.

# A Powerful Lever

The first seeds of this book were planted after the three of us visited Roberts Elementary School several years ago and observed how teachers at every grade level had deliberately and thoughtfully infused opportunities to nurture students' critical consciousness into their curriculum.

We vividly remember a 3rd grade lesson in which students were reading aloud a biography of historian Carter G. Woodson. The teacher paused the story after a scene where an older White professor at Harvard scoffed at Woodson's goals of studying and writing about Black history. The professor told Woodson that African Americans had no history. The Roberts teacher asked her students why Woodson's life's work of making sure that Black people's history *did* get told was important, and we listened as 3rd graders articulated numerous ways in which opportunities to learn about and understand Black history represent an important way of challenging a society that has long denied Black people's humanity.

When we started asking teachers questions about these lessons that were simultaneously building students' content knowledge, academic skills, identity, and critical consciousness, we heard about the school's adoption of a justice framework that explicitly included these areas. Teachers also told us about the arc of professional learning that had helped them incorporate the concepts into their planning and teaching. Because the three of us have seen relatively few schools use curriculum as a foundation for justice work, and even fewer schools establish structures and practices to do this work schoolwide, we got excited about the possibility of sharing these approaches with a wider audience of educators.

But of course, educators should not have to do this work alone. In the next chapter, we turn to the role that community partners can play in the development and delivery of justice-centered curriculum.

##  Questions for Reflection

1. To what extent do you think your school community currently centers justice in its curriculum?
2. What structures and practices are already in place at your school to support educators in centering justice in curriculum and instruction?
3. What structures and practices in your school can be re-envisioned to support educators in centering justice in curriculum?

4. What structures and practices do you need to create in your school to support educators in developing and delivering justice-centered curriculum and instruction?
5. What obstacles do you anticipate in leaning into this principle? How can you mitigate these obstacles to move the work forward?

## Additional Resources

California Department of Education. (2022). *Ethnic studies model curriculum.* https://www.cde.ca.gov/ci/cr/cf/documents/ethnicstudiescurriculum.pdf

Conway, B. M., IV, Id-Deen, L., Raygoza, M. C., Ruiz, A., Staley, J. W., & Thanheiser, E. (2022). *Middle school mathematics lessons to explore, understand, and respond to social injustice.* Corwin.

Cooperative Children's Book Center, School of Education, University of Wisconsin-Madison. (n.d.). *Booklists.* https://ccbc.education.wisc.edu/booklists/

Duncan-Andrade, J. M. R., & Morrell, E. (2008). *The art of critical pedagogy: Possibilities for moving from theory to practice in urban schools.* Peter Lang.

Gutstein, E., & Peterson, B. (Eds.). (2013). *Rethinking mathematics: Teaching social justice by the numbers.* Rethinking Schools.

Hammond, Z. (2015). *Culturally responsive teaching and the brain: Promoting authentic engagement and rigor among culturally and linguistically diverse students.* Corwin.

Kokka, K. (n.d.). *Social justice mathematics resources for K–12 educators.* MathSocialIssues.com. https://mathsocialissues.com/sjm-resources

Ladson-Billings, G. (1995). Toward a theory of culturally relevant pedagogy. *American Educational Research Journal, 32*(3), 465–491. https://doi.org/10.3102/00028312032003

Muhammad, G. (2020). *Cultivating genius: An equity framework for culturally and historically responsive literacy.* Scholastic.

Paris, D., & Alim, H. S. (2017). *Culturally sustaining pedagogies: Teaching and learning for justice in a changing world.* Teachers College Press.

Picower, B. (2012). Using their words: Six elements of social justice curriculum design for the elementary classroom. *International Journal of Multicultural Education, 14*(1). https://doi.org/10.18251/ijme.v14i1.484

Sleeter, C. (2017). *Designing lessons and lesson sequences with a focus on ethnic studies or culturally responsive curriculum* [Working paper]. TeachingWorks. https://www.teachingworks.org/images/files/TeachingWorks_Sleeter.pdf

# Foster Powerful Partnerships

# 2

# Collaborate with Justice Partners

Systems of oppression are complex, and the reality is that few of us in education attended K–12 schools, colleges, or even graduate schools that adequately prepared us to engage with this topic, much less to develop and execute curriculum that helps our students to do so. Education scholars have described this failure of teacher preparation programs as a "significant problem" in education (Maloney et al., 2023, p. 1).

In the same way that we needed explicit teaching to learn disciplinary content (e.g., biology, algebra, U.S. history) and then coaching from mentor teachers, supervisors, and other educators on how to teach the content, we need explicit teaching about injustice and resistance to injustice *and* coaching on how to teach it to our students.

In Chapter 1, we explained the necessity of identifying a justice framework and launching an arc of professional learning to incorporate justice work into curriculum planning. Chapter 5 describes ways to make space for adult professional development and for teachers to become more comfortable talking and learning about systemic injustice. Although these steps are a strong foundation, they are not sufficient. School leaders and teacher leaders need to continue to foster their staff's learning, growth, and development. Like every learner, young or old, teachers need repeated, deliberate practice with concepts and skills to develop mastery. They need opportunities to strengthen their pedagogical practice of weaving issues of injustice and concepts of power into their lessons.

Fortunately, schools and educators need not tackle such curricular change alone. Local and national organizations and nonprofits focused on critical consciousness development can often support teachers and schools in this work. We use the term *justice partner* to refer to an external partner whose core expertise is in equity and justice and whose work and training can inform, deepen, and challenge educators' teaching about these topics. Justice partners can be found in nonprofit organizations, local universities, individual community leaders, local community collectives, and so on. Your own school district may even have an office or personnel that can proactively partner with you.

Justice partners can support teachers' efforts to nurture students' critical consciousness in multiple ways:

- Observe teachers in action and offer feedback about classroom practice.
- Conduct an audit of a school's practices or curate data to illuminate oppressive practices embedded in a school's operations.
- Help identify curriculum materials to use for justice-driven teaching and learning, or model culturally and linguistically affirming pedagogical practices that engage a wider range of students.

- Sit in on planning meetings and offer suggestions about how to seamlessly embed nurturing students' critical consciousness into units and daily lessons.
- Offer feedback to school leaders on professional development plans designed to build teachers' content knowledge on topics related to class, ability, language, race, gender, and so on.
- Serve as guest teachers for lessons on justice and resistance to injustice and invite other individuals to do the same.
- Support school leaders in crafting a multiyear strategic plan for building and sustaining a school that supports students to recognize, analyze, and challenge injustice.

These collaborations between teachers and a justice partner are no different than those between teachers and a literacy coach or inclusion specialist. Teachers possess deep and valuable expertise about their students, content, and school context that can be supported and enhanced by connecting with others' expertise. Moreover, collaborating with a justice partner models the importance and necessity of partnership in challenging injustice. Partnership and collaboration play pivotal roles in social change by amplifying collective wisdom, resources, innovation, and strategic thinking.

> Partnership and collaboration play pivotal roles in social change by amplifying collective wisdom, resources, innovation, and strategies.

In this chapter, we describe how deep, sustained, and proactive collaboration with a justice partner can contribute to a schoolwide effort to nurture students' critical consciousness. We will offer examples of such collaboration between Roberts Elementary School and its justice partner, Little Uprisings, as well as offer guidance on what to look for when selecting your school's own justice partner.

We recognize that access to an external justice partner may not be possible for every school because of limited resources, geographic location, or other prohibitive factors. Even if these factors affect you, we urge you to read on to learn about what justice partners can bring to schools and how those benefits might be obtainable through internal school practices or professional development. Consider also how some justice partner roles might be assumed by students' families, caretakers, or even students themselves. Finally, we will close the chapter with key principles for teaching with a focus on critical consciousness developed collaboratively by Little Uprisings and Roberts Elementary School.

## Justice Partner Work at Roberts Elementary School

Little Uprisings is a collaborative education service focused on liberation work with children. Co-founder Tanya Nixon-Silberg describes herself as a Black mother, educator, artist, and radical dreamer. Her sister, co-founder Octavia Nixon, previously worked as a special education teacher, English teacher, instructional coach, and curriculum designer. They founded Little Uprisings out of a deep belief that children can understand and grapple with topics such as injustice and systemic racism, and that teachers who use their classrooms and curriculum to do this work help communities heal.[1]

---

[1] At their request, Tanya Nixon-Silberg, Octavia Nixon, and Little Uprisings are not referred to by pseudonym.

As we noted, collaboration between a justice partner and a school can take different forms. At Roberts Elementary School, Nixon or Nixon-Silberg join grade-level teams on their quarterly planning days for a one-hour consultation in which they work with teachers to develop, adapt, or update units with opportunities to nurture students' critical consciousness and incorporate the school's culturally and historically responsive literacy framework. Nixon-Silberg explained to a new 1st grade teacher at the start of one of these sessions: "What we do is, we work together to look at the curriculum and think about how we can expand it to include the justice framework. How do we include kids' identities? How do we take the curriculum as clay and mold it to what we want to see?" These consultations complement the work teachers are doing with their instructional coach to make sure their planning and teaching are addressing all of the school's areas of intent: identity, intellect, joy, skills, and critical consciousness.

## Multiple Ways of Partnering

Deep knowledge about how a justice partner can help strengthen a school's capacity to teach about and challenge injustice can help school leaders and teacher leaders choose a partner of their own. At Roberts, Little Uprisings plays four central roles for teachers:

- Quelling fear and anxiety
- Providing thought partnership on curriculum
- Sharing resources
- Offering honest feedback

As you read about the different roles a justice partner can play, think about which are most needed in your own school community to make progress in centering critical consciousness development schoolwide. For those at the very beginning of this work, the most essential roles may be quelling teachers' anxiety and reservations about taking on this work and offering honest feedback to teachers and school leaders about their efforts. School communities that are further along in their efforts may be more interested in help connecting with community resources. Keep your school's needs in mind as you consider potential justice partners in your own community.

## Help Quell Fear and Anxiety

One of the most prevalent concerns for educators about centering topics of injustice in their curriculum is that they will say the wrong thing, not know how to respond to a student's question, or unintentionally explain something in a way that harms their students or upsets their families. None of these concerns is outrageous or surprising. We live in a society that has socialized us since we were children to believe that topics such as race, class, racism, and systemic injustice are taboo. Moreover, relatively few of us have engaged in deep learning about these topics in our own education, and even fewer of us have received substantive coaching or mentoring about teaching these topics. We are also living in a historic moment when many conservative pundits and policymakers have sought to heighten educators' anxiety about engaging their students in these and other "controversial" topics.

A justice partner cannot change our socialization or sociopolitical context to fully eradicate these concerns, but coaching and consultation can help assuage them. Roberts teacher Maysa Karam explained: "Especially when we first started this work, Little Uprisings was so helpful in sharing [that] if you don't have the answer, that is OK. You don't have to have all the answers. None of us have all the answers. Just be honest with students." Teachers in schools who are just beginning to take steps to center critical consciousness development in their curriculum and teaching benefit from this reassurance from experts. In fact, it can be empowering for students when teachers position themselves as learners about these important topics.

An example of this messaging comes from a 1st grade team planning meeting at Roberts. As the team worked with Nixon-Silberg to adapt a district-mandated curriculum unit on identifying resources in one's own community, they were excited about emphasizing the importance of fair trade and teaching students how some of the merchandise that shows up in local grocery or shoe stores contributes to the exploitation of workers around the world. When one teacher expressed concern about her own limited knowledge of this topic, Nixon-Silberg reassured her, "If you do that [research] in community *with* the kids, you don't have to know the whole story. And if you do the research with the kids, you can work together to figure out what fair trade means and really share your knowledge with each other. And that's what I think a good school should be doing." Reflecting on messages like this one, teacher Maysa Karam added: "They helped us understand what we could say if we don't know . . . that we're all learning and unlearning and we're doing that together, and I think presenting that to students is also really affirming to them—like we're all learning constantly."

Justice partners can also help address teachers' fear and anxiety by helping them get past deeply ingrained beliefs that they're not supposed to be talking with their students about topics like racism, sexism, and ableism. And in fact, researchers have found that children are harmed by the failure of adults in their lives to help them take pride in their own identities and to acknowledge and discuss injustices based on race, gender, class, and other identity markers that are already evident to them (Elenbaas et al., 2020; Tatum, 2017). For this reason, when teachers question whether they should be talking about challenging topics such as racism with their students, Nixon-Silberg likes to respond, "Well, what's your goal? If your goal is liberation and seeing the genius of every Black and Brown person in front of you, then absolutely, yes, you should be doing this!"

Instructional coach Andrea Reynolds, who supervises the K–2 classrooms at Roberts Elementary School, credited her school's justice partner with "really affirming for us [that] a huge part of this work in early childhood is just seeing things, naming them out loud for kids, and teaching them that it's not taboo or inappropriate [to discuss them], or that it's not normal or not fair. Kids at 5 and 6 [years old] have these huge convictions about what's fair and not fair, but we kind of don't let them say it, or we just read on and read past it." Another Roberts teacher, Alexandra Martinez, explained that their school's justice partner encouraged her and her colleagues not to be afraid to name injustices in discussions with their 3rd graders. She added, "That has been one of the most influential things in our teaching, because we stopped holding onto this fear of 'We can't say this; we shouldn't say that.' And we just started talking to the kids in a very matter-of-fact way."

### *Quelling Fear and Anxiety in Action*

Let's look more closely at what it can sound like for a justice partner to quell teachers' fear and anxiety about centering justice in their curriculum and teaching. Consider a consultation between the Roberts preschool team and Little Uprisings about an upcoming curriculum unit on wind and water. One of Nixon-Silberg's suggestions for the unit was to let students try on the identity of scientist:

> *Nixon-Silberg:* The idea around identity is not just that I can identify the wind and rain and stuff, but I can tell you the cycle. I can be a scientist. Maybe that's the identity you want to build. Kids are natural scientists.
>
> *Teacher 1:* There is even [the story] *Ada Twist, Scientist*, which talks about what scientists do.
>
> *Teacher 2:* We could talk about meteorologists and how they track the weather.
>
> *Teacher 3:* We can have a scientist Skype with us.
>
> *Nixon-Silberg:* When you show scientists, make sure they're not all White with white coats on. There was a hashtag recently trying to bust that stereotype.
>
> *Teacher 1:* Do you think we should name that with the kids?
>
> *Nixon-Silberg:* Yes, always take advantage of an opportunity to bust a stereotype.

Stereotypes—such as the idea that scientists are White men in lab coats—can limit children's beliefs about what roles and positions they can aspire to one day (Savitz-Romer & Bouffard, 2012). Justice partners can encourage teachers to seek out opportunities in their curriculum to name these stereotypes, dispel them, and offer counterexamples to empower children to consider all the different avenues available to them. Doing so requires teachers to dive into these discussions with their students in direct, developmentally appropriate ways. Justice partners can play a powerful role in helping teachers feel ready, willing, and able to take this work on.

# Bring Additional Thought Partnership

Thought partnership is another key role that a justice partner can play. They can supplement teachers' expertise in their content areas, students, and school context with their own content knowledge about injustice and resistance to injustice as well as their pedagogical content knowledge about how best to engage youth in exploring and reflecting on these topics.

## *Thought Partnership in Action*

What does such thought partnership look like? One consultation at Roberts between the kindergarten team and Little Uprisings focused on a curricular unit on construction. The kindergarten teachers expressed dismay that all 10 of the children's books required by the district-mandated unit were written by White authors. The consultant and team went through each book together and identified themes or ideas raised in each book and paired them with texts written by a more diverse set of authors. This helped teachers follow the district-mandated curriculum but supplement it with more inclusive and community-responsive texts.

An additional suggestion from Little Uprisings was to expand the definition of construction beyond the erection of buildings (as the mandated curriculum defined it) and add to the unit the book *Martin's Big Words* (Rappaport, 2007) so that the kindergartners could learn about and discuss Martin Luther King's role in the *construction* of the civil rights movement. This suggestion offered the kindergarten team an entry point for content that nurtured children's critical consciousness about the fight for civil rights. More broadly, it helped the team learn how to create their own opportunities for integrating the school's justice framework into a mandated curriculum featuring a racially homogeneous set of core texts. Instructional coach Reynolds remarked, "Each time we [consult with our partner], like, our [justice] muscles get bigger. That whole conversation about those 10 books on construction is going to stick with us through every planning session."

During this same planning meeting, Reynolds also sought Little Uprisings's perspective on another part of the construction unit, the classic story *The Three Little Pigs*, asking, "Has this got some bias? Something feels not right about this book, but I don't know how to name it or say it out loud." In response, Nixon-Silberg pushed the teachers to think about one of the story's central messages: that houses made out of sticks and straw are weak, and that people who make those kinds of houses are lazy or unintelligent. She suggested pairing *The Three Little Pigs* with a nonfiction children's text about houses around the world built out of sticks and straw because that's what is wise and prudent in their environment.

Based on this conversation, the kindergarten team adjusted their lesson plan for *The Three Little Pigs* to make time for students to discuss and consider why people build houses in different ways while still reinforcing the target standards and skills of the unit. In other words, the lesson expanded to engage students in questioning one of the central presumptions of the classic story—that a house made of brick is better than a house made of sticks or straw. This presented an age-appropriate opportunity to nurture in kindergartners the skills for challenging ethnocentrism, the conviction that the values, traditions, and ways of being of one's own group are better than others, which is a common foundation for bias, discrimination, and racism.

This glimpse into the kindergarten team's planning meeting offers several valuable insights into how a justice partner can help educators strengthen their capacity to nurture students' critical consciousness. Partners can recommend texts that bring in a greater diversity of voices and perspectives than the anchor texts in a mandated curriculum and assist with integrating them into the curriculum unit in meaningful ways (Tatum, 2014). They can also help teachers identify and reflect on assumptions and beliefs underlying the anchor texts and design learning activities that raise and question those assumptions. Importantly, such collaboration develops educators' planning and pedagogical muscles so that they can do justice-focused work on their own. This type of thought partnership and scaffolding can be invaluable for school communities in the beginning stages of their work to center justice in their curriculum and teaching.

## Share Community-Responsive Resources

It can be hard for busy teachers to find the time to seek out new materials. Beyond helping educators identify curricular opportunities to nurture students' critical consciousness, justice partners may be able to recommend developmentally appropriate resources to engage students in learning and reflection about topics relevant to their community. Such curricular and resource recommendations can be vital to teachers' efforts to integrate justice work into the curriculum. Importantly, classroom teachers should not simply hand off the responsibility for discovering community-responsive resources to someone else but should collaborate with justice partners to identify and seek out these resources.

### *Community-Responsive Resources in Action*

At Roberts, Little Uprisings consulted with the 2nd grade team on the immigration unit described in Chapter 1. During the consultation, Nixon-Silberg encouraged teachers to infuse joy (one of the tenets of their justice framework) into the curriculum unit by emphasizing ways immigrants make important contributions to the countries and communities that they join. She then offered: "I have a friend who is from Cape Verde, and she is the first immigrant elected to the City Council. I just texted her to see if she would come to the class and talk about her experiences, and she said yes. So having kids possibly interview her collectively might be a way to think about being an immigrant in this city."

Not all justice partners will draw upon their own networks to connect educators and school leaders directly to in-person resources, but many community-embedded partners can and do facilitate these types of connections. It is important for school leaders and teacher leaders to consider whether such connection making and resource gathering are key elements of what they hope for from a justice partner, and if so, make sure to raise the question with potential partners about their ability to contribute in these ways.

# Give Honest Feedback

Developing a commitment to nurturing students' critical consciousness and living up to that commitment daily is challenging work. Given the continuously evolving, complex, intertwined nature of injustice, every one of us has learning to do, and even the most knowledgeable, self-aware, and committed educators will make mistakes from time to time in their efforts to develop and carry out justice-centered curriculum. Although many of us were socialized to think of mistakes as failures, mistake making is a part of this work for *every single educator*.

Providing feedback about such mistakes is a key role for a justice partner. Because they bring substantial expertise to the work of centering justice in the curriculum and are outsiders to the school community, justice partners are well-positioned to communicate with educators about errors or problems with practices or curriculum (and perhaps suggest ways to address them). They don't have to worry about repercussions from overstepping boundaries with colleagues or question whether it's even their role to offer that type of counsel.

> **Even the most knowledgeable, self-aware, and committed educators will make mistakes in their efforts to develop and carry out justice-centered curriculum.**

### *Honest Feedback in Action*

Let's look at an example of honest feedback and correction using an example from Little Uprisings and Roberts. One year, Little Uprisings expressed concerns about the 2nd grade immigration unit's culminating task, which asked each student to interview an immigrant to the United States and write their biography. According to 2nd grade teacher Tina Pollock, "Little Uprisings [said], 'It feels like you're taking from these people that you're interviewing without giving back. You're using them almost as a token immigrant. So how do you change that to where it's like a partnership rather than a taking from?'" Another 2nd grade teacher, Yvonne Dean, added: "The feedback we got last year was about not 'othering' other people [by implying] 'You immigrated here; how can we use you?'"

The 2nd grade team took the feedback to heart and revised the assignment for the next school year. They wanted students to conduct interviews, but their new plan called for partnering with a high school English as a second language teacher who was excited about his teenage students having an opportunity to practice their English language communication skills. Teacher Lena Thomas described the adaptation as mutually beneficial, with younger students learning from the stories of older students, and older students sharing their life stories and working on their English. The team's justice partner applauded their efforts to revise the portions of the original assignment that felt "extractive" as well as their explicit efforts to integrate interview questions about the beauty and assets of the teens' home countries, rather than just the strife and challenges they may have encountered there or in the United States. A year later, Little Uprisings offered additional critical feedback, asking the team whether they could go even further in framing the students' interviews as recognizing and honoring the immigrant community as a vital city component.

This example illustrates the value of a school community establishing a long-term, sustained collaboration with a justice partner. Justice partners and educators can work together over multiple years to adapt curriculum units to support the development of students' critical consciousness. After implementing recommended adaptations, teachers can report how they played out in the classroom, obtain feedback from the justice partner, and continue iterating and improving the curriculum.

Another benefit of long-term collaboration is the development of a trusting relationship where educators can share their curriculum ideas and suggestions without feeling like they are trying to ace a "justice test," and the justice partner can offer honest and direct feedback without fearing the educators will take it personally. When these types of collaborations have the time and space to develop, there can be genuine dialogue about the curriculum all participants are invested in improving. With these deeper relationships, the willingness of educators and justice partners to be wrong sometimes allows powerful work (and learning) to happen. Accordingly, we recommend that school leaders and teacher leaders seeking collaboration with a justice partner evaluate whether their school community has the resources to support the collaboration long-term and whether a potential partner is interested and can commit to such a relationship.

Honest feedback from a justice partner that a particular project, lesson, or text is not in the best interests of students or conducive to nurturing justice work can also lead educators to move away from problematic learning materials entirely. For example, the 3rd grade team at Roberts taught a unit on J. M. Barrie's 1904 play *Peter Pan* for years. Perhaps not surprising for a literary work that is over a century old, the play contains numerous examples of sexism and outdated gender roles—issues called out by the district's curriculum. However, the curriculum said little about the play's problematic representation of Indigenous people.

Over a period of time, the 3rd grade team made a number of different adaptations to the curriculum to try to counteract and disrupt these troubling representations and to provide counter-narratives of past and present Indigenous communities. They also developed a sequence of writing lessons focused on argument writing in which they engaged students in learning about the use of Native Americans as mascots for athletic teams, and why these representations are disrespectful. To strengthen the curricular connection, the team delivered these lessons concurrently with the *Peter Pan* unit during another instructional block.

Little Uprisings applauded the 3rd grade team's efforts to name and counteract the problematic stereotypes in *Peter Pan*, but during a planning session, Nixon-Silberg observed that there comes a point at which, as educators, we have to ask whether this book is one that we want students to read at all. She offered the following series of questions to help the team consider how to proceed with texts or lessons whose limitations might outweigh their benefits:

1. Do you want your students to read and absorb this damaging narrative about a marginalized group of people?
2. Is there another way to share some of the key themes and standards raised in this text?
3. Is reading this text nurturing students' critical consciousness of problematic actions or stereotypes, or is it just reinforcing those practices or stereotypes?

The answers to these questions might lead a teacher or team of teachers to jettison a project, lesson, or text altogether rather than to continue to try to adapt and revise it. Ultimately, that's what the Roberts team did, replacing the *Peter Pan* unit with "Water Around the World," another unit approved by their district. They also worked with their justice partner to critically assess the new curriculum unit for opportunities to nurture students' critical consciousness.

## Messages on Repeat

We hope our glimpse into how the teams at Roberts Elementary School work with their justice partner, Little Uprisings, has offered useful insights into the different roles that a justice partner can play in a school's efforts to nurture students' critical consciousness. We want to close by sharing four distinct but interrelated messages communicated by Little Uprisings coaches over and over again in the course of the partnership:

1. Celebrate genius and joy.
2. Emphasize resistance.
3. Unveil counternarratives.
4. Connect past injustice to the present.

Let's look at how these key ideas provide invaluable guidance for teacher leaders and school leaders.

## Message #1: Celebrate Genius and Joy

The first message draws directly from Gholdy Muhammad's (2023) work. Muhammad emphasizes that teaching about the injustices facing people from oppressed and marginalized groups must always be paired with celebrating the genius and joy of people in these groups. Little Uprisings coaches pushed Roberts teachers not to assume that the district's mandated curriculum included this type of celebratory or humanizing work and not to wait for a "heritage month" to honor certain groups' legacies of joy and genius. Instead, they spurred Roberts teachers to seize every opportunity to incorporate texts and ideas featuring strengths-based narratives so that students both within and outside these identity groups hear them continuously, not just during a specified month. Nixon-Silberg explained, "The first idea that people have when you think about critical consciousness is, 'Oh my gosh, we have to talk about the 1619 Project; we have to talk about the ravages of slavery.' And that is important, but what we don't talk about in our curriculum and in our schools is that when we do talk about Blackness, it's always [about] a kid suffering." Accordingly, Roberts teacher Emma Ward recounted that one of her primary takeaways from collaborating with Little Uprisings has been "making sure that we have counternarratives right. We're not just telling stories of struggle, we're also including stories of joy and resistance."

### Celebrating Genius and Joy in Action

This stance was evident in Little Uprisings's consultation with the 2nd grade team about the immigration unit. At the very outset of their meeting, Nixon-Silberg shared, "What I don't want to force upon 2nd graders is this narrative about the plight of the immigrant [to the United States]. It's the story that keeps getting generated, and I want to find a way not to do that." Nixon-Silberg and the team identified texts and supplemental resources centering the genius and contributions of immigrants to the country and to their own city, specifically. Second grade teacher Yvonne Dean reflected, "If the kids take one thing from this unit, I want them to know that immigrants have enriched our community and that their story has power." Adapting the immigration unit was not just about using different texts but also about thinking strategically about making genius and joy a conduit for content knowledge and skill building.

### Message #2: Emphasize Resistance

As teachers educate their students about injustice, they must also teach their students about the movements, people, and groups that have consistently resisted and challenged these injustices over time. Offering students both historical and contemporary examples of resistance to systems, structures, institutions, and interpersonal forms of injustice has many essential outcomes. First, young people are reminded each time they learn about resistance that systems of oppression were constructed and created and, therefore, have the potential to be unseated. This framing contributes to students feeling motivated and empowered by their learning about injustice rather than solely discouraged or demoralized by the extent to which unjust forces such as racism, sexism, and ableism shape our lives and communities (Watts et al., 2011). Second, examples of resistance to injustice can provide models for young people of the many different forms and methods available for taking action and challenging injustice. That is, students learn firsthand that there isn't just one way to push back or reimagine. This awareness can enhance students' sense of agency and broaden their perspective on the possibilities and visions for their own roles in advancing justice.

### *Emphasizing Resistance in Action*

Consider, for example, the 5th grade team's planning meeting with Little Uprisings for their humanities unit on Jackie Robinson. Fifth grade teacher Rachel Bryant asked Little Uprisings co-founder Nixon-Silberg for her advice about a culminating assignment for the unit.

> *Bryant:* We've had them write an essay about which factors helped Jackie be successful. I'd love to add into that. Giving kids a bank of ways you can resist and fight injustice. I'd love the focus to be on—this is a toolkit we can use for today.
>
> *Nixon-Silberg:* What you're thinking about is "when we fight, we win." Kids need to see the examples of how that happened.

Then Nixon-Silberg followed up with a suggestion, not from history, but from the Roberts community itself. For many years,

Roberts Elementary School had enrolled students from grades preK through 5. However, the previous year a group of parents and students had petitioned the district to add a 6th grade to the school just like it had done for a number of other elementary schools in the district. When the district initially turned down their request, these parents and students formed a 6th grade taskforce and began advocating in a number of different ways for the addition of a 6th grade to their school. Nixon-Silberg observed to the 5th grade team: "It'd be good for the 5th graders to know that the district said no, the [current] 6th graders said we're not accepting that, and they did a letter-writing campaign, they met with folks and said you're not doing the things you said you'd do. There was an architect at the school who made a blueprint of what this thing could look like. When the district said, 'You can't knock down that wall,' a parent said, 'I'm 99 percent sure that's not a load-bearing wall.' So it's important to think about what knowledge is in the community and how to use that to make change." Ultimately, these efforts by students and their families persuaded the district to take a more timely and innovative approach to solving the space constraints that were a barrier to adding a 6th grade to the school.

Nixon-Silberg went on to suggest some specific texts and a game that might help 5th graders learn and think more about the power that individuals possess. She added. "Grounding this idea of power—people power, our own personal power—is important." She reminded Roberts teachers over and over again that lessons introducing students to injustice should be rooted, not in struggle or deficit-thinking, but, rather, here's the genius and joy of these groups we are learning about, and here's how we use our power to make change.

> If we don't offer young people examples of change or models of efforts toward change, how will they believe or know that social change is possible?

As a reminder, the end goal of critical consciousness development is social change. If we don't offer young people examples of this change or models of efforts toward change, how will they believe or know that social change is possible? It is our job to make sure that young people's awareness of injustice doesn't outpace their learning about how to resist and challenge injustice (Huguley et al., 2019).

## Message #3: Unveil Counternarratives

A third key idea that Little Uprisings emphasizes is the importance of shining the light for students on counternarratives. A counternarrative refers to stories, ideas, and understandings that challenge taken-for-granted stories, ideas, or beliefs that have been established by members of a dominant group and are repeated throughout society (Perry et al., 2003).

A common dominant narrative in the United States is that Christopher Columbus discovered America. A counternarrative and the more accurate re-telling of history about Christopher Columbus might focus on his invasion, destruction, and enslavement of Native Americans. Another dominant narrative is that seamstress Rosa Parks single-handedly catalyzed the Montgomery Bus Boycott protesting segregation in Montgomery, Alabama, in 1955 when she refused to leave her seat at the front of a segregated city bus because she was tired after a long day of work. This dominant narrative obscures the accurate counternarrative that Rosa Parks had been a longtime activist and leader within her local chapter of the National Association for the Advancement of Colored People and that her act of civil disobedience came about as a result of significant planning and collaboration with fellow activists. The ensuing boycott was not one that sprang up spontaneously, but was a result of African American activists working explicitly and affirmatively to push for social change. Counternarratives play a vital role in the development of critical consciousness as they unravel or disrupt false understandings propagated by dominant narratives. With access to counternarratives, young people can more accurately see the world around them, including the diverse groups, communities, and identities often erased by dominant narratives.

## *Unveiling Counternarratives in Action*

When Little Uprisings coaches joined grade-level teams in their planning meetings, they liked to ask Roberts teachers three questions about the curriculum units they were working together on: *Whose voices are we hearing? Whose voices are being omitted? What are the opportunities for counternarratives?*

In a planning meeting with the 4th grade team, for example, the 4th grade teachers sought Nixon-Silberg's feedback on a social studies unit focused on the women's suffrage movement in the United States and the 1920 constitutional amendment that gave women the right to vote. After looking over the 4th grade team's planning documents, Nixon-Silberg observed that a substantive portion of the unit focused on the efforts of suffragette Susan B. Anthony but gave little time or attention to the contributions of Black women during this time such as Sojourner Truth and Mary Church Terrell. Nixon-Silberg offered to lead a workshop with the 4th graders focused on the contributions to the suffragette movement of these and other Black women.

On the day of this workshop, Nixon-Silberg captivated the 4th graders with several stories about the contributions of Black women suffragettes to the activism for women's rights. At the conclusion of this workshop, Nixon-Silberg asked the students why no one in the classroom had heard of these women before today. "Because they were Black?" one student volunteered, and several other students nodded in agreement. Nixon-Silberg looked back at them thoughtfully. "It wasn't because *they* were Black," she said slowly, "but because the people who got to tell this history were White." Nixon-Silberg explained later that she wanted the 4th graders to be able to make this shift in their thinking "because we keep looking at the victims and not looking at the oppressors. I always think of the system as like [magician] Harry Houdini, right? Like smoke and mirrors. Let's hide this, but let's highlight that."

Nixon-Silberg also encouraged the 4th grade team not to let the dominant narrative about suffragettes such as Elizabeth Cady Stanton and Susan B. Anthony obscure that these same suffragettes explicitly distanced themselves from the movement seeking the enfranchisement of Black Americans and were wary about allying with Black women suffragettes. Worth noting is that this work didn't entail throwing out the texts about the contributions of Elizabeth Cady Stanton and Susan B. Anthony but, rather, pairing these texts with others that discuss these suffragettes' limitations. Cumulatively, this collection of texts not only offered 4th graders a more complete view of history but also empowered them to call out biases and shortcomings in the texts they were reading. When students get opportunities to develop this type of critical analytic lens, they begin to notice on their own what voices and stories are centered in all of the texts they are reading, and what voices and stories are being omitted. This deepening recognition is an important step in students' critical consciousness development and can pave the way for students' commitment to not replicating these patterns in their own lives and work.

## Message #4: Connect Past Injustice to the Present

Finally, Little Uprisings encouraged teachers to connect their study of past injustices to the present day (Emdin, 2016). Research shows that it is common for young people, particularly in elementary school and on to middle school, to think that injustices such as sexism and racism are historical realities no longer present in our everyday lives. Our own research has found that even high schoolers raised during the height of Black Lives Matter struggled to link contemporary police brutality to historical choices and patterns that pre-dated this movement.

Connecting past injustices to the present emphasizes for students that oppressive forces such as racism and sexism are not issues that have been solved and squared away, but obstacles that continue to exist, even if in a different form, that they and their peers need to understand, resist, and challenge. Making these connections between past and present injustices also helps young people to understand oppressive forces as a *system*. Nixon-Silberg liked to encourage teachers and students to think about racism and other unjust forces like a bicycle. Something moves the pedals in one part of the bicycle, which moves a chain, which starts the wheels turning in a whole other part of the bicycle, and now the whole bicycle is moving down the street. Just like that bicycle, past injustices move across time and impact the present day.

## Connecting Past Injustice to the Present in Action

For this reason, Little Uprisings encouraged the 4th grade team at Roberts Elementary School to connect students' learning about the suffragette movement to the efforts of activist and politician Stacy Abrams in the 2020s to challenge voter suppression efforts in Georgia targeted primarily at Black voters. The 5th grade team also took up Little Uprisings' guidance when they connected their lesson on how different news outlets in 1947 portrayed Jackie Robinson's first game in the major leagues to the ways in which different newspapers in 2020 reported on the protests following the murder of George Floyd. And as we describe in upcoming chapters, other grade-level teams helped their students to make connections between past injustices and present-day issues such as hair-based racial discrimination and the banning of children's books featuring queer and nonbinary characters and families. Teacher Maysa Karam described these connections to the present day that she and her colleagues built into their curriculum units as "a lot of things that I would never have thought to do, honestly," without the urging and guidance of their justice partner.

These four principles—celebrate genius and joy, emphasize resistance, unveil counternarratives, and connect past injustice to the present—are well documented as essential to critical consciousness work (e.g., Bell, 2010; Muhammad, 2023). While justice partners may use different language or phrases, schools are likely to encounter ideas such as these as well as other research-based principles for this work from any research-driven justice partner they work with.

## The Power of Sustained Partnership

In this chapter, we have sought to describe the multiple roles that a justice partner can play in supporting a school community invested in nurturing students' critical consciousness in its curriculum and teaching schoolwide. The type of proactive, deep, and sustained collaboration we describe in this chapter between a justice partner and school community is quite different than the partnerships we have found in many K–12 schools that consist of an expert consultant being hired to lead a single workshop—or even a handful of workshops—on topics related to equity, diversity, justice, and inclusion. School leaders arranging these workshops often do so with the best of intentions, and the expert consultants may be deeply knowledgeable about the topics on which they are speaking. Yet, while these "one-stop-shop" workshops can be useful for learning, they are simply too brief—and the interactions with a school's staff too superficial—to have a *substantive* impact on participating teachers or their work in the classroom with students.

What we have sought to illustrate in this chapter is the powerful collaboration that can emerge between educators and a justice partner when there is time and space for these partners to develop genuine relationships with each other that are grounded in trust and a shared commitment to nurturing students' critical consciousness. When these types of genuine relationships develop, educators and justice partners can treat the curriculum units they are working on together as continual works-in-progress that they improve and strengthen over time. The educators and justice partners can grow comfortable bringing their genuine selves into this work, and their willingness to be vulnerable with each other and trust each other can facilitate powerful work together in a domain that most of us have been socialized to treat as taboo since we were school children ourselves.

Schools cannot act as silos in this work. Although educators play a crucial role in positioning young people to recognize, analyze, and challenge injustice, it's critical for school leaders to honor the power of meaningfully collaborating with others. By working closely with partners, schools can amplify their impact and enhance their capacity to foster meaningful change.

## Questions for Reflection

1. Which justice partner roles (e.g., anxiety queller, thought partner, resource gatherer, deliverer of honest feedback, etc.) seem most useful and relevant for your own school community?
2. What structures and practices in your school could you maintain, adjust, or establish to support the work of a justice partnership?
3. Which of the "messages on repeat" (e.g., celebrate genius and joy, unveil counternarratives, etc.) could your own school community benefit from emphasizing more strongly?
4. How might you identify a local organization, group, or individual that could be a good fit for your school community as a justice partner?

## Additional Resources

Aguilar, E. (2020). *Coaching for equity: Conversations that change practice.* Jossey Bass.

Bell, L. (2020). *Storytelling for social justice: Connecting narrative and the arts in antiracist teaching*. Routledge.

Little Uprisings. (n.d.). https://www.littleuprisings.org

Muhammad, G. (2023). *Unearthing joy: A guide to culturally and historically responsive teaching and learning*. Scholastic.

Perry, T., Steele, C., & Hilliard, A. (2003). *Young, gifted, and Black: Promoting high achievement among African American students*. Beacon Press.

# 3

# Elevate the Wisdom of Families and Caretakers

Partnership and collaboration are fundamental to social change. No one school's efforts will be the sole force that topples broader systems of oppression. Building a school community that nurtures students' critical consciousness requires powerful relationships not only with community partners (as described in Chapter 2) but also with students' families and caretakers. Educators must reach beyond school walls and create space for students' families and caretakers to participate in planning, learning, and teaching their children how to recognize, analyze, and challenge injustice, as well as evaluating and improving a school's efforts to carry out this work. Research confirms the power of deep engagement with students' families. Studies consistently show that high levels of school–family engagement are predictive of better learning and achievement for students. These findings hold for students of all ages, race/ethnicities, and economic backgrounds (Mapp et al., 2017). In other words, *all* children benefit from educators and schools engaging their families and caretakers in meaningful ways.

# The Importance of Families for Nurturing Students' Critical Consciousness

Family members and caretakers are students' first and most influential teachers (Branje, 2018). The conversations that students have with their families about current events, local political issues, and personal experiences with injustice can set the stage for their critical consciousness development and influence their capacity to recognize, analyze, and challenge injustice (Bañales et al., 2021). When schools and families work together, they reinforce and amplify student learning.

> The conversations that students have with their families often set the stage for their critical consciousness development.

Imagine, for example, an African American middle schooler learning about the discriminatory practice of redlining in social studies class who then initiates a conversation over dinner with her parents about experiences they have had with racial discrimination related to renting apartments or purchasing a home. Such a conversation is an opportunity for the student to make a personal connection to the content offered at school. Her parents' descriptions of their experiences with discriminatory housing policies amplify her understanding of the impact of redlining on communities and the historical choices that have led to that impact. Moreover, this reinforcement could be enhanced if schools proactively invite families to contribute their historical and sociopolitical knowledge, experience, community connections, and emotional support to students as they navigate this learning.

Family members can also bring a valuable intergenerational perspective to the work of nurturing students' critical consciousness. For instance, imagine a White 2nd grade boy who learned about resistance to sexism and gender discrimination when his class read *Send a Girl! The True Story of How Women Joined the FDNY* (Rinker, 2021), which describes Brenda Berkman's efforts in the early 1980s to change New York City's policies of excluding women from serving as firefighters. He then has a series of conversations with his great-grandmother about social change efforts she remembers from before that time that helped pave the way for Berkman's successful fight. These earlier efforts include the Equal Pay Act in 1963, which required equal pay for men and women, and Title IX in 1972, which outlawed gender discrimination in educational settings and programs. The conversations at home help the 2nd grader gain a deeper understanding of the multiple generations of activism that contributed to challenging sexism and other forms of injustice. Inviting the student's great-grandmother to share her perspective with the entire 2nd grade class could further reinforce learning for even more students.

Family members and caretakers may also have local and contextual wisdom to share about social and political issues facing a community, as well as information about active efforts to advance justice. Family members connected with the elementary school where Aaliyah taught in Atlanta had memories of the sit-ins in 1960 that led to Martin Luther King's arrest, and family members in the elementary school where Julia served as principal could recall Massachusetts becoming the first state to legalize same-sex marriage in the early 2000s. Exposing students to the experiences and perspectives of firsthand witnesses to history can deepen their learning about topics ranging from environmental racism to Islamophobia to nonviolent resistance. Sharing local and contextualized knowledge and connections to the present-day community makes topics of injustice and justice movements tangible and real, particularly for students whose day-to-day lived experiences may feel removed from a particular issue (Sullivan et al., 2021).

Partnering with family members should not be a haphazard process or an afterthought. Rather, a school community must design engagement structures that encourage family members and caretakers to share their knowledge, lived experiences, and wisdom with the broader school community. In addition, such contributions should be infused into the school's curriculum, instruction, and professional learning practices.

The following sections offer guidance and resources for intentionally designing structures that involve and uplift the expertise of families in critical consciousness development initiatives. This work begins by evaluating existing family engagement structures and modifying or establishing new structures to enhance family involvement in four areas:

1. Shaping justice-related curriculum and instruction
2. Building trust and buy-in for justice work across the school community
3. Deepening student learning at home
4. Evaluating and improving the school's justice efforts

Throughout the chapter, we will share examples, resources, and tools from our observations at Roberts Elementary School and, in particular, the school's actions to engage families and caretakers in student learning during Black Lives Matter at School Week of Action.

We recognize that some family members and caretakers will have decidedly different opinions from teachers and school leaders about whether schools should play a role in nurturing their children's critical consciousness, and that some might feel concern about schools addressing a range of topics. The chapter will wrap up with suggestions on how to address resistance from families.

## Evaluating the Family Engagement Structures in Your School

Powerful partnerships don't just happen. They require intentional, diverse, continuous structures to bloom and flourish (Abt Associates & Philadelphia Youth Network, 2016). A school's family engagement structures must be set up to welcome a diverse group of family members with different knowledge, lived experiences, and wisdom. This is sometimes easier said than done.

In our home state of Massachusetts, every public K–12 school must form a school site council comprising the school principal and an equal number of parents and educators elected by their respective constituencies. The council plays an important role in shaping the school's policies, programming, and culture by approving and monitoring school rules, budgets, hiring decisions, and so on. The membership of school site councils is supposed to be representative of the community's diversity, but this is often not the case.

> A school community must encourage family members and caretakers to share their knowledge, lived experiences, and wisdom.

Family members from systemically privileged groups—White parents, wealthier parents, English-speaking parents, and so on—sometimes act quickly to occupy spaces of power and influence, which positions them to advocate for their vision for the school community (Quinlan, 2016). At the same time, many family members from marginalized and minoritized groups may be leery about becoming more deeply involved with schools after experiencing years (or even generations) of inequitable treatment for themselves or their children in public school systems (Diamond & Gomez, 2004). Family members and caretakers with inflexible work hours and fewer childcare supports also experience greater barriers to participating in family engagement structures. These dynamics can contribute to a school's failure to include family members with the most personal and salient experiences of injustice. In other words, schools are often unsuccessful at soliciting participation from families who possess the knowledge, lived experiences, and wisdom most relevant to centering justice in the work and life of the school (Fenton et al., 2017).

## *Evaluating Family Engagement Structures in Action*

This dynamic was very much the case at Roberts during the first several years of Bethany Drake's principalship. Two-thirds of the student body were children of color, and half of the students came from low-income families, yet nearly all the parents on the school site council were White and middle class. Drake had significant concerns about this disproportionality in parent participation as a form of injustice itself. She recognized that the school could not powerfully nurture students' critical consciousness without the participation and leadership of a more diverse group of family members and caretakers.

In the face of inadequate family engagement practices, teacher leaders and school leaders are responsible for adapting existing structures or creating new ones. At Roberts, Principal Drake and her staff did both. First, they changed the way their school held elections for the school site council, encouraging a more diverse group of families to join. They also established a brand-new structure, a family engagement team, to solicit more racially and economically diverse participants in school leadership. Finally, when the school district mandated the formation of another engagement structure—the justice roundtable—Drake took the opportunity to elevate the voices of family members from minoritized groups in charting the school's path forward. We will explore the practices of the family engagement team and justice roundtable further as we proceed through the chapter.

## Shaping Justice-Related Curriculum and Instruction

Students' family members often hold valuable insights about how to teach their children about injustice and strategies for social action in ways that will resonate with students and support their developmental needs. For example, Scott has biracial Black-White children in the elementary grades, and he and his spouse now have almost a decade of experience talking with their children about race and racism in ways that account for their children's multiracial identities in a society with monoracial understandings of race. Their insights can benefit their children's teachers and may be applicable to the experiences of other students as well.

Principal Drake created the family engagement team to solicit these types of insights and guidance from diverse members of the community. Whereas the school was required to hold elections for seats on the school site council, Drake populated the family engagement team by reaching out to families from diverse racial, cultural, and linguistic backgrounds and inviting them to join the newly established leadership group. She also invited Roberts staff to join, particularly those who had expressed frustration with the ways that White and wealthier families perennially dominated the school site council. The family engagement team was co-chaired by a family member and a teacher and met one evening per month using an online platform. Their charge was to bring a wider range of family voices into the life of the school community by re-envisioning what family engagement looks like in a racially, culturally, and linguistically diverse school community.

The family engagement team helped shape student learning about injustice and resistance to injustice by offering feedback on learning opportunities such as Black Lives Matter at School Week of Action, a national week of intentional engagement with the experiences of Black children, families, and communities in schools. The observance is meant to invite self-reflection aimed at advancing the global liberation of Black people (visit https://www.blacklivesmatteratschool.com/woa.html for more information).

As you read through the following description of the Roberts family engagement team meeting on the Black Lives Matter at School Week of Action program, notice how family members and caretakers participated alongside school staff as equal partners in generating ideas. Are these kinds of rich collaborations happening in your own school community? If not, begin to brainstorm how you could introduce and facilitate similar approaches.

## *A Family Engagement Team Meeting in Action*

At a meeting in mid-January, family engagement team members learned of the school's upcoming participation in the Black

Lives Matter at School Week of Action. Principal Drake asked the committee for feedback and advice on how to involve families more deeply in the week's programming and activities. One teacher shared with family members that teachers planned to discuss the principles and demands of the Black Lives Matter at School movement with their classes and that the school had purchased copies of two texts, *Hair Love* (Cherry, 2019) and *Saving American Beach* (King, 2021), for teachers at every grade level to integrate into their curriculum during the week.

The teacher added that the activities coincided with the 5th grade's social studies unit on Jackie Robinson and asked the committee for advice about how to partner with families. One parent offered a suggestion: "Having links to books you can get at the public library would be one small thing. I'm sure the librarians at the public library would pull together a book list and set them aside for families. That's a good partnership to think about. I'd be happy to reach out to them."

Another parent followed up by adding, "There are also YouTube videos of parents or celebrities reading the books, so that would be even easier." She also proposed arranging an online meeting with the illustrator of *Saving American Beach*, Ekua Holmes.

A third parent recommended sharing team plans with families in advance for feedback and ideas, saying, "There are families at every grade that have been engaged in racial equity and justice work in varying places and spaces. They might be willing to take a look, offer suggestions, or even partner."

"Yes!" responded a teacher enthusiastically. "I love the idea of reaching out to grade-level families." Principal Drake agreed.

Throughout the meeting, school staff received valuable and specific suggestions about unexplored means of encouraging family involvement in the school's efforts to nurture students' critical consciousness during the Black Lives Matter at School Week of Action. Specifically, Principal Drake and the teachers on the family engagement team learned from participating family members about the importance of both making students' learning materials more accessible to families and caretakers and leveraging the racial justice expertise of members of the school community and the broader local community. Taking up these suggestions led to richer learning experiences for students that were amplified and reinforced at school and at home.

## Building Trust and Buy-In

Family members are sometimes a school community's best ambassadors to reach out to, communicate with, and solicit the involvement of other families (Murray et al., 2020). This may be especially true when it comes to a school's efforts to develop and deliver curriculum that nurtures students' critical consciousness. The more families are invested in supporting and reinforcing a school's vision for justice work, the greater the impact on students.

### *Roberts Family Engagement Team in Action*

At Roberts, the family members serving on the school's family engagement team played an essential role in promoting the school's efforts to nurture students' critical consciousness and widening its reach. For example, when Principal Drake shared a draft of a letter to families and caretakers describing the school's participation in the Week of Action and what it would mean for students, members of the family engagement team offered feedback ranging from linking to the texts students would read to providing more specific information about the curriculum plans at each grade level. The final letter was then cosigned by the principal and the family engagement team (see Figure 3.1).

The co-signed letter helped assuage concerns of some White families that the school's participation in the Week of Action was solely championed by an activist principal, as well as concerns of some Black families about the ability of a White principal to carry off such an event in a thoughtful and productive way. In short, family members in the school community needed to hear *from other family members* that the weeklong event would be worthy of their children's participation. The family engagement team members felt willing and able to offer their endorsement because they had a genuine hand in the design and construction of the event.

The family engagement team played a similarly critical role in building schoolwide family investment in other justice-based initiatives. For example, in Chapter 5, which focuses on building adult capacity, we describe how Roberts uses affinity spaces to deepen adults' content knowledge on topics of injustice. The family engagement team worked closely with Principal Drake to establish racial affinity spaces for both family members and teachers. Before launching that initiative, committee members led focus groups with other family members and caretakers to solicit a wide range of perspectives on the benefits and concerns related to such a program.

Just as teachers might be more comfortable confiding in their fellow teachers than in their school leaders, family members may prefer to share their thoughts with each other instead of their students' teachers. During the family-to-family focus group discussions, it became clear that some White families and families of color felt uneasy about the idea of a White affinity space, even one focused on promoting antiracism. Armed with this information, the family engagement team urged Principal

## FIGURE 3.1
## Letter Introducing Black Lives Matter at School Week of Action

Dear Roberts families,

As a school community committed to growth and development as a multicultural, antiracist institution, we strive to counter dominant, Eurocentric narratives by intentionally shining the light on the strength, power, and brilliance of Black and Brown lives all year long. Therefore, we are thrilled to share that we will participate in the national Black Lives Matter at School Week of Action.

During this week, we will introduce the guiding principles of the Black Lives Matter movement through morning announcements, classroom discussions, and the shared reading of two central texts: *Hair Love* by Matthew A. Cherry and *Saving American Beach* by Heidi Tyline King, illustrated by artist Ekua Holmes. Both texts touch on themes related to Black physical, emotional, environmental, and social health and wellness.

The specific goals of this Week of Action are to raise awareness about and support for Black students, families, and educators and the communities that serve them. Throughout the week, each class will focus on *at least* one of the 13 guiding principles of the Black Lives Matter movement:

- Restorative justice
- Empathy
- Loving engagement
- Diversity
- Globalism
- Queer affirming
- Trans affirming
- Collective value
- Intergenerational
- Black families
- Black villages
- Unapologetically Black
- Black women

The Black Lives Matter at School Week of Action will launch our school's observance of Black History Month, during which each grade-level team and specialist will explore Black health and wellness, with an interdisciplinary focus on spiritual, physical, emotional, intellectual, environmental, social, and career aspects. In keeping with our goal to normalize the study of Black history as American history and to reinforce the idea that shining the light on Black people, ideas, and contributions is year-round learning, these topics will complement and enhance our general curriculum content.

Throughout the month, students will engage in book studies, videos, art projects, interviews, virtual field trips, and more, culminating in a schoolwide showcase the first week of March. The showcase will provide a platform for

*(continued)*

## FIGURE 3.1
**Letter Introducing Black Lives Matter at School Week of Action**
*(continued)*

> students to share their learning with their peers, educating one another and publicly and collectively celebrating contributions to Black health and wellness. We will also share artifacts and pictures of student learning online and through emails. If you have an idea or resources to support this learning, please reach out to your child's teacher.
>
> We recognize that the Black Lives Matter movement is bigger than a day, a week, or even a month of study and celebration. As a community committed to antiracism, we are *all* responsible for identifying and uprooting our biases, elevating voices of color, and confronting and dismantling systems of oppression that exist within our nation, our city, and even our own school community. Who and what we teach—and of equal importance, who and what we omit—have a deep and lasting impact on our students and their identity development. For that reason, we will work together during this important week and month to intentionally center, affirm, and uplift the voices and contributions of the Black community, past and present, to whom we all owe so much.
>
> For more information on how you can support the Black Lives Matter movement, visit www.blacklivesmatteratschool.com.
>
> Thank you for all of your teamwork,
>
> Bethany Drake, Principal     Roberts Family Engagement Team

Drake to launch the affinity spaces for family members of color and teachers of color first and then follow up with affinity spaces for White family members and White teachers.

Equally important, every member of the family engagement team co-authored and cosigned a letter to the school community explaining why they were establishing both affinity spaces, how they would work, and how to get involved (this topic is addressed further in Chapter 5). This joint effort was crucial to the wider school community recognizing that a range of stakeholders agreed that the affinity spaces were an adult learning strategy worth trying. Simply put, far fewer family members would have considered participating in the racial affinity spaces—or been confident about the good intentions behind the plan—without the participation, support, and endorsement of the family members on the family engagement team.

## Deepening Student Learning at Home

Because family members and caretakers are often students' first and most important teachers, they can engage their children in conversations that reinforce and amplify students' learning about injustice and resisting injustice. Conversations that purposefully integrate knowledge gained at home with knowledge acquired at school are more likely to happen when schools have established systems for keeping families informed about their children's learning (Epstein et al., 1999). Some students come home from school and share every detail of their school day, but many do not—and the proportion of students in the latter category increases as students age (Pickhardt, 2014). To enlist the aid of family members in deepening students' understanding of justice-related topics (or any other subject), educators may need to get the ball rolling themselves.

As is the case at many schools, Principal Drake and her staff keep parents informed about what students are working on and learning about through a weekly electronic newsletter. The newsletter was instrumental in offering family members and caretakers multiple entry points into students' engagement with the Black Lives Matter at School Week of Action as well as explicit tools for extending their learning at home (see Figure 3.2).

FIGURE 3.2

## Black Lives Matter at School Week of Action Follow-Up Newsletter

Dear Roberts families,

This week, the Roberts community celebrated Black Lives Matter at School Week of Action. We introduced students to the guiding principles of the Black Lives Matter at School movement through morning announcements, classroom discussions, and the shared reading of two central texts: *Hair Love* and *Saving American Beach*.

Grade 4 students built on their reading by learning about the history and significance of Black hair, dating back to how different braids and hairstyles held great meaning in African kingdoms and other communities. They explored how this rich history is still celebrated today, such as when the hairstylist for the movie *Black Panther*, Camille Friend, used inspiration from African tribes for some characters' hairstyles.

Students examined examples of hair discrimination and appropriation and learned about the advocacy aimed at preventing it, such as the CROWN Act. They then listened to *Hair Love* with new appreciation for the character's experience, based on all they had learned.

The most meaningful piece of this learning was the opportunities it created for our students to be the teachers. One 4th grade student's mom has a braiding salon, and we got to see pictures of her amazing work as her daughter described the process of different braiding techniques.

Next week, students will read *Crown: An Ode to the Fresh Cut* by Derrick Barnes and hear from educator Eliana Diaz about her own experience with natural hair discrimination. Students will be responding to the following writing prompts:

1. Why is it important to embrace our own uniqueness and be proud of who we are?
2. How do you think the main character in *Crown* views the other people he sees in the barbershop?
3. What makes his experience at the barbershop so special?
4. When do you feel most proud of your appearance? How does it make you feel on the inside?

Consider inviting your child to join you in a conversation exploring this important topic.

Family members could draw on the information in this newsletter to talk with their children about a range of issues and topics supporting their children's developing critical consciousness. The preview of the writing prompt students would be asked to respond to seemed particularly tailor-made for home conversations. Although not every family member or caretaker will have the time or desire to engage in these learning opportunities every week, we know as caretakers ourselves the value of being able to chat with our kids during dinner or in the car or on the way home from errands. If our children went to Roberts, we could invite them to share with us: "Tell me about the CROWN Act" or "What did you learn this week about the history of braiding hair?" This is much more effective than the usual "What did you do at school today?"

## Evaluating and Improving Justice Work

Injustice and effective strategies for social action are dynamic and evolving topics. The language we use to describe social experiences, identities, and movements shifts over time, and teacher leaders and school leaders must continuously evaluate and improve how their school community engages students in recognizing, analyzing, and challenging injustice. Inviting family members and caretakers to assist with evaluation and improvement efforts can surface opportunities and possibilities that educators might miss on their own.

At Roberts, a second family engagement structure was established to assess and strengthen the school's justice work: the justice roundtable. Although the formation of the justice roundtable was mandated by the district, Principal Drake recognized it as a perfect space for educators and family members to work together to evaluate and improve efforts toward justice.

## *Evaluating and Improving Justice Work in Action*

When the COVID-19 pandemic upended K–12 education in the United States, the superintendent of the district in which Roberts Elementary is located instructed school leaders to form justice roundtables made up of parents, teachers, and community members. Throughout the pandemic, these groups met online monthly with the goal of helping their respective school leaders make decisions that centered the needs of students and families most impacted by historical and systemic injustices in our city and country. Specifically, justice roundtables were charged with ensuring that students of color, students with disabilities, students who are multilingual learners, and unhoused students received equitable access to learning experiences, resources, and support from their schools.

Some principals felt overwhelmed by this mandate, but Principal Drake recognized an opportunity. Because the roundtable positions were not elected and the meetings could be held in the evenings (i.e., outside of typical working hours), she could bring a more diverse set of parent voices and perspectives into the governance and leadership of the school. Accordingly, Drake invited parents and family members she believed could help her and her staff really hear and understand the needs of their school community to join the justice roundtable.

The parent members serving on Roberts Elementary's justice roundtable played a significant role in steering their school community through the pandemic. They knew the community and understood the contexts of many families' experiences in a much deeper way than Principal Drake and school staff did, and they were savvy about coming up with strategies to respond to circumstances in real time, such as figuring out what types of resources families needed to support their children's online learning, what to do about students who stopped showing up for online classes, and how to build rapport with families who weren't responding to communications from the school. Members of the justice roundtable offered actionable guidance and support to Roberts educators on all of these questions. Principal Drake also started asking the justice roundtable to review content she planned to share with students and their families during online community meetings. "That's too much information," members told her at times. "It's overwhelming." They let her know which information families most needed to know and urged her to focus her communications on those topics.

## Collecting "Street Data"

Insight, support, and strategizing from a diverse group of parents offer value that extends far beyond crisis management. As the school emerged from the worst of the pandemic, Principal Drake asked the justice roundtable to partner with her leadership team to evaluate the school's efforts to embed Muhammad's CHRL justice framework into students' learning experiences.

Members accepted this invitation but decided that such an evaluation required collecting what educators Shane Safir and Jamila Dugan (2021) call "street data"—qualitative, on-the-ground data collected from interviews and conversations that illuminate students', staff's, and family members' experiences. Such data can help educators and family members learn more about questions like whether students see themselves in the school's curriculum, whether students' learning feels joyful, and whether there are opportunities in school for students to challenge injustice in their communities.

Because Roberts had chosen CHRL as its guiding justice framework (see Chapter 1), the justice roundtable used several questions developed by Muhammad to investigate how students felt their school was doing at shaping their identity, skills, intellect, critical consciousness, and joy. They adapted these questions for age appropriateness for students in grades K–2 and 3–5.

Teachers read the following questions out loud to students in grades K–2; students responded by checking "yes," "no," or "not sure" on a paper survey:

1. Do you think it's important to learn about other people who don't look like you? (identity)
2. In school, do you learn about other countries and parts of the world? (intellect)
3. Would you like to learn about how to make the world a better place? (critical consciousness)
4. Do you experience joy/happiness in our school? (joy)

Students in the upper elementary grades responded to the same four questions as well as several additional questions via an anonymous online form:

5. Do you see yourself in what you learn at school? (identity)
6. Do you feel you can be yourself at school? (identity)
7. Do you feel safe and empowered at school? (critical consciousness)
8. Do you talk about race and justice in class? (critical consciousness)
9. Do you feel like you learn about the truth in history? (critical consciousness)
10. Does your learning connect to the real world? (intellect)
11. Do your teachers bring joy to your classroom? (joy)

Two educators on the justice roundtable compiled students' responses into charts that disaggregated students' responses by grade level and race/ethnicity.

### *Justice Roundtable Meeting in Action*

At their next meeting, the roundtable divided into small groups to examine the disaggregated data by grade level more closely. One group considered the grade 5 responses to questions related to critical consciousness and identity (see Figure 3.3).

Students' responses on two survey items raised questions for the members of the justice roundtable. They were pleased that the majority of students reported engaging in learning and discussions about race and justice in school but were surprised and concerned about the relatively high number of students (and, in particular, Black students) who responded negatively or with uncertainty about whether they could express their authentic identities at school. They also observed that some students who adults perceived to be Latine must have identified as White on the survey.

"Are they confused about race?" asked one family member.

"Could students be identifying as White as survival?" asked another.

A Latine community member on the justice roundtable suggested that some Latine students might be taught by their families to identify as White.

"Are we overlooking Latine issues?" asked a third parent. "I believe that teachers are being inclusive, but maybe students are not feeling that."

"Maybe students need to have more conversations about identity," offered another family member. "We might be making assumptions about how students would identify their race."

FIGURE 3.3

## Sample Street Data, 5th Grade

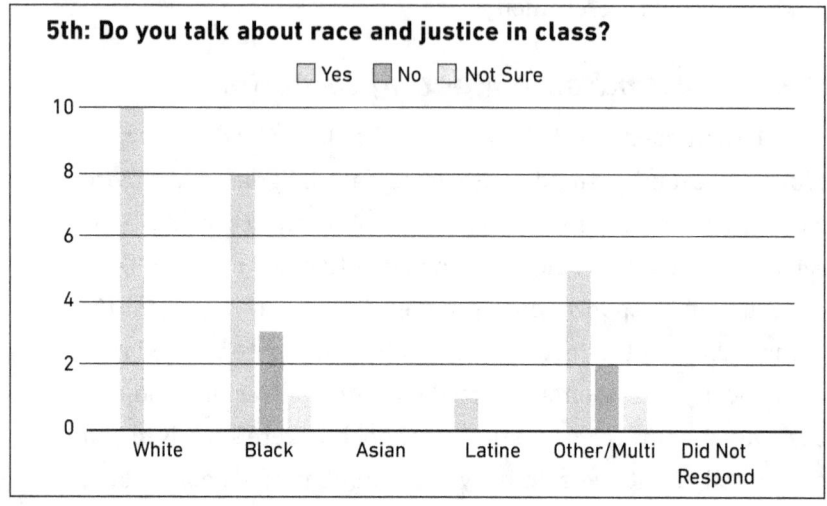

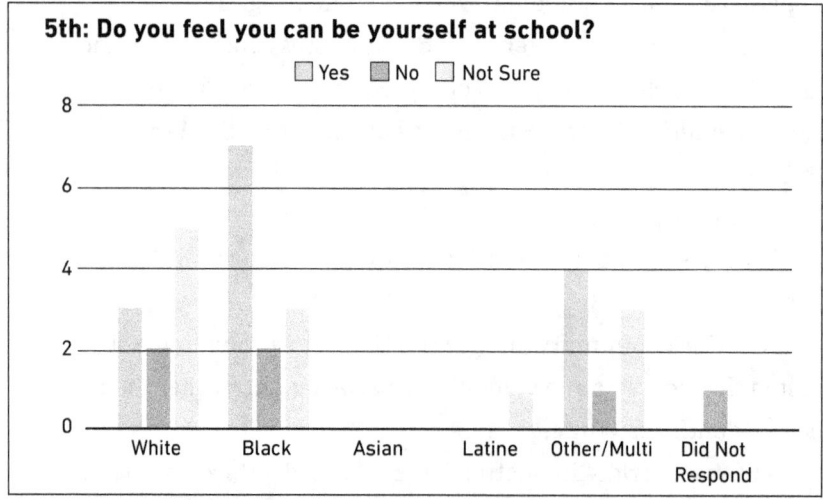

"I really want to know more about student belonging and how they are feeling in the classroom," added another family member.

Because there were so many questions about what the survey data did (and did not) reveal about the school's justice efforts, the roundtable asked the school's principal and leadership team to collect richer, more nuanced data from students. Accordingly, two staff members who were not classroom teachers held focus groups during several different lunch periods with a diverse, representative group of 3rd, 4th, and 5th grade students. The goal of these focus groups was to learn more about how students were thinking about their own development of skills, intellect, identity, critical consciousness, and joy, and the ways in which their school was (and was not) contributing to this development.

A month later, the justice roundtable reconvened to consider the new data. The focus group facilitators had documented students' responses to their questions in real time, then identified key trends and put together a slide presentation of these trends accompanied by representative comments from students (see Figure 3.4). For example, in response to a question about how students would like to make an impact on their school community, one trend that emerged was students' interest in improving their school's facilities, participating in more schoolwide community activities, and reducing the application of stereotypes and differential treatment based on a person's economic status. Another focus group question asked students about issues in society that need to change. Key trends in response to this question included the importance of challenging anti-Black racism and eliminating homelessness.

The members of the justice roundtable dove into this second round of street data and remarked on students' evident awareness of the shortcomings of their school's facilities as well as their awareness of racism as a societal problem that needs to be addressed. Members also wondered aloud about what racism and change mean for students on a deeper level, how the school can elevate and empower students to move forward with

FIGURE 3.4

## Sample Street Data from Focus Groups

---

### Q2: What are some issues in society that need to change (to be better)? (intellect)

**Trends:**
- Many students named the importance of challenging racism and affirming Black rights.
- Some students articulated a need for tougher gun laws.
- Some students named eliminating homelessness (which is compounded by COVID).

*Student 1 (Black, female, grade 5):* "In society, we need to change racism and thoughts of superiority."

*Student 2 (White, male, grade 5):* "We need to challenge abuse of power."

*Student 3 (White, female, grade 4):* "We need to support Black people's rights."

*Student 4 (Latine, female, grade 4):* "More listening to people who want to say something in this world. Also more homeless people getting a place to live. It's not helpful if they are living on the streets and can't find a place to live, eat, and with COVID too. I know there are shelters, but that's not helping."

---

### Q3: How would you like to make an impact on our community? (critical consciousness)

**Trends:**
- Most students identified their hopes for modifications to the physical limitations of our school facilities, specifically related to play.
- Many students articulated a hope to bring respect, kindness, and love to our community.
- Some students advocated for more "schoolwide" community building and engagement activities (e.g., field trips, field day).

*Student 1 (White, female, grade 5):* "Me and my friends thought that the bathroom passes here show girls with long hair and dresses. We don't like dresses. It promotes stereotypes."

*Student 2 (Black, female, grade 5):* "[I would show] respect, and if someone is not as rich as you or not as smart as you, you shouldn't treat them like they aren't a human being."

*Student 3 (White, male, grade 3):* "I would like to see an actual soccer goal, bigger schoolyard, and instead of concrete it could be like turf. And more balls—they get kicked over the fence."

*Student 4 (Black, male, grade 5):* "[I think it would help the community] to be quieter, limit banging [of steam radiators and when students are frustrated], enter the school as one [not have to wait], and have science experiments."

their suggestions for improving the community, and whether students may have felt shy about offering critiques or feedback to staff members.

The roundtable encouraged Principal Drake to work with the school climate team to come up with some concrete actions that would demonstrate to the students that their feedback and perspectives had been heard and responded to. We will explore the climate team's subsequent efforts to work with students to actualize their ideas in Chapter 6.

Powerful improvement efforts can emerge when educators and families collaborate to evaluate a school's efforts to center justice and nurture students' critical consciousness. Members of the justice roundtable at Roberts urged the school's leadership team to collect two rounds of data that prioritized students' perspectives and then offered insight on the meaning of emergent trends that educators may have lacked the lived experience or social position to recognize on their own. They also encouraged school leadership to turn the student feedback into concrete, justice-centered improvements.

## Responding to Resistance

Although many family members and caretakers will be enthusiastic partners in nurturing students' critical consciousness, some may express concern or outright resistance to their children learning to recognize, analyze, and challenge injustice. It's important to be prepared to respond to such resistance in ways that strengthen and support the school's justice work.

### Common Root Causes of Family Resistance

When family members protest their children learning about and challenging injustice, there are typically a few recurring themes underlying their concerns. Some, from both dominant and marginalized identity groups, believe their children will feel overwhelmed and discouraged by learning about the injustices shaping our lives, communities, and the wider world. In conversations with these family members, we find it helpful to emphasize that researchers have found that children as young as 3 and 4 already notice, think about, and talk with their peers about injustices related to race, class, gender, language status, (dis)ability status, and so on (Elenbaas et al., 2020; Miller et al., 2018; Rogers et al., 2021). The question, then, is not whether we want children to notice, think, and talk about injustice, because they already are. The question is whether we want trusted adults in their lives—family members, teachers, and other mentors—to be part of those conversations.

> The question is not whether we want children to notice, think, and talk about injustice, because they already are.

This is not to say that learning about injustice doesn't have the potential to be saddening, but it also has the potential to empower young people, particularly when the adults facilitating these conversations take care to focus on not only the injustices but also all the different ways people have resisted and challenged them (Seider & Graves, 2020). James Huguley and colleagues (2023), who research how Black parents prepare their children to encounter and resist racial bias, recommend that parents talking with their children about racism take care to pair their teaching of "analysis skills" with the teaching of "coping skills" so that children feel confident about their ability to respond to racism rather than overwhelmed or discouraged by its perniciousness (Huguley et al., 2023). This is good guidance for educators as well, and it resonates with advice offered by justice partner Little Uprisings in Chapter 2.

Another concern family members sometimes raise is that they do not want children who belong to dominant identity groups (e.g., White, cisgender, male, Christian, heterosexual) to feel guilty or ashamed of their identity (Hodge et al., 2022). In response, we have found it helpful to share that we also don't want children to feel guilty or ashamed about their identity. As Audre Lorde (1984) observes, "I have no creative use for guilt, yours or my own. Guilt is only another way of avoiding informed action" (p. 130). Rather than wallowing in guilt, we want our White students to see themselves as having an important and substantial role to play in challenging racism, our cisgender boys to see themselves as having an important and substantial role to play in challenging sexism, our heterosexual students to see themselves as having an important and substantial role to play in challenging heterosexism, and so on. In conversations with concerned families, we encourage you to similarly stress that your goal is for students from dominant identity groups to see themselves as following in the footsteps of the many people from these groups who have worked to challenge and disrupt injustice (Helms, 2019).

Another concern we sometimes hear is that school is simply not the right place for conversations and learning about injustice. In response, we like to share that goals for nurturing young people's civic development have been a part of public education in the United States from the very beginning. In fact, several of our country's founding fathers made the case for public education by arguing that a democracy requires citizens who have learned how to fulfill their civic responsibilities (McClellan,

1999). Two hundred years later, Benjamin Mays—the president of Morehouse College for nearly three decades—reiterated that the central purpose of education is "to strengthen the will to act in the interest of the common good" (1942, p. 408). Likewise, contemporary educator and author Ron Berger—who spent nearly three decades as an elementary teacher—observes, "Public schools were not founded in this country to prepare kids for tests. They were founded to prepare them to be good citizens. We're talking about being a good human being who stands up for what's right, who respects all human beings, who stands up against racism, against sexism, against what's wrong in the world. That has to be part of what education is" (Gonser, 2021, para. 19). Like Mays and Berger, we believe that K–12 schools have an important role to play in—and are following a long tradition of—preparing young people with the knowledge, skills, and motivation to build a better, more just world.

We certainly do not guarantee that these perspectives will win over every concerned or resistant family member. People are complex, hold unique beliefs and motivations, and of course, are rightfully protective of their children's well-being. There is no single response to resistance that will convince all the people, all the time, of the importance of centering justice in a school's curriculum and teaching. That said, we have found that these explanations—in concert with the proactive approaches we describe below—can go a long way toward assuaging family members' concerns.

## Anticipating and Planning for Pushback and Resistance

Realistically, we cannot expect to engage in work that aims to upend systems and structures that perpetuate privilege and power for so many in our country without some resistance. As a school leader or teacher leader, it is important to anticipate this resistance, including potential pushback. When you expect resistance, you can prepare for it.

As part of your initial planning to take on this work, we strongly suggest taking the time to anticipate where and from whom you might get pushback and making an action plan for how to engage with and address the sources. Remember that you are not alone in this endeavor; you should involve trusted families in this process as well. The following proactive strategies are ones that, in our experience, have been meaningful and effective in engaging families with concerns or outright resistance to teaching students how to recognize, analyze, and challenge injustice in schools.

**Provide clear and consistent communication about what will be taught and why.** One initial step in assuaging concerns is proactive and transparent communication from the school about its justice work. Consider how the examples from Roberts Elementary School in Figures 3.1 and 3.2 shared information with families before and after the event, offered a detailed description of the goals underlying the learning activities, and provided examples of student work. This type of messaging will not automatically assuage every family's concerns, but it does open an avenue for family members to engage with school leadership or their children's teachers about the learning taking place, rather than succumb to rumors, assumptions, or fears.

**Leverage support from other families.** Establishing an adult learning space where families can interact with one another about topics of injustice can offer space for families and caretakers to talk through questions, concerns, and resistance among themselves. Just as young people can often convince other young people to shift their viewpoints even when adults have been unsuccessful, family members may empathize and push back on other families in ways that school leaders and teachers may not be able to. Chapter 5 offers two structures for such cross-family learning.

**Ensure all teachers and staff can respond clearly and with conviction to questions about why the school is engaging in topics of injustice and how this work matters.** Often, families' first point of contact after learning about a school's focus on topics of injustice will be their child's teacher. A concerned or questioning family member who interacts with a teacher who does not express confidence in the school's decisions and justice efforts will likely not have their concerns quelled—and might have them intensified. As a part of ongoing professional development, teachers need direct time and space to practice responding to concerned parents. They should be able to clearly and confidently articulate why a school has chosen to embed topics of justice and strategies for challenging injustice in their curriculum and why this commitment is important for students' well-being, their academic development, and for social change. For each topic, Carolyn Stoughton and colleagues (2022) suggest ensuring teachers can answer: (1) "Why am I teaching this specific topic?"; (2) "Why am I using this specific material?"; and (3) "Why is this important for students to learn about?" Teachers also require clear protocols for handling situations where family resistance becomes particularly intense or intricate: Who can teachers turn to for support? What steps should they take if a parent threatens external action or requests to withdraw students from a class?

**Prepare staff for the emotional toll of managing ongoing resistance.** Constantly encountering resistance from families about teaching topics related to injustice can be emotionally taxing for school staff committed to nurturing students' critical consciousness. It can feel disheartening and demoralizing to face opposition to efforts aimed at promoting social awareness and empathy in students. Navigating these conflicts requires managing difficult conversations and potential confrontations, which can evoke feelings of stress and anxiety. Additionally, fear of backlash beyond the school walls (e.g., in the local community, media) may create a sense of vulnerability, which could be particularly heightened for staff who hold systemically marginalized identities. School leaders committed to this work who anticipate moderate to high family and caretaker resistance should proactively engage in conversations with staff about the possibility of emotional fatigue. Consider creating debrief spaces for educators to discuss family responses and engagement after rolling out new initiatives such as affinity groups or new curricula, having clear protocols for particularly challenging conversations, and facilitating feedback loops on how family engagement is going—including allocated time to celebrate positive responses.

**Create spaces to engage one-on-one or in small groups with families who might be most resistant.** One-on-one or small-group settings offer unique advantages for addressing resistance to students learning about topics of injustice. Individual conversations help establish a personal connection, demonstrate care and empathy despite disagreement, and often allow for deeper exploration of the root causes of pushback or resistance. Additionally, sometimes the opportunity to be heard can build trust with family members, even if their concerns aren't immediately resolved. School leaders and teacher leaders preparing to implement justice work should proactively schedule time to hold one-on-one meetings with families and caretakers as needed. These could be facilitated through family engagement nights, open classroom hours, or scheduled appointments. Anticipating and allocating time for personal engagement, rather than reacting hastily to questions, concerns, and resistance, can significantly reduce stress for teachers and school leaders.

**Accept that some families may not come on board.** Despite all these proactive steps and actions, you may still encounter family members who vehemently oppose specific lessons and learning on injustice and strategies for challenging injustice. These family members deserve the opportunity to express their apprehensions and to have these concerns heard and responded to thoughtfully by teacher leaders and school leaders. But responding respectfully does not mean abandoning or adjusting your commitment to nurturing students' critical consciousness.

## Families and Caretakers Are Essential Partners

We chose to conclude this chapter with a substantive discussion of responding to resistance because we know that this topic is very much on educators' minds. But we also believe this consideration of resistance should not distract from the overarching theme of this chapter—that family members and caretakers are essential partners in a school's efforts to nurture students' critical consciousness.

The National Parent Teacher Association—an organization dedicated to engaging family members in the work of their children's schools—reports that children are more successful in school when their parents are participants in their education (National PTA, n.d.). We believe the reverse is also true: When family members and caretakers are invited to play an active role in their children's education, schools do better by their students. In Chapter 4, we turn our attention to the ways educators, students, and their families can work together to engage in collective social action challenging injustice.

## Questions for Reflection

1. To what extent are your school's existing structures for family engagement drawing in a diverse group of family members and caretakers? Do you need to think differently or more flexibly about those structures?
2. What does this chapter get you thinking about in terms of honoring and integrating the wisdom, assets, and resources that families and caretakers hold?
3. What do you need to stop doing, and what do you need to start doing instead?

## Additional Resources

Black Lives Matter at School. (2024). *What we do and how we done it: A guide for BLM at school.* https://www.blacklivesmatteratschool.com/guideforblmas.html

Hodge, E. M., López, F. A., & Rosenberg, J. M. (2022). How to respond to community concerns about critical race theory. *Phi Delta Kappan, 104*(3), 48–53. https://doi.org/10.1177/00317217221136599

Mapp, K. L., Carver, I., & Lander, J. (2017). *Powerful partnerships: A teacher's guide to engaging families for student success.* Scholastic Professional.

Safir, S., & Dugan, J. (2021). *Street data: A next-generation model for equity, pedagogy, and school transformation.* Corwin.

Stoughton, C., Lynch, M. E., & Lee, M. (2022). Family engagement and conflict about teaching for social justice. *Phi Delta Kappan, 103*(7), 23–27. http://doi.org/10.1177/00317217221092230

# Engage Students in Social Action

# 4

# Empower Students to Take Action

The end goal of critical consciousness is social change. Change doesn't happen simply by thinking about it. As adults, we know this. Yet educators often provide their students with more opportunities to engage in critical reflection (notice and verbally analyze injustice) than critical action (work to challenge injustice) (Watts & Hipolito-Delgado, 2015). One possible reason is that the typical school structure makes it hard for educators to envision ways students can engage in meaningful social action as a part of an academic agenda.

But schools can support and nurture students' ability to challenge injustice in myriad ways. In the opening vignettes of the book, we described a 12th grader organizing a community dialogue on gentrification in her neighborhood and 3rd graders writing letters to their state representatives about legislation to prohibit hair-based racial discrimination. At other schools, we have seen students testifying in front of a state legislature subcommittee about supporting English learners in public schools and organizing efforts to prevent utility companies from shutting off people's heat during the winter. All these experiences not only engage students in social change efforts but also further academic learning goals.

This chapter focuses on the practices of challenging injustice and supporting critical action, with guidance and examples of how schools can and do nurture this component of students' critical consciousness. Our decision to dedicate a whole chapter to engaging students in social action reflects its importance. If we raise a generation of young people capable of recognizing and analyzing injustices yet leave them without the skills to change anything in response to their observations, we ultimately sustain the status quo. Paulo Freire referred to this as cultivating a generation of "armchair activists"—individuals who spend their time thinking and talking about injustices in their lives and communities but do nothing to address the issues. If we envision a world better than the one that currently exists, we cannot fall into this trap.

> If we raise a generation of young people capable of recognizing and analyzing injustices yet leave them without the skills to change anything in response to their observations, we ultimately sustain the status quo.

Before jumping in, we need to distinguish between service and social action called up by critical consciousness. The previous examples deliberately feature students engaging in social action challenging sexism, racism, and classism rather than service that helps individuals affected by unjust practices and policies. Service experiences—such as tutoring an English learner, serving meals in a soup kitchen, or cleaning up a community park—are valuable learning opportunities that many K–12 schools have incorporated into their programming, and they can have a powerful impact on communities and people's lives. But these efforts often treat the symptoms of injustice rather than the roots. Nurturing students' critical consciousness demands thinking of social action in a slightly different way—we must ask ourselves: What has led to the disparities and injustices that my students and I see? What are the underlying systems and structures that sustain them? And how do I give students the opportunity to challenge those systems and structures directly?

## Are Some Students Too Young?

In our work with educators, school leaders, family members, and policymakers, we have seen that some stakeholders find it difficult to comprehend how schools can engage younger children in social action challenging injustice. Factors that may contribute to this difficulty include adultism (societal belief that adults are more capable than younger people), fears about younger children's ability to comprehend complex social issues, and uncertainty about whether challenging injustice is developmentally appropriate.

Yet the reality is that our youngest students are both capable of and interested in pushing back against injustice. Anyone who has ever spent time with elementary-age children knows that they are deeply preoccupied with fairness. How many of us have brought a present for a younger sibling to an older sibling's party to ensure the parents are not met with cries of "That's not fair!" Or perhaps have had to redistribute snacks because one child pointed out that someone else got more? Early childhood is a time where questions of fairness dominate young people's interactions. Specific to social injustice, researchers have found that children as young as 8 are angered and offended by the idea of some children being excluded from opportunities based on their family's economic means (Dys et al., 2019), and they will propose laws and policies to try to remedy past and present inequalities (Elenbaas, 2019). Scholars have also found that when you offer young children explicit guidance on how to challenge injustice, they are inclined to do so. For example, one study found that when children as young as 5 receive explicit instruction on challenging sexist comments such as "Girls aren't good at sports" from their peers, they are more likely to stand up against sexism going forward (Lamb et al., 2009). For similar reasons, the American Psychological Association (2012) advocates a proactive approach to children learning about race and racism, noting that "a preventive approach (early socialization and learning) is more effective than a remedial one (unlearning deeply ingrained prejudice) in combating prejudice and discrimination" (p. 63).

Schools can and should create opportunities for elementary-age children to challenge injustice. For example, Judy Wu and her 1st graders at a Los Angeles elementary school turned their classroom into a museum of Chinese American history to challenge the erasure of Asian Americans from many U.S. history curricula and to raise their community's consciousness of this history (Agarwal-Rangnath, 2020). The museum consisted of several exhibits focused on reasons Chinese immigrants come to the United States, the contributions of Chinese immigrants to the building of the transcontinental railroad and westward expansion, and the passage of the Chinese Exclusion Act restricting further immigration from China. The students invited both family members and older students to visit their museum and learn about the experiences, contributions, and injustices faced by a group in the United States that have been actively excluded from many history courses and textbooks. And this is just one example of our youngest learners challenging injustice.

## Do Schools Have the Time?

We have worked with educators and school leaders who believe they don't have time to engage their students in social action in the context of so many competing academic demands. However, as we have emphasized throughout the book, critical consciousness development is not a competing demand. Nurturing students' critical consciousness is a key dimension of engaging students in powerful learning that can be aligned with state learning objectives across all subjects, including the arts. It is not a separate goal or a side goal that distracts from students' academic growth and development. Just as supporting students to recognize and analyze injustice can be tightly linked to existing academic objectives, so too can supporting students to challenge injustice.

The next sections describe and illustrate five key practices that can help educators and school leaders develop students' will and skill to challenge injustice and reinforce existing academic standards. The first two practices build students' knowledge of the many different ways individuals and communities can resist and disrupt injustice and strengthen students' sense of agency about engaging in social action. The next two practices help students develop the skills to effectively engage in action through authentic opportunities. Finally, the fifth practice builds students' skill in continually reflecting on the impact of their interventions and refining their critical action skills.

## Practice #1: Introduce Varied Activist Models

To build students' knowledge of different approaches to resisting and disrupting injustice, educators need to share examples of people and groups challenging injustice who represent a wide range of ages, ideologies, geographies, cultures, and identities. Students particularly benefit from opportunities to learn about activists whose identities—age, race/ethnicity, class, neighborhood—resonate with one or more of their own identities. Psychologists have found that people's ideas about roles they can take on in the world (e.g., self-efficacy) are greatly influenced by what they believe is possible for people like them—whoever the "them" is (Savitz-Romer & Bouffard, 2012). That means students need opportunities to read about, learn about, listen to, and talk with individuals engaging in social action with whom they share interests and identities. More colloquially, "you have to see it to be it."

## *Introducing Varied Activist Models in Action*

An example of Roberts students learning from and about activists like them occurred in the context of a 2nd grade district-mandated curriculum unit on immigration. As part of the unit, students read books that portrayed the experiences of immigrants to the United States from many different home countries and cultures. Throughout, teachers emphasized to students that some books are "window books" that help you look into someone else's life, and others are "mirror books" that remind you of yourself and help you to think about your own life (Bishop, 1990a, 1990b). In one lesson during this unit, 2nd grade teacher Lena Thomas showed her students a slide with the covers of books they had read such as *Islandborn* by Junot Díaz, *My Name Is Celia* by Monica Brown, and *The Name Jar* by Yangsook Choi. "How did reading these books make you feel?" Thomas asked her students.

One student raised her hand and said, "It made me feel proud, because not many books have main characters of color, so it's nice to see all these books and feel proud."

"I agree," Thomas replied. "We know these books aren't all published at the same rate, so it's great to have them here." She asked the whole class, "Do you think these books belong in our classroom library?" The response was a chorus of yeses.

Another student raised her hand: "Yes, because they're window and mirror books."

Thomas showed her students a new slide with a map on it featuring New York, Ohio, Pennsylvania, and New Jersey. One county in Pennsylvania was highlighted in yellow. "This is York County, Pennsylvania," Thomas told her students. "And last year York County decided that all of these books did not belong in classroom libraries."

"Why?" asked one student.

Thomas continued, "They put them on a banned book list. Most of the books featured characters of color like *Islandborn* or the Sofia Martinez series. A lot of the books featured LGBTQ+ characters, like *Pride*, which we'll read in June. And others featured students with disabilities." Thomas looked at her students. "Imagine you're a kid in York County, and all of a sudden your teacher gets an email that these books don't belong. What's your response?"

"Angry," said one student.

"I'd yell at the top of my lungs," said another.

"I would leave the school forever and not come back."

"I would be triggered."

Thomas explained further: "York County calls this their banned diversity book list, which says to me that they're not valuing people's diversity and experiences in their community, or the people who might benefit from these window books. Like you, a lot of people in York County were furious, and they decided to take some action, and this is what they did." Thomas clicked to a slide showing York County teenagers protesting the book ban. One young woman held a sign that read "Education is not indoctrination." A young man held a signing reading "Reverse the ban!"

Thomas explained that the photograph had come from a local newspaper covering the student protests, and she read a comment from one of the protesting teenagers: "'We saw books that would help with self-love, inclusion, and representation, so we really needed to get our message out so people would know the importance of these books.'"

"We should buy those books!" volunteered one student.

"It's funny that you said that," said Thomas. "When I looked at this book list, I was shocked and horrified, but I also said, 'They compiled a list of really amazing books,' and some of these books were books that I decided to buy."

This lesson introduced the 2nd graders to young people like themselves who believed that banning diverse books is wrong and who engaged in individual and collective social action to resist and challenge the school committee's book ban. They were amazed and excited that the individuals engaging in social action were students, and that several of the banned books were books they had recently read. This recognition that "people like me" can and do participate in activism to challenge injustice is essential to students developing the skill and will to engage in social action themselves.

As the lesson continued, the 2nd graders were thrilled to learn that the teenage activists' efforts ultimately contributed to the school committee voting to reverse its ban and that they then shared their experiences and perspectives with the U.S.

House of Representatives Subcommittee on Civil Rights and Civil Liberties (Figueroa, 2022) and spoke out against book bans in interviews with media outlets ranging from CNN to *Seventeen* magazine. Moreover, learning about these inspiring young activists deepened the 2nd graders' investment in the books they were reading during this immigration unit and helped them to see their own academic learning in this unit as a form of resistance against injustice in and of itself.

## Practice #2: Introduce Students to Varied Strategies for Social Action

Just as it's important to offer students varied models of *who* engages in activism, it's also important to help students understand that social action takes many different forms. When we hear terms like activism or social action, many of us—including our students—think of protests or demonstrations, but of course there are countless ways to challenge injustice, such as sharing and spreading information through teach-ins and learning spaces, building connections and collaboratives through organizing, writing letters, and speaking up in board meetings or other public spaces. Misunderstanding challenging injustice to be only a few specific actions can lead students to think participation opportunities are limited or that they, given their personalities, identities, age, or interests, aren't suited for it. Students need exposure to multiple forms of social action so they can identify ones that resonate with their own unique skills, strengths, personalities, and interests and so they can understand that there is

> It's important to help students understand that there are countless ways to challenge injustice.

always something a person can do to contribute to building a better, more just world.

## *Introducing Students to Varied Strategies for Social Action in Action*

During a 3rd grade unit focused on equitable access to books, Roberts students had an opportunity to speak over the internet with children's author Innosanto Nagara, author of books that introduce children to social action, including *A Is for Activist* and *Counting on Community*. Their conversation created an opportunity for students to reflect on various forms of social action and consider what types of activism work they might be most interested in.

When Nagara asked the students if they had questions for him, a boy raised his hand and said, "Hello, my name is Putnam. What do you do to stand against racism?"

Nagara answered, "There are so many different ways to stand up against racism and for a better society in general. I think I'm best at writing books and lifting up stories that have not been told about real people who help us understand the way that racism and oppression have affected people and in what ways people have been able to stand up against that, and how that is inspiring to people and kids in particular." He added, "And the main way I participate in my community is to be engaged. If there is a protest in the streets, I will go to that. Sometimes I'm part of organizing that. I think it's important to go to protest for the things I'm against, and I also think it's important to advocate for the policies and things that we want. So that's my answer."

A girl raised her hand to ask a question she had written down on her paper: "What advice do you have for students who want to be activists in their community?"

Nagara nodded again. "This is a question I get asked a lot, and it's an interesting one because I'm reluctant to stand here and tell you what to do. There are so many different ways that you can engage. So I always say that no one knows you as well as you do. You know yourself the best, and the question to ask yourself is where you have the most influence, where you're the most confident, what are the spaces that are yours to have an influence on. ... In terms of getting involved, that can be wherever that space is. For my son, it's the rock climbing space. He's 11 years old, and in that space, he has some influence. He may not be able to influence what the president of the United States does, but where he has the most influence is in the group of friends in the climbing community he is in, and within that group, there are lots of questions about who is in that community, why it looks the way it does, [and] who is allowed to be part of that community. And that is a place where he has some influence."

This conversation with Nagara underscored for the young learners the varied forms social action can take. He explicitly noted that he often participates in protests in his community but thinks that he is best suited to writing books, and that writing has become an important form of activism for him. Explanations like these reinforce for young people that social action is not just the purview of a few select heroes during momentous historical moments, but something that ordinary people do as part of their regular lives. Although online conversations with authors may not be everyday learning activities, teachers can absolutely look for opportunities to raise this point or to uncover instances of social action in the texts their students are reading and historical events and scientific discoveries they are studying.

Students can also be introduced to ways that people have used a given subject area or domain of expertise to challenge social injustice. For example, songs and music have often served as levers for consciousness raising, building solidarity, and challenging injustice. Likewise, statistics and mathematical processes have been important tools for raising awareness about systemic marginalization. There are countless ways to introduce students to authentic examples of the many ways that people have and can challenge injustice.

## Practice #3: Partner with Students in School-Based Social Action

Once students have learned about and explored different pathways for engaging in critical action, schools can offer young people opportunities to try out some of these pathways by addressing issues that shape their own lives. One authentic setting for this activist work is their own school community. As we described in the introduction, schools are often sites of injustice. Addressing these "in-house" injustices—which students are aware of and affected by—is a natural starting place for educators and students to engage in social action together. In partnering with students, it is important to encourage students to take the lead in identifying the issues that feel most salient to them and most worthy of their time and energy.

### *Partnering with Students in School-Based Activism in Action*

Several years ago, we did a research study that compared the critical consciousness development of teenagers attending six different high schools, from their first day of freshman year to their final day of high school (El-Amin et al., 2017; Seider & Graves, 2020). Students at one of the high schools—Espiritu

High School in New England—reported significantly higher confidence in their ability to challenge injustice than their peers at the other schools. We spent more than 50 days observing at the school to learn more about *why* students at this particular school were graduating with so much confidence in their ability to effect social change.

What we discovered was that Espiritu offered students many more opportunities to engage in social action *within the school community* than the other schools did. As just one example, an 11th grade social studies course involved students conducting youth participatory action research (YPAR), a form of critical, collective inquiry that engages young people in a process to identify problems affecting their lives, collect and explore data about these problems, and generate ideas for actions that can effect change (Brion-Meisels & Alter, 2018; Cammarota & Fine, 2008). Students can apply this iterative process of inquiry and action to problems and injustices in their own schools (Hipolito-Delgado & Zion, 2017).

In the Espiritu social studies course, students pored through their school's handbook to identify rules, regulations, and policies that they believed to be unfair, unjust, or not right and identified a policy they wanted to work to change as a class. One year, the class targeted the school's electronics policy that essentially prohibited the use of smartphones and tablets during the school day. The students felt like this policy was out of step with the positive role that technology can play in student learning, and they spent several weeks engaging in research to explore various perspectives more deeply.

Drawing on their research, they developed a new technology policy that included a "media pass," which enabled students to use technology during designated portions of the school day.

Ultimately, the students authored a presentation that knit together their research efforts and the proposed new policy, which they delivered to the faculty. After several rounds of negotiation, the Espiritu community agreed to test out the new policy for the rest of the school year and collaborated to establish metrics to evaluate its success. The students reacted to their successful social change efforts with genuine jubilation; they had worked hard to engage in both the academic research and social action necessary to bring it about—and as a consequence, they graduated from high school with tremendous confidence about their ability to effect change in any community they are a part of in the future.

What we learned from that research study is that, for young people, their school community is as real and relevant as any other community they are a part of, and that conditions inside schools often replicate the world outside schools. Similar injustices emerge along race, class, and gender lines, as well as on the basis of students' language status, (dis)ability status, sexual orientation, and so on. Consequently, opportunities for students to effect change in their school community strengthen their confidence in their ability and motivation to effect change in other communities. As psychologist Albert Bandura (2006) has observed, these types of learning experiences in school help "to instill a belief [in children] that political systems are also responsive and influenceable" (p. 30).

## Practice #4: Partner with Students in Local Activism

Students' local communities can offer additional meaningful sites for students to practice and strengthen their skills for challenging injustice. Young people are often highly motivated to participate in social action in their local community to address injustices that affect their friends, family members, and neighbors. Research has found that youth become more invested in engaging in social action that is relevant to the settings and people they interact, connect, and feel solidarity with in their everyday lives (Wray-Lake & Abrams, 2020). Importantly, even social action opportunities located outside the school building can be tied to learning goals, curriculum, and classroom assignments.

## *Partnering with Students in Local Activism in Action: High School*

Espiritu High School embraces community involvement as a key value for student learning. Accordingly, all students participate in four Community Improvement Projects (CIPs), which focus on different community social issues, over their four years of high school. Each CIP, led by an Espiritu teacher, meets twice a week during the school day. CIP topics range from housing and homelessness to prisoner health to urban gardening.

Importantly, a number of these CIPs partner with local advocacy organizations and nonprofits to engage students in meaningful local social action work in ways that resonate with research on the powerful impact of youth organizing (e.g., Ginwright et al., 2006). For example, one year, Espiritu's Housing and Homelessness CIP collaborated with a local advocacy organization to campaign against winter heat shutoffs for households behind on their bills. The dilemma of not having enough money to pay all the bills was one that many students' families knew about firsthand. The issue felt relevant and meaningful to Espiritu students, and they were highly motivated to research the issue, generate persuasive arguments for their position, and make phone calls urging people to attend an upcoming community meeting with state representatives and the utility companies. The teacher leading the CIP shared that the work was personally meaningful for him because he had both grown up in public housing and worked for a state housing authority prior to becoming a teacher.

Working alongside teachers, local adult activists, and advocacy organizations on local community social action can teach students numerous lessons about social action, including the following:

- **Strategy is key to challenging injustice.** The students participating in the phone banking campaign against winter heat shutoffs met with one of the local community organizers leading the campaign, Camilo, a Latine man in his early 20s. Camilo explained to students that although he didn't believe utility companies should be allowed to shut the heat off for *anyone* during the wintertime, the advocacy organization had decided for strategic reasons to focus on prohibiting heat shutoffs for families with children under 6 years old. If the campaign worked, they intended to work to extend the prohibition against heat shutoffs to individuals with medical conditions. Students learned the importance of strategizing and planning to achieve success with activist efforts.
- **Challenging injustice can require multiple steps.** The discussion of strategy with Camilo also taught students that challenging injustice is not always a one-step process but rather one that may entail multiple steps and unfold over several years. In fact, many Espiritu students came away from their conversation with Camilo with a

newfound recognition of the ways in which challenging injustice is a process instead of a single act.
- **Activism can be hard.** Camilo also communicated to the students that organizing and social change work is hard work and that it can be frustrating when progress comes in incremental steps. He warned them that some of the people they called during the phone banking sessions would immediately hang up on them, and others would decline to make time for a conversation. His words catalyzed students' thinking about the tough emotions that can accompany engaging in social action and, in particular, the frustration and disappointment with the seemingly slow pace of progress. Lessons like these can sustain young people's current and future involvement in social action work by preparing them to experience strong feelings, recognize that these emotions come with the territory, and understand that they are not alone in these feelings but rather part of a long chain of activists and citizens committed to pursuing justice.

In short, intergenerational conversations and collaborations with community members committed to social action can be formative for students who are developing their social action skill sets.

## Partnering with Students on Local Activism in Action: Elementary School

As we mentioned in Chapter 2, for several years, 3rd graders at Roberts Elementary School engaged in a district-mandated English/language arts unit that included reading J.M. Barrie's 1904 play *Peter Pan*. Because the play includes problematic stereotypes of Native Americans, 3rd grade educators worked with justice partner Little Uprisings to design lessons that offered students opportunities to analyze and discuss these stereotypes in the play and why they are problematic.

As part of the unit, students read and learned about the formal request in 2021 by leaders of the Cherokee Nation that automobile manufacturer Jeep remove the tribe's name from its vehicles (i.e., the Jeep Cherokee). Jeep declined to comply with this request, citing their automobile's powerful name recognition as too valuable to give up. The students also learned that more than 20 communities in their home state used a Native American name or mascot for their high school athletics teams, including a nearby community that used a derogatory term. The 3rd graders and their teachers read op-eds and blog posts by Native American leaders about these types of uses of their identity as well as portions of an academic study about how such naming practices negatively influence contemporary Native American youth.

The 3rd grade teachers offered students an opportunity to engage in local community social action by writing letters to the school committee of the nearby town expressing their thoughts and perspectives on its Native American mascot. One student wrote:

> Dear School Committee:
>
> I'm writing to you because I want to ask you to change the mascot for the high school. The mascot is a racial slur, and I am asking you to change it to something that is not connected to the Native American people.
>
> The first reason I am asking you to change the mascot is because it is harmful and offensive. Our evidence from the National Congress of American Indians shows that it appears Native American

mascots yield negative effects for Native American students. These mascots are making people feel sad because this is rude to them.

The second reason is Native Americans do not agree with these mascots in most cases. Our evidence is that we read about five letters from different Native tribes and nations disagreeing with mascots. It is not right to have these mascots.

The third reason is these mascots create and continue stereotypes. The NCAI says, "The use of racist and derogatory Indian mascots, logos, or symbols is harmful and perpetuates negative stereotypes of America's first peoples."[1] Stereotypes are a problem because not everyone is the same person.

The mascot needs to change.

Sincerely, Julissa

## A second student wrote:

Dear School Committee,

The high school needs to change their mascot. My first reason why the mascot should be changed is because Native Americans say it's not honoring them. I know this because in a paper from the NCAI it says, "Specifically rather than honoring Native peoples, these caricatures and stereotypes . . . contribute to a disregard for the personhood of Native people."[2] This means that Native Americans say that this causes stereotypes, and it is definitely false that these logos/mascots are honoring Native Americans. This matters because you are using a Native American mascot and saying that it's honoring them when you're not the Native Americans. It is not true because it's not their opinion.

My next reason that this mascot needs to change is that it is harmful to youth and it lowers self-esteem. I know this because in a study by Laurel R. Davis-Delano, Joseph P. Gone, and Stephanie A. Fryberg it says the mascots caused "depressed self-esteem."[3] This means that Native American mascots lower

---

[1] Material quoted comes from National Congress of American Indians (NCAI), 2013, p. 5.
[2] Material quoted from NCAI, 2013, p. 5.
[3] Material quoted from Davis-Delano et al., 2020, p. 617.

youths' self-esteem. This is a problem because if you are lowering their self-esteem you are also harming them. How would you like it if you were a kid and someone lowered your self-esteem?

My last reason that the mascot needs to change is that it is offensive to Native Americans. I know this because representatives from the Nipmuc Nation said so in a recent newspaper article. This means that if you use mascots with Native Americans, it is very offensive. This is offensive because you are using their culture as a mascot. Also, how would you feel if someone put your culture into a mascot? You have read that because of Native American mascots, kids' self-esteem has been lowered and Native Americans have been offended. In summary, please change your mascot.

Sincerely, Alix

This assignment, which integrated existing state writing standards, gave 3rd graders an authentic opportunity to engage in social action. Although the school committee never responded to the students' letters, the students were heartened when several state legislators subsequently proposed a bill prohibiting the use of Native American mascots in public middle and high schools across the state.

Opportunities for young children to engage in social action challenging injustice offer the same benefits as they do for high schoolers. Authoring these letters contributed to students' beliefs that they can be changemakers. Moreover, the reading and research that went into authoring the letters helped them start developing their own perspectives on topics such as cultural appropriation, microaggressions, and whether state governments should limit a school community's choices. The research work reiterated for students that strong knowledge about an issue is a necessary precursor to thoughtful action.

Finally, authoring a letter about a topic of injustice that they genuinely cared about significantly deepened students' investment in their end-of-unit argument writing assignment. Students worked hard to integrate their research and collected evidence into their letters and to use rhetorical strategies skillfully. The focus on injustice deepened and enhanced students' academic learning and skill development rather than distracting from it in any way.

## Practice #5: Follow Up with Reflection

Offering young people opportunities to engage in social action opens up valuable pathways for growth and learning, but we should not assume that such growth and learning happen automatically. Reflection is key. As adults, after we participate in new or important experiences, we often reflect on how the experience went, which enables us to learn from the experience moving forward. Those reflective moments are even more powerful when we talk through our experiences with a trusted friend, family member, or mentor. Likewise, students are best able to learn and grow from social action when they can debrief their experiences with families, teachers, and peers. What did they learn about the injustice they were seeking to challenge? How did their strategy for disrupting this injustice work? What will they do differently next time? What did they learn about themselves? Reflecting on these and other questions helps students strengthen the knowledge and skills necessary to do social action work effectively and to process the work's accompanying emotions.

It's also important for educators and schools to recognize that many students are engaged in social action activities outside school through religious institutions, community groups, extracurricular organizations, and their own families. There is great value in creating space for students to share and reflect on these experiences and the expertise they've gained with classmates.

### *Following Up with Reflection in Action*

Another high school that participated in our research study on adolescents' critical consciousness development was Community Academy, a small public high school in the Northeast that serves predominantly Black and Latine students. At Community Academy, teachers took the time to engage students in reflecting on their social action work even if the activities were not school-sponsored. For example, one day approximately half of Community Academy's students participated in a citywide student walkout to protest proposed budget cuts to public high schools.

Although nearly all of Community Academy's teachers and staff were personally supportive of the campaign, they were not supposed to publicly endorse it or permit their students to walk out of school. Nonetheless, when students returned to school the next day, some teachers created the time and space during class to ask students to share their experience participating in the protest and what they had learned. Several students shared with us that their teachers had helped them to see how the specific issue they were protesting—proposed budget cuts to city high schools—connected to the larger Black Lives Matter movement. These reflective, in-class discussions played an important role in helping them learn and grow from the event they participated in.

Reflecting on social action is important for younger children as well. Every April, Roberts students participate in the Racial Justice Challenge, an annual national campaign by the YWCA to raise awareness of the impact of systemic racism in our lives and communities. During the four-week campaign, students hear and learn from community leaders engaged in promoting racial justice and reflect in class on the actions they already take to challenge racism in their lives and communities.

To encourage this reflection, the school's family engagement team identified four questions for teachers and students at every grade level to think about. They asked grade-level teams to decide how they wanted to engage their students in sharing, reflecting, and connecting around these four questions:

1. What does it mean to stand against racism?
2. Why do you think it's important to stand against racism?
3. How do you stand against racism in your school, community, and beyond?
4. How do others stand against racism?

The 5th grade team asked students to write responses to a Tweet from YWCA: "Tell us: Why do you #StandAgainstRacism? What are things you and other people can do in their daily lives to stand against racism?" (YWCA USA, 2018). Students produced the following responses:

- "I stand against racism because I believe that everyone should be treated fairly."
- "I stand against racism because it is not OK to use offensive language to someone of color."
- "I stand against racism because people should be treated equally at all times, and it's not OK when someone gets treated better than others!"
- "To me, standing against racism means to never, ever discriminate based on race or make fun of someone's culture. It means to help those who are being discriminated against based on race or culture. It means to learn more about when and why racism happened so we can learn how to stand against it."

- "[Standing against racism] means that you are willing to use your power to fight for justice and brave enough to take risks that could really make change happen."
- "[Standing against racism] means actually standing up for injustices you see and not reminiscing on what was. Stand against racism should mean action now. There is still plenty of racism out in the world. There is a system built around White supremacy that makes getting a job and having a family harder for Black people. Also I would say that Black profiling is still alive and well, and that it adds to a lot of things. I want people fighting against these injustices because people think that we have solved this. But not yet. I know that we will. That is what standing against racism means to me."

This learning activity gave students the opportunity to reflect upon and articulate *why* they were committed to challenging racism and *how* they were already engaging in social action to do so. It also offers an important reminder that students' social action need not be limited to their school or local context but can connect to national and global movements. Guiding students to consider their own investment in challenging injustice and transforming society absolutely plays a role in shaping the commitments they carry with them into adulthood.

> Children who participate in social action at a young age are more likely to grow up to be active and engaged citizens who see themselves as responsible for helping to build a better world.

In the same way that individuals introduced to sports, reading, or art as young children are more likely to grow into adults with identities as athletes, readers, or artists, children who participate in social action at a young age are more likely to grow up to be active and engaged citizens who see themselves as responsible for helping to build a better world (Rymond-Richmond, 2023).

## Push, Challenge, Strategize, Persevere

We can't move forward if we don't *move* forward! Our students need to learn how to recognize and analyze injustice, but they also need to learn how to move, how to push, how to challenge, how to strategize, and how to persevere.

Children's Defense Fund founder Marian Wright Edelman (2014) once observed, "You just need to be a flea against injustice. Enough committed fleas biting strategically can make even the biggest dog uncomfortable and transform even the biggest nation" (p. 10). Offering students various examples of activists and strategies for social action, arranging opportunities to partner with teachers and other adults to effect change in their communities and society at large, and engaging them in reflection about their efforts are integral to students developing the will and skill to "bite" strategically, challenge injustice, and transform the world.

 ## Questions for Reflection

1. To what extent do students in your school community have opportunities to engage in social action?
2. How do the chapter's descriptions of youth engaging in school-based and local social action catalyze your own thinking about social action opportunities for students in your school community?
3. How might you offer—or build on—opportunities for students in your school community to reflect together about their participation in social action?

## Additional Resources

Agarwal-Rangnath, R. (2020). *Planting the seeds of equity: Ethnic studies and social justice in the K–2 classroom.* Teachers College Press.

Albert Einstein Institution. (n.d.). *198 methods of nonviolent action.* https://www.brandeis.edu/peace-conflict/pdfs/198-methods-non-violent-action.pdf

Berkeley YPAR Hub. (n.d.). *Why YPAR?* https://yparhub.berkeley.edu/why-ypar

Figueroa, A. (2022, April 8). York, Pa. students who fought book ban tell their story to U.S. House panel. *Pennsylvania Capital-Star.* https://penncapital-star.com/arts-culture/york-pa-students-who-fought-book-ban-tell-their-story-to-u-s-house-panel/

Gasch, R., & Reticker-Flynn, J. (n.d.). *Youth activist toolkit.* Advocates for Youth. https://advocatesforyouth.org/wp-content/uploads/2019/04/Youth-Activist-Toolkit.pdf

Keene, A. (n.d.). *Native appropriations* [Blog]. https://nativeappropriations.com/

Kirshner, B. (2015). *Youth activism in an era of education inequality.* New York University Press.

Nagara, I. (2019). *Innosanto Nagara* [Website]. https://aisforactivist.org/

Schulten, K. (2018, March 7). The power to change the world: A teaching unit on student activism in history and today. *The New York Times.* https://www.nytimes.com/2018/03/07/learning/lesson-plans/the-power-to-change-the-world-a-teaching-unit-on-student-activism-in-history-and-today.html

YWCA. (n.d.). *About the Racial Justice Challenge.* https://justice.ywca.org/challenge/

# Build Adult Capacity

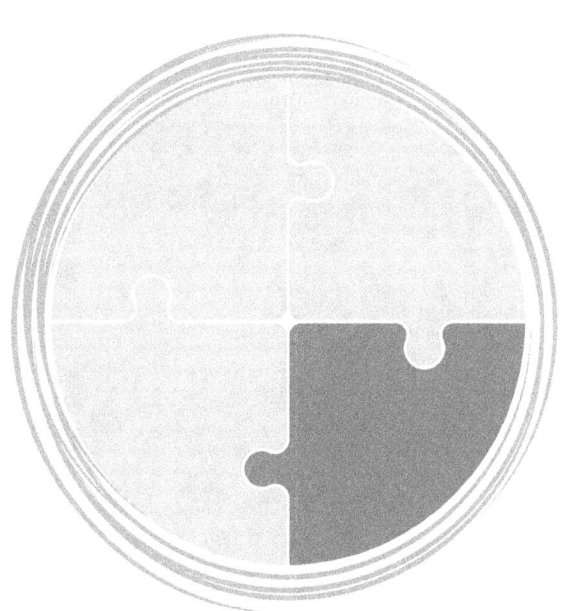

# 5

# Let Teachers Be Learners

Now that you have engaged with the previous chapters on curriculum development, justice partners, family engagement, and social action, you are primed to determine the types of capacity building your staff needs. Because it's hard to teach what we don't know, staff need access to concrete professional learning opportunities to deepen their knowledge base about the roots and consequences of socially oppressive forces. They also need time to explore their own questions, examine their personal relationship to injustice, and develop proficiency in talking about these topics. Putting structures in place to address these needs is critical to enacting the vision laid out in the previous chapters.

In the K–12 schools we visit, we often find a handful of teachers who can draw on their educational and lived experiences to feel confident about leading students in discussions and learning activities focused on injustice. But most teachers we meet describe themselves as hesitant to lead such discussions. This hesitance can come from multiple places.

First, in the United States, we are socialized from a young age not to talk about topics such as race and class, much less racism, classism, and interlocking systems of oppression. When Onnie Rogers and colleagues (2021) interviewed Black, White, and Asian children about their racial identities and asked them to describe their race or races, several responded that it was racist of her to ask them that (e.g., "You know, you're being really racist right now!"), signifying that young children have already absorbed the lesson not to talk about race (p. 1823). Relatedly, many adults—particularly teachers whose social identities are conferred the most power (e.g., White, cisgender, middle and upper class)—spend decades learning to avoid speaking about injustices associated with race, class, gender, and sexual identity (Pollock, 2004).

Second, research highlights that people in the United States experience psychological barriers that inhibit our engagement with topics of injustice (Seider, 2011). For teachers from privileged identity groups, engaging in discussions of injustice often requires grappling with their own unearned advantages, conscious and unconscious support of unjust systems, and internalized problematic beliefs (Tatum, 2017). This type of reckoning with how one's own actions perpetuate injustice, or how one benefits from unearned privilege, can be challenging to acknowledge, which means that such discussions are often initially met with resistance, anger, and denial (Seider, 2011; Tatum, 2017).

For teachers from systematically oppressed and marginalized identity groups, participating in discussions of injustice can surface painful, uncomfortable, and enraging personal experiences or observations and force them to relive or re-experience pain from everyday confrontations with racism, classism, homophobia, and so on. Discussing these lived experiences may also open them up to ridicule, pity, minimization, or condemnation (Arao & Clemens, 2013).

Institutional and structural reasons can also hold educators back from discussing topics of injustice. In recent years, some states have passed legislation explicitly designed to constrain teachers from engaging their students in learning about topics such as racism, sexism, and heterosexism. As a result, many educators across the country are increasingly reluctant to bring up any topics related to race, gender, or sexuality for fear of reprisals from their school district or the criminal justice system. Even in the absence of restrictive policies, educators may worry about negative reactions from parents, families, or the community.

Of course, there are also educators from both privileged and oppressed groups who are more than happy to engage in discussions of injustice. Kentucky's 2022 Teacher of the Year, Willie Edward Taylor Carver Jr., recently led more than 200 state teachers of the year in publicly condemning laws that restrict conversations about specific identities, histories, and topics of injustice in schools for putting politics above the needs of students. Carver explained that, for many students, school is "the singular place where they can experience any modicum of freedom to be their authentic self or even to try to figure out what their authentic self is" (Jones, 2022, para. 8). But other teachers similarly eager to dig into these topics in schools may not feel sufficient relational trust—with their colleagues, school leaders, students, or families—to have these conversations with their school community.

In short, numerous forces—social, psychological, and political; both outside and within schools themselves—discourage teachers from engaging their students in learning about oppressive forces such as racism and how to challenge them. Yet, as we explained in the Introduction, students need this type of knowledge and skills if they are going to challenge the roots and pernicious effects of these forces and build a better world (Heberle et al., 2020).

To extend confidence in educating for justice beyond the handful of teachers who feel personally comfortable doing so requires active, explicit, and strategic effort from school leaders as well as strong, consistent professional learning for the entire faculty. Specific goals for adult learning will differ by school, but adult learning (and unlearning) in this domain should create space for the following:

- **Building content knowledge**—Building knowledge about the history, structures, systems, and individual choices that sit at the root of injustice across multiple axes of identity
- **Practice conversations**—Developing fluidity with talking about topics of injustice, including unearned privilege and power, and intervening in injustice
- **Collaborative problem solving**—Problem solving and puzzling about questions, concerns, fears, and misunderstandings related to this work
- **Visions of new possibilities**—Imagining and designing new ways forward

In this chapter, we describe how school leaders and teacher leaders might launch adult learning about injustice and strategies for social action using four different professional learning structures. We also identify and unpack the key commitments essential to the success of these professional learning structures: space for adults to learn, shared leadership in establishing these learning spaces, and listening to participants about what is and is not working for them. Throughout the chapter, we highlight the practices at Roberts Elementary School, Centre Heights Public Charter School, and Mountain City Elementary and Middle School to illustrate the launch and execution of these adult learning structures. All the approaches we describe below rely on two foundational conditions: Teachers know it is OK to be learners, and teachers have relational trust with each other and their leaders. Although it is outside the scope of this book to comprehensively address how you create these two conditions, we urge you to consider the extent to which they are in place before launching professional learning in this domain.

## Lay the Groundwork for Adult Learning

Before implementing adult learning practices, leaders have to consider what it means and looks like to launch them. How do we invest our colleagues in new learning structures, particularly ones designed to engage participants in difficult conversations? What should we avoid?

One approach to avoid is to unilaterally declare, "This is what we're doing and the direction we're heading!" Another is to try to do all the work of building knowledge at once. Both approaches tend to panic staff members; they grow fearful and defensive, and may respond by revolting, explicitly or inwardly.

Instead, begin this work in collaboration with your colleagues, at a pace that gives them time to metabolize their learning. This more deliberate approach is understandably challenging for school leaders and teacher leaders who are keenly attuned to the injustices and opportunity gaps in our society and feel urgency to address them. But in our experience, leaders who unilaterally initiate professional development in justice-centered education will struggle to have this learning take hold.

Another approach to avoid is being overly reliant on professional learning opportunities that bring an entire school's staff together for a short workshop (or even a series of workshops) from outside experts. Although whole-staff professional development sessions are valuable for creating common purpose and shared understandings, researchers have found that whole-group professional development sessions do not consistently translate into shifts in teachers' planning or instruction or in the broader work of the school community (Borko, 2004). Teachers or adults learning or unlearning for the first time benefit from small groups and differentiated learning spaces in addition to whole-group learning spaces.

So how can teacher leaders and school leaders move forward collaboratively and deliberately? We recommend beginning this process by seeking out conversations and dialogue with as many different members of your school community as possible. During these conversations, try to learn more about what your colleagues know about injustice and resistance to injustice, what role they see these topics playing in their classrooms, and what fears and hopes they have related to this work. Have the same conversations with families, caretakers, and students. Dialogues can take place in formal spaces such as professional development sessions, parent–teacher organization meetings, or student council sessions, as well as more informal spaces such as the school playground during dismissal time or on the sidelines of extracurricular activities. It is crucial to connect with students, teachers, and caregivers who reflect the full diversity of the school community, not just those who are the most visible, active, and vocal within traditional school engagement structures. Learn more about how different community members experience the school, how they believe student learning can be strengthened and improved, and how nurturing students' critical consciousness fits into their own vision of powerful teaching and learning.

Learning about and reflecting on different individuals' perspectives will allow you to craft a plan for adult knowledge building that will serve your community and build trust and good will with different stakeholders—individuals you will likely need to draw on for the harder parts of this work. As the saying goes, you can only move at the speed of trust.

## *Learning Before Launching in Action*

When Principal Drake became the principal of Roberts Elementary School, she initiated a listening and learning tour, soliciting feedback about the school's vision statement from all of its stakeholders. Nearly everyone she spoke to believed the school's existing vision statement to be too generic to guide critical consciousness work with students, so she began to solicit inspiring themes and ideas that could serve as a north star to guide this work during professional development sessions. The responses formed the basis of Roberts's revised vision statement and core values, as well as the rationale for launching adult learning opportunities focused on justice and resistance to injustice. Principal Drake also treated these conversations about the vision statement not as a one-time exercise but as an ongoing project that the school community should spend time on year after year to reflect their evolving goals. This type of ongoing dialogue allows the entire school community to build a unified sense of purpose about why they are doing this work together.

Collectively drafting a vision statement that includes a commitment to challenging injustice is an important start, but common language does not in and of itself build the trust necessary for successfully launching adult learning opportunities focused on injustice and resisting injustice. School leaders and teacher leaders invested in this work also need to invest in building relationships with their staff and colleagues. One way leaders can do this is to prioritize space for in-person observation debriefs and faculty check-ins. These one-on-one conversations allow for more organic discussions about how nurturing students' critical consciousness and integrating topics of injustice and strategies for resistance into teaching and learning might impact students' engagement, intellectual curiosity, and sense of purpose. At Roberts, regular, personal, and honest conversations between Principal Drake and her teachers in multiple configurations—sometimes one-on-one, sometimes with grade-level teams, sometimes with the whole staff—slowly built up the trust necessary for staff members to be willing to participate earnestly in adult learning structures.

Leaders who carry out this type of listening and learning tour are likely to learn that educators on their staff have different levels of knowledge, expertise, and needs when it comes to topics of injustice and strategies for resistance. Therefore, one size cannot fit all in creating space for adult learning on these topics. Adult learning structures need to be varied and flexible enough to meet staff members where they are and help them move forward.

> One size cannot fit all in creating space for adult learning on topics of injustice and strategies for resistance.

We have seen school communities effectively use four learning structures (in conjunction with whole-group professional development) to support and differentiate adult professional learning related to topics of injustice, power, and resistance to injustice:

- Cross-identity dialogues
- Affinity spaces
- Justice groups
- Professional learning communities

These four structures are by no means the only effective adult development approaches, but we believe them to be promising ones for building content knowledge, practicing conversations, collaboratively problem solving, and envisioning new possibilities. Two structures—cross-identity dialogues and affinity spaces—focus primarily on building adults' content knowledge about injustice and resistance to injustice and their relationship to each other, while the other two—justice groups and professional learning communities—focus primarily on supporting educators as they bring these topics into their classrooms and work with students. Descriptions of each structure appear below, as well as examples of how different K–12 schools have used them to work toward nurturing students' critical consciousness. Although each structure can be deployed in support of a range of topics, we primarily focus on them in the context of exploring racism and antiracism.

## Adult Learning Structure #1: Cross-Identity Dialogues

*Cross-identity dialogues* are facilitated discussions among members of two or more identity groups that seek "to create new levels of understanding, relating, and action" (Zúñiga, 2003, p. 9). In school communities, the goal of cross-identity dialogues is often to build trust and connection by helping teachers and family members learn from and with each other about key concepts related to identity groups, identify differences and commonalities in people's lived experiences across identities, and engage participants in working to improve inclusion within their organization. Research on cross-identity dialogues has found that participants come away with a deeper capacity to understand other groups' perspectives, higher levels of critical consciousness about structural and institutional inequities, and greater investment in acting as an ally and interrupting injustice (Frantell et al., 2019).

A common form of cross-identity dialogues is cross-race dialogues. In contrast with a whole-staff professional development session, cross-race dialogues offer an opportunity for members of a school community to work together more intimately and alongside families to learn about race and racism, consider how their own race-based experiences relate to those of others, and strengthen trust and relationships within the broader school community. In sum, this learning structure connects adult partners who will be instrumental in supporting students' critical consciousness development.

Cross-race dialogues should be entirely voluntary, but school leaders and teacher leaders can work proactively to encourage the participation of as many staff and family members as possible. One way to encourage participation is to offer cross-race dialogues at least once a year for several years in a row, each time providing free childcare and refreshments to participating parents and teachers.

To foster participants' comfort and honest engagement, it often makes sense to bring in a community partner or outside facilitator with expertise in leading such dialogues. One example is the YWCA, which offers in many local chapters a program called Dialogues on Race and Ethnicity, a series of five evenings of conversations. These types of community partners—the focus of Chapter 2—can also provide guidance about how to structure dialogues, such as striving to include roughly even proportions of participants who identify as people of color and who identify as White.

## *Cross-Race Dialogues in Action*

At Roberts, Principal Drake partnered with the YWCA to hold cross-race dialogues several years in a row for teachers and family members. During the five nights of dialogues, teachers and families with different racial/ethnic identities talked together about where they came from, what was important to them, and traditions they did and did not share. Kelly Federico—a White-identifying parent of two students—explained that she participated in the dialogues because she wanted to build relationships with more Roberts families of color. Leondra Jones—an African American–identifying parent of two students—explained: "They started dialogue literally beyond the race dialogues. There is a mom who I'm friends with to this day—our sons were in kindergarten together, and we became friends, but I don't know that she and I would have connected in the way that we did if we didn't have that time together to really share. She could share who she was, and I could share who I was." Both parents pointed to the cross-race dialogues as valuable in helping adults in the school community see and recognize everyone else's humanity. Another participant, Maysa Karam, a Roberts teacher and person of color, described the dialogues as "super helpful" because they offered her and other teachers a valuable space to think critically about the role of race in their own and other people's lives.

As we say many times throughout this book, one size never fits all in education, so there will certainly be school community members who have little interest in participating in cross-identity dialogues. Yet we have also seen firsthand that both teachers and family members are willing to share their own experiences, perspectives, and questions in these smaller, more intimate dialogues that they would never feel comfortable sharing in a whole-staff professional development session or whole-community meeting.

## Adult Learning Structure #2: Affinity Spaces

*Affinity spaces* (or affinity groups) are spaces for individuals who share an identity to come together, share experiences, and consider the unique affordances or challenges they experience in their organization (Hirsch, 2021). School communities can establish affinity spaces based on race/ethnicity, sexual orientation, nationality, language, and other identities.

Our work primarily involves schools that host race-focused affinity spaces. Beverly Daniel Tatum—author of *Why Are All the Black Kids Sitting Together in the Cafeteria?* (2017)—explains that racial affinity spaces are valuable in part because people from different racial groups in the United States have different relationships to racism and therefore different roles to play when it comes to challenging racism. People of color are by no means a single or monolithic group, but racial affinity spaces can offer people of color a protected space to share, reflect upon, and receive support for encounters with different types of racism without those encounters being minimized, questioned, or rejected by White colleagues.

Likewise, racial affinity spaces can offer White people a space to share, reflect on, and discuss with each other their developing understandings of the workings of racism and their own role in disrupting racism. Tatum adds that White racial affinity spaces give White people a chance to speak with candor and honesty about their developing commitment to antiracism in a way that might feel impossible in mixed-race settings. She continues: "Even when White people feel comfortable sharing these feelings with people of color, frankly, people of color don't necessarily want to hear about it" (p. 205).

## Forming an Affinity Space

There is no single right way to form or facilitate an affinity space. School leaders might start by either seeking an outside facilitator for the space or inviting a teacher leader within the community to facilitate. We believe that it can work for school leaders to *participate* in a racial affinity space—and, in fact, such participation sends a powerful message to staff about the importance of these spaces—but teachers may be more comfortable verbally contributing in spaces that are facilitated by someone who does not manage or evaluate the teachers.

Second, participation in affinity spaces should be completely voluntary. In the same way that some educators in your school community will find cross-race dialogues a useful structure for adult learning and others will not, some educators will be drawn to affinity spaces and others will not. It is not helpful to mandate participation in either of these adult learning spaces, in contrast with other types of professional development experiences.

How frequently should educators meet in affinity spaces? We acknowledge that time is always the most precious commodity in a school community. Some schools we have worked with see success with hosting affinity spaces once a month, but if possible, we recommend meeting twice a month for an hour or 90 minutes. A twice-monthly meeting allows educators to connect and deepen their thinking more easily and prevents unavoidable cancellations from leading to a two-month gap between meetings.

We recommend that facilitators of affinity spaces develop a proposed structure for meetings, run their ideas by their colleagues, and modify and adapt their plans based on feedback. Not only will different approaches work better at different schools, but different affinity spaces in the same school might prefer different approaches to their work together. For example, at Roberts Elementary School, the affinity space for White educators and the affinity space for educators of color established distinct structures and goals for their respective meetings. The next section illustrates the diverse pathways that different affinity spaces—even within the same school community—can pursue.

## *A White Affinity Book Study in Action*

Principal Drake enlisted a White educator with expertise in racial justice work from her district's central office to facilitate an affinity space open to White teachers. The affinity space focused on *antiracism and allyship*. Participation was completely voluntary, and the group of 7 to 10 teachers—approximately half the White teachers at Roberts—met every other week for an hour after school. They read articles and watched videos about topics ranging from the stages of White racial identity development to the history of segregation in their own school district to inequities in how students of color are classified as having special needs.

The district facilitator agreed to lead the group for one year, as long as another member of the Roberts community would take over thereafter and keep the group going. The next year, participants in the group agreed to rotate the responsibility for facilitating discussion, with one group member leading the discussion and another serving as "guardian," whose job was to stay attuned to the tone of the conversation and refocus the group if it felt like tension was arising in an unhealthy way.

Participants also decided to choose a single text each year to center their work together. One year they chose Layla Saad's (2020) *Me and White Supremacy: Combat Racism, Change the World, and Become a Good Ancestor* to discuss chapter by chapter over the course of the school year. The following year, they took the same approach with Bettina Love's (2019) *We Want to Do More Than Survive: Abolitionist Teaching and the Pursuit of Educational Freedom.*

*Me and White Supremacy* was a particularly useful text for this affinity space because Saad concludes each chapter with reflection questions and a protocol for discussing them that participants used to guide their meetings. They responded to a journal prompt in writing before each session but did not have to share their reflective writing with their peers; the only expectation was that members would do the reading, respond to the prompt, and show up ready to be part of the conversation. This scaffolding, built into both the group's work and the book they chose, meant that facilitators didn't need to position themselves as a resident expert on the topics discussed but could instead attend to moderating the discussion. A resource that could play a similar role for an affinity space is Ibram X. Kendi's *The Antiracist Deck,* a deck of 100 cards featuring conversation starters designed to catalyze meaningful conversations on power, equity, and justice.

Third grade teacher Emma Ward explained that the work in the White affinity space felt like an important complement to teachers' efforts to nurture students' critical consciousness through their curriculum and instruction because "if we're going to talk about these things with our students and we're going to commit to this work, then this is a piece we also need to do within ourselves." Ward added that one aspect of the group that she particularly appreciated is that discussions were "very honest. It's a space where you can own up to the not-so-great things that we've had in place without even knowing it, but now we're like, 'Oh, crap!'"

## An Educators of Color Affinity Space in Action

Because Roberts is a small school—just 300 students and fewer than 30 full-time staff members—Principal Drake established a single affinity space for all staff of color. In contrast, Centre Heights Charter School, a K–12 school located in a mid-Atlantic city with more than 1,000 students and 100 staff members, holds separate affinity spaces for teachers who identify as White, Black, Latine, Asian American, and international. Schools interested in forming affinity spaces for their educators of color will need to decide how many distinct affinity spaces to form based on their own size and context.

The affinity space for educators of color at Roberts also met every other week and used an outside facilitator—an equity coach from a nearby district who had previously worked at the school. Whereas the affinity space for White educators focused on antiracism and active intervention in self and the world, participants in the affinity space for educators of color decided to use their time together to focus on *relationships, connectedness, and belonging*. Some group meetings entailed reading an article or watching a video related to issues of race and racism, but more often, the group came together to have fun, celebrate, vent, and enjoy being with one another in a space that felt like theirs—one where they did not have to concern themselves with code-switching.

This focus on connection meant that group members formed genuine and lasting relationships that extended beyond the Roberts Elementary School walls. In fact, several times, the group chose to meet at a local restaurant or someone's home so that members could connect outside the school building.

The educators of color affinity space at Roberts also focused on *identifying school-related issues facing faculty of color* to bring to the attention of Roberts's principal and other administrators. For example, staff shared that they often felt like their teaching practices were scrutinized and critiqued by White parents in a way rarely experienced by White teachers. Several teachers of color described receiving emails from White parents questioning their (district-mandated) curriculum and pedagogical decisions with a frequency and vehemence that bordered on harassment. Other teachers described requests from parents for lengthy and regular reports on their children's academic work that went beyond reasonable expectations. The facilitator for the affinity space met regularly with Drake and other Roberts administrators to share experiences that the group decided they wanted her to pass along. Principal Drake then used this information to begin conversations with the predominantly White parents contributing to these issues.

## Adult Learning Structure #3: Justice Groups

The purpose of *justice groups* is to bring together a small group of staff members from a school community on a regular basis to talk about issues or questions relevant to their work with students (i.e., problems of practice). Like cross-identity dialogues, justice groups comprise members with diverse identities. However, their specific emphasis is not on understanding one another's experiences and lives but on recognizing, analyzing, and addressing dilemmas related to justice work in their shared school community.

As always, there is no single way to form or facilitate justice groups, but there are some practices worth considering for school leaders and teacher leaders. First, we recommend forming a justice planning group of educators from across the school who are invested in taking a leading role in the school's justice work. This planning group can help to divvy the entire staff into justice groups of six to eight staff members apiece. Members in each group should come from different grade levels, content areas, and identity groups. Try to avoid placing any staff member in a group with their direct supervisor (e.g., department chair, grade-level coordinator). Unlike cross-identity dialogues and affinity spaces, which we recommend be voluntary opportunities for adult learning, justice groups can take the form of required whole-school professional learning, with every staff member expected to participate.

The justice groups can meet monthly or every other month for 90 minutes, and each group can be facilitated by a member of the justice planning committee. In schools where we have seen this structure implemented, the justice planning committee holds a separate meeting each month to determine the focus of the justice group meetings. Often, the starting point for the justice group meetings will be an article, podcast, or video on a particular topic or question raised in the school community, such as antiracist grading practices or unconscious bias in teacher–student interactions. Staff members will spend the first part of their professional learning time reading the article, listening to the podcast, or watching the video, then convene to discuss what they read, listened to, or watched and how they perceive the topic or issue to be manifesting in their own school community.

Other times, the starting point for justice group meetings may be a short vignette written by a staff member in the school community about a situation or circumstance they recently encountered that brings up topics of injustice, power, identity, or resistance to injustice. For example, justice groups at Centre Heights Public Charter School recently discussed a vignette written by a White teacher about her challenges in responding to Black and Latine students in her classes using the N-word with one another. Another vignette focused on a physical education teacher's uncertainty about how to support elementary school students who identify as nonbinary with regard to which locker room to use to change. Staff in each of the justice groups discussed these problems of practice and shared how they would have addressed the issue in the moment and whether the teachers' experiences point to the need for broader school policy changes.

One Centre Heights teacher, Sandy Smith, explained that the justice groups are a great chance for teachers across the school to come together to talk about an issue relevant to their work with students and to "kind of get on the same page or share information." Another teacher, Jackie Albion, expressed her appreciation that the scenarios the justice groups discuss are "things that have actually happened in our building," and felt that it was useful to get input from other colleagues about handling the situations. She also valued having these conversations with colleagues rather than a supervisor, allowing teachers to be more vulnerable about sharing mistakes or uncertainties.

Interestingly, Centre Heights structured its adult professional learning calendar to alternate justice groups and affinity spaces by month. This schedule allowed teachers to participate in one structure focused on adult learning about injustice and experiences with injustice or privilege (affinity spaces) and another structure focused on how educators can bring their understanding of injustice into their classrooms and work with students (justice groups).

This alternating approach is a good reminder that you do not have to pick just one approach to adult learning for your school community. Different adult learning structures will work differently for different adults, and it can be advantageous to offer several concurrent adult learning structures to accommodate your colleagues' preferences and needs.

## Adult Learning Structure #4: Professional Learning Communities

*Professional learning communities*, or PLCs, are collaborative spaces that offer sustained support for educators to critically analyze and improve their practice (McConnell et al., 2013). If justice groups represent a space for educators to talk through and address justice-related dilemmas and problems of practice within their school community, PLCs represent a space for more proactive and planful deep learning about a particular justice-related topic.

PLCs strive to offer teachers the opposite experience of traditional models of teacher professional learning consisting of isolated workshops that fail to attend sufficiently to their particular school contexts. In contrast, PLCs should be context-specific, be sustained over time, include shared responsibility for planning instruction, and draw on the varied expertise of participating educators (Dobbs et al., 2017). PLCs can focus on any instructional or pedagogical topic (e.g., equity-based grading, supporting LGBTQ+ students, STEM and critical consciousness building) and can be a powerful learning structure for strengthening teachers' capacity to nurture students' critical consciousness in numerous ways. A school can offer several PLCs based on educators' diverse interests or needs, giving teachers the option to choose a PLC that resonates most with them.

PLCs typically consist of a group of 3 to 10 educators working on a shared problem of practice or learning about a topic that affects their teaching in their respective classrooms. Some PLCs meet weekly for 60–90 minutes for an entire school year (or even over multiple school years) so that teachers can sustain momentum in addressing a particular problem of practice or deepening their content knowledge. We recommend that PLCs meet at least once per month for at least half a school year, because sustained involvement is one of the structure's key features. PLCs often meet in person, but many educators are growing increasingly comfortable with virtual PLCs that meet online, which allows for the participation of educators who might otherwise not be able to join in.

PLCs typically have a facilitator or co-facilitators who take the lead in organizing the schedule and developing meeting agendas. But importantly, PLCs do not position the facilitator as the instructor or knowledge-holder for the group. Unlike traditional models of professional learning, PLCs acknowledge and honor the expertise of every participant, and every participant can and will contribute to the group's learning.

Recently, Scott co-facilitated a yearlong virtual PLC for middle school teachers at Mountain City Elementary and Middle School, a K–8 public charter school in the southwestern United States. Scott and the five teachers at Mountain City, who led advisory groups comprising 10–15 middle schoolers, formed the PLC to explore a specific question: How can advisory be a space for nurturing middle schoolers' critical consciousness of injustice and resistance to injustice?

The PLC met online for 60 minutes each month for the entire school year. To each meeting, Scott brought several learning activities related to recognizing, analyzing, or challenging injustice that he thought might be effective with the participating teachers' students. For example, one learning activity helped students think about why racial joking and teasing can be problematic and explored how to respond to such joking and teasing (Umaña-Taylor & AERID Lab, 2020). Another engaged students in learning how to detect, reflect, and reject racist and sexist stereotypes that appear routinely in advertisements and social media (Carnes et al., 2012).

Scott and the Mountain City teachers chose to participate in these learning activities as if they were middle school students. Then the teachers took the lead in brainstorming adaptations that would maximize the effectiveness of the activities with their students. Next, individual teachers volunteered to implement the adaptations and prepare materials to carry out the lessons in the next month's advisories. Finally, the teachers offered guidance to Scott on the types of learning activities they wanted him to seek out for the next PLC meeting.

When the PLC reconvened a month later, the teachers began by describing how the learning activities had gone over with their students, and Scott shared with the group the next batch of learning activities. In reflecting on this work at the end of the school year, one Mountain City teacher, Mae Santos, explained: "I think it's been awesome to have that collaboration time on Zoom, where we're looking at the risks and talking through things." Mae added that participating in the monthly PLC meetings "made me want to work harder at being comfortable with having those conversations [about injustice] with kids. . . I've been exposed to so many more of those conversations this year than ever before, and I do think that my comfort level is growing, and I hope to keep working on that." The monthly PLC meetings not only gave participating teachers an opportunity to craft and hone the lessons on injustice they would subsequently lead with their students, but also helped them deepen their confidence in engaging their students in these lessons and discussions.

## Key Elements of Supporting Adult Learning

These four different learning structures—cross-identity dialogues, affinity spaces, justice groups, and PLCs—are not the only adult learning structures that can help a school community move forward in its work to center justice in its curriculum and teaching. But they highlight several elements that are key in implementing effective adult learning: shared leadership, space to learn, and listening to people.

### Shared Leadership

Establishing opportunities for adults to deepen their understanding of topics such as justice, power, and strategies for challenging injustice is a complicated undertaking. As noted earlier in this chapter, individuals in the United States have been socialized from incredibly young ages *not* to talk about these topics. Moreover, our investment and approach to engaging in these topics are deeply impacted by our own positionality, lived experiences, and belief systems. No single individual within a school community should take full responsibility for designing and implementing the adult learning necessary for a school community to center justice in its curriculum and teaching. This work is simply too complex and too fraught to be handed off to a single teacher leader or school leader, no matter how invested, wise, or dedicated that educator may be.

A diverse group of individuals who hold different roles within a school community can jointly raise questions and concerns about plans for establishing adult learning opportunities that may not be apparent to a single individual. Moreover, if this diverse group works together to plan, establish, and roll out adult learning opportunities, their support and endorsement can motivate a wider swath of the school community and reassure them about the value of engaging in the opportunities.

At Roberts Elementary School, Principal Drake collaborated with the family engagement team to establish racial affinity spaces. As we described in Chapter 3, the family engagement team is a diverse group of parents and teachers in the school community invited by Drake to help bring a wider range of family voices into the life and leadership of the community. The team, co-chaired by a teacher and a parent, worked closely with Principal Drake to think through the role that racial affinity spaces could play in keeping parents and teachers in the community moving forward in their conversations and learning about race and racism.

As a group, the family engagement team raised questions for the principal:

- What is the purpose of racial affinity spaces?
- Who should provide the messaging about this purpose to the school community?
- Is there a role for a White affinity space around antiracism, and how will that role be explained to the community?
- Who will facilitate these groups, and what happens if the White affinity space gets misconstrued as a White power group?

Importantly, the team not only asked these questions but collaborated with Principal Drake to think through the answers—and the deliberately diverse composition of the family engagement team meant that these planning sessions represented a type of cross-race dialogue themselves.

Ultimately, the entire family engagement team worked together to co-author and sign a letter to the school community explaining the purpose of forming racial affinity spaces, why they believed this strategy made sense, and why they were excited to see how the groups would contribute to the Roberts community (see Figure 5.1). A crucial aspect of this letter is that Roberts parents and teachers needed to see that the racial affinity space initiative wasn't coming solely from the school's White principal but from a racially diverse group of parents and educators who were working together to wrestle with the best ways to keep the Roberts community talking explicitly and specifically about issues of race, racism, and justice. We have included a reproduction of the letter because of its importance to the entire endeavor and as a guide (but not a template) for other schools communicating with stakeholders about establishing adult learning opportunities on topics of justice and injustice.

FIGURE 5.1

## Letter from Family Engagement Team Introducing Racial Affinity Spaces

Dear Roberts families,

Our family engagement team, a group of Roberts staff and families committed to fostering the Roberts vision of building a more welcoming, equitable, and actively antiracist school community, has been reflecting on recent feedback from the Roberts community. Specifically, we have identified a theme of advocating for the creation of safe and protected spaces for community members to come together within self-identified affinity groups to build relationships, reflect on their experiences at Roberts, and develop targeted action steps to support our shared vision of inclusivity and antiracism.

We are writing to invite you to join one of two affinity groups, described below, to be launched this fall. While we anticipate most members of the groups will be parents and guardians, Roberts teachers, administrators, and other staff are also encouraged to participate. Childcare and food will be provided for all participants.

We look forward to continuing to transform our learning community through this and other antiracism efforts!

**Affinity Group for People of Color**

We invite parents, guardians, teachers, administrators, and staff whose identity is non-White and who are interested in coming together to co-construct our purpose, vision, and goals. Our launch meeting will take place November 18 from 4:30–6:00 p.m. in Room 21. At that meeting, we will collectively define the scope of our time together, including meeting times and places. To sign up for this group, or if you have questions or concerns, please contact your family engagement/school site council representative.

**Affinity Group for White People Challenging Racism**

This group is open to White parents, guardians, teachers, administrators, and other staff at Roberts. The group will aim to educate, support, and respectfully challenge one another as White people to face the historical and current realities of racism, particularly as it has impacted and continues to impact Roberts and all city schools, and take bold steps to eliminate our own racism and, through our individual and collective leadership, the impact of racism on Roberts and all students, families, and staff.

> A central office leader with three years of experience facilitating similar groups for White central office staff and school leaders will facilitate the meetings. The group will initially meet for five consecutive Monday nights beginning November 18 from 4:30–6:30 p.m. in Room 211.
>
> **Please note that you must attend the first session of the White People Challenging Racism group to attend the rest of the series.**
>
> To sign up for this group, or if you have questions or concerns, please contact the family engagement team co-chair.
>
> Sincerely,
>
> Bethany Drake, Principal
> Roberts Family Engagement Team

The clarity of this letter—and its inclusion of signatures from Principal Drake and every member of the family engagement team—went a long way toward reassuring both teachers and parents about the motivation and goals for racial affinity spaces. But both faculty and parents still raised questions and concerns about whether the affinity spaces would further divide the community, whether these conversations were best held together rather than in affinity spaces, and whether there was something inherently racist about having White faculty and parents meet on their own. No one can completely control the narrative for an initiative focused on such fraught topics, and some parents and teachers remained skeptical. However, the thoughtful and intentional effort Drake and her family engagement team put into designing and rolling out the initiative contributed greatly to its successful lift-off. Leadership shared among a diverse range of colleagues and collaborators is essential for educators and school leaders invested in ramping up adult learning in their own school communities about race, power, and justice.

## Space to Learn

The learning structures described in this chapter are grounded in the belief that for educators to be able to engage their students in learning to understand and challenge injustice, they need concrete professional learning opportunities to deepen their own knowledge base about the roots and consequences of injustice. Accordingly, school leaders and teacher leaders invested in bolstering their staff's capacities in this area need to carve out meaningful time and space to engage in professional learning.

> Educators need concrete professional learning opportunities to deepen their own knowledge base about the roots and consequences of socially oppressive forces.

Schools make different decisions about how to carve out this time and space based on their unique contexts. The cross-identity dialogues at Roberts Elementary School took place in five evenings over the course of the school year, the affinity space for White teachers at Roberts met every other week before school, and justice groups at Centre Heights Public Charter School were held every other month on early-release days. You will need to make decisions about what works for your particular schedule, calendar, and staff members, but *all* schools invested in centering justice in their curriculum and teaching need to make time for adults in their community to deepen their knowledge and understanding of injustice and strategies for challenging injustice.

It is equally important for school communities to establish settings and spaces for this adult learning that enable participants to learn in productive ways. The factors that contribute to a particular setting or space feeling healthy and safe to participants will vary, but one question to consider is whether educators will participate in adult learning alongside their direct supervisors, and if so, whether this situation will interfere with educators' comfort and willingness to speak candidly.

At Roberts, Principal Drake participated in the racial affinity space for White educators because she felt that doing so signaled the importance of affinity spaces to the entire school community. In contrast, the justice groups at Centre Heights separated educators and their supervisors because the justice planning committee feared that the presence of supervisors could compromise educators' willingness to admit vulnerability or uncertainty related to topics of injustice. You and your colleagues may need to decide which of these rationales is most compelling for your own school context and circumstances.

Another issue to consider is whether the demographics of these adult learning spaces prevent individual staff members from feeling "spotlighted" based on their race/ethnicity, gender, sexual identity, and so on. Spotlighting refers to a member of a minoritized group feeling as if their thoughts and contributions to a discussion are being received by their colleagues as representative of an entire identity group, rather than a single individual's perspective (Carter, 2008). A justice group or cross-identity dialogue that includes only a small number of individuals from a minoritized identity group may contribute to individuals feeling spotlighted during the group's conversations. Accordingly, school leaders and teacher leaders should strive to place multiple members of a particular identity group together, rather than dispersing members of a particular minoritized group across multiple justice or cross-identity groups.

## Listening to People

Finally, school leaders and teacher leaders establishing learning opportunities about injustice for adults in their school community must listen to members of their community at every step in the process (Scanlan, 2023). Community members have valuable feedback to share with educators leading this work about topics they want to focus on, their own and others' concerns about participating in adult learning opportunities, who should and should not be invited to participate in the learning opportunities, and so on. School leaders and teacher leaders can use this feedback to consider adaptations and modifications to their plans.

> Leaders establishing learning opportunities about injustice for adults must listen to members of their community at every step in the process.

At Roberts, Principal Drake and the family engagement team originally established racial affinity spaces that were open to both staff members and families. However, in their first year, teachers shared that they sometimes felt inhibited by the participation of parents and caretakers. Drake and the team listened carefully to these concerns and ultimately restructured the affinity spaces to allow families and teachers to participate in separate racial affinity spaces. This change enabled all interested individuals to continue participating in the school's affinity spaces in a way that allowed participating teachers to share their thoughts and experiences more freely.

School leaders and teacher leaders need to be good listeners so that they can adapt and adjust plans for adult learning opportunities to best meet the needs of their community. It can be tempting to dig in your heels and stick with your original vision for an endeavor, but ultimately, the success of any adult learning opportunity depends on the continued participation, investment, and enthusiasm of community members.

## From Reflection to Action

There is tremendous value in learning and reflection for its own sake, but a central goal of creating spaces for adult learning in a school community is to deepen teachers' capacity to serve their students. The adult learning structures described in this chapter can lay a powerful foundation for educators' work in the classroom with students—both by deepening educators' knowledge of injustice and by providing differentiated spaces to consider how to bring this work into teaching. Specifically, these adult learning spaces and experiences can help ready educators to implement the curriculum planning, instructional practices, family engagement strategies, and social action work described in the preceding chapters.

 ## Questions for Reflection

1. Do you have a culture of adult learning at your school? Why or why not?
2. Do structures exist in your school community for you and other adults to learn about topics of injustice, power, and resistance to injustice?
3. Which of the structures for adult learning described in this chapter could be useful in your school community?
4. Which of the key elements for supporting adult learning (shared leadership, space to learn, listening to people) are in place in your school community? Which elements need to be developed further?

5. How can the voices, experiences, and preferences of family members and caretakers in your school community inform adult capacity and knowledge building?

## Additional Resources

DiAngelo, R., & Burtaine, A. (2022). *The facilitator's guide for White affinity groups: Strategies for leading White people in an anti-racist practice*. Beacon Press.

Ford, K. A. (Ed.). (2018). *Facilitating change through intergroup dialogue: Social justice advocacy in practice*. Taylor & Francis.

Great Schools Partnership. (n.d.). *Racial affinity groups: Guide for school leaders*. https://www.greatschoolspartnership.org/resources/educational-equity/racial-affinity-groups-guide-for-school-leaders/

Johnson, M. C. (2023). *A space for us: A guide for leading Black, Indigenous, and people of color affinity groups*. Beacon Press.

Saad, L. (2020). *Me and White supremacy: Combat racism, change the world, and become a good ancestor*. Sourcebooks.

Sue, D. W. (2015). *Race talk and the conspiracy of silence: Understanding and facilitating difficult dialogues on race*. John Wiley & Sons.

# Put It All Together

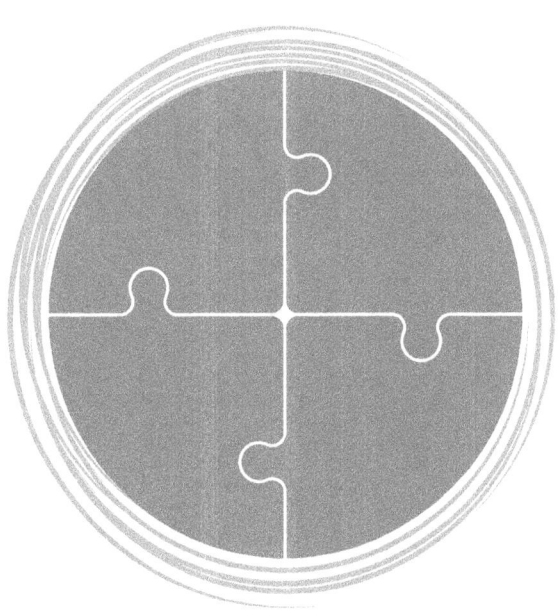

# 6

# Amplify the Impact of Heritage Months

We like to think of the structures, practices, and professional learning involved in educating for justice as a jigsaw puzzle. A puzzle isn't complete if a piece is missing, nor is the picture clear until the pieces are connected with one another. The four principles described in the previous chapters—build adult capacity, center justice in curriculum and pedagogy, foster powerful partnerships with families and community partners, and engage students in social action—need to be similarly linked to have the greatest impact. Here are a few examples:

- Teachers are better equipped to develop curriculum that nurtures students' critical consciousness when they are continually building their own knowledge of the roots and consequences of injustice and historical and contemporary strategies for action (center justice in curriculum and pedagogy; build adult capacity).
- Justice partners can better support teachers to nurture students' critical consciousness when protected time for planning and collaboration is built into teachers' calendars

(foster powerful partnerships; center justice in curriculum and pedagogy).
- Family members and caretakers can better support their children's studies related to justice when structures have been established to facilitate a strong partnership between school and home (foster powerful partnerships; center justice in curriculum and pedagogy).
- Students are more likely to engage in meaningful social action work when they are supported by teachers, family members, and caretakers who are working together (engage students in social action; foster powerful partnerships).

School leaders and teacher leaders need to proactively cultivate all four principles to lovingly, carefully, and deeply do this work. Chapters 6 and 7 show how the combined cultivation of all four principles enriches the work of educating for justice in schools. Chapter 6 describes how a federally sanctioned opportunity available to all schools—heritage months—can be leveraged as a rich learning experience that fosters students' ability to recognize, analyze, and challenge injustice. These months are explicitly intended to challenge injustice in our country's history, books, popular media, and curricula, and they can serve as powerful ways to nurture students' critical consciousness when all four principles are at play.

## Defining Heritage Months

Heritage months seek to amplify the history, literature, culture, contributions, and experiences of groups in the United States who have been systematically marginalized, excluded, tokenized, and misrepresented and whose history, literature, knowledge systems, and contributions continue to be underrepresented or intentionally left out of popular culture, K–12 curricula, history textbooks, academic scholarship, and so on. Figure 6.1 lists heritage months commonly celebrated in the United States.

During heritage months, schools often affirm and celebrate underrepresented identities, honor and teach about the cultures of the communities of focus, and support students in acknowledging and challenging the injustices that these community members experience. School participation in heritage months in robust, authentic, and meaningful ways can be an important

FIGURE 6.1

**Heritage Months Established by the U.S. Federal Government**

| Month | Recognized Group |
|---|---|
| February | National Black History Month |
| March | Women's History Month<br>Irish-American History Month |
| April | Arab American Heritage Month |
| May | Asian American, Native Hawaiian, and Pacific Islanders Heritage Month<br>Jewish American Heritage Month |
| June | Lesbian, Gay, Bisexual, Transgender, Queer, and Intersex Pride Month<br>National Caribbean-American Heritage Month<br>National Immigrant Heritage Month |
| July | Disability Pride Month* |
| September–October | National Hispanic Heritage Month |
| November | National Native American Heritage Month |

*Source:* The White House, n.d.
* Worldwide recognition but not declared by U.S. federal government.

opportunity to nurture critical consciousness and counter unjust exclusion of groups from history and curriculum.

## A "Both/And" Approach to Heritage Months

Many educators rightly worry about schools using heritage months to silo the histories and contributions of oppressed and marginalized groups rather than integrating content about these groups into the regular curriculum. There is further concern that schools participate in these months in shallow ways and, in so doing, perpetuate the flattening of the rich histories, identities, and experiences of the groups students are learning about.

Teacher leaders and school leaders who are committed to nurturing students' critical consciousness schoolwide must understand that heritage months are not singular opportunities for student learning about a particular group of people but rather *one piece* of a larger commitment to exploring a group's history, contributions, and ways of being. At Roberts Elementary School, Principal Drake addresses this concern at the start of the school year in her annual letter to staff introducing the first heritage month of the year (see Figure 6.2).

> Leaders committed to nurturing students' critical consciousness must understand that heritage months are just one piece of a larger commitment to exploring a group's history, contributions, and ways of being.

Principal Drake's letter makes several important points. First, she emphasizes that heritage months are not an alternative to integrating the experiences and wisdom of marginalized and diverse groups in the United States into their regular

## FIGURE 6.2
**Letter to Roberts Faculty About National Hispanic Heritage Month**

> Dear Roberts faculty,
>
> National Hispanic Heritage Month takes place from September 15 to October 15. This is an important opportunity to shine the light on the diverse legacy of strength, beauty, and brilliance within the Latine and Hispanic communities in our school, our neighborhood, and our country.
>
> We want to begin by reinforcing something we discussed this summer during our Summer Institute Unit Planning Session. Heritage months exist because we are not yet in a place where racially, culturally, and linguistically diverse communities (specifically communities of color, the LGBTQ+ community, women, individuals with disabilities, etc.) are fully seen, heard, and affirmed in the curriculum and content we study on a regular, consistent, and meaningful basis, both at Roberts and more broadly in society. This oversight applies to both excellence and everyday examples. Therefore, we intentionally elevate their voices, ideas, and contributions during specific months of the year.
>
> However, we also recognize that i*dentity is intersectional and dynamic and does not evidence itself only one month a year.* We also know that learning about racial, cultural, and linguistic diversity is more meaningful when it is thoughtfully and authentically embedded in content you are already studying (e.g., using text collections instead of single stories to provide a comprehensive and holistic representation of content and ideas). To be truly antiracist and inclusive, we must thoughtfully integrate stories, ideas, voices, and contributions from diverse sources all year long. Celebrating heritage months is truly a both/and situation!
>
> Sincerely,
>
> Bethany Drake, Principal

curriculum but rather an *additional* opportunity to emphasize the experiences and contributions of groups who are not yet fully seen, heard, and affirmed. She also conveys that sharing the stories, ideas, voices, and contributions of a particular group during a heritage month should *not* entail designing standalone lessons or activities that students will experience as a tangent from their "regular" curriculum work.

In other words, a class learning about World War II when February and Black History Month come around should not pause their work for a standalone lesson on Rosa Parks and the Montgomery Bus Boycott. Instead, the teacher could integrate lessons on the contributions of Black soldiers to the U.S. military during the time, the impact of WWII on racial segregation in the United States, or ways Black soldiers were systematically excluded from the G.I. Bill after the war. In other words, teachers and teaching teams should leverage heritage months as chances to identify and develop lessons that thoughtfully integrate the history, literature, and contributions of the featured identity group into existing curriculum.

In the following sections, we will explore how each of the book's four principles can be applied to heritage months. For clarity, each principle will be addressed individually, but the interlocking nature of these principles will be evident throughout the illustrations.

## Build Adult Capacity: Shared Leadership and Curating Resources

Remember, adults cannot teach what they do not know. Teachers greatly benefit from having support and resources from their school community to honor heritage months. Research suggests that many teachers, particularly White teachers, lack sufficient education and training on the history and lived experience of cultural groups consistently excluded from school curriculum (Cruz et al., 2020) and may need intentional support to learn more and uncover how best to share this learning with students. Without such support, teachers may feel ill-equipped to do this important work. A school leader or teacher leader can take on the bulk of this support work, but this may also be an opportunity to implement shared leadership by providing teachers with opportunities and a structure to support their peers and their school.

## *Shared Leadership and Curating Resources in Action*

In earlier chapters, we described how principal Bethany Drake invited teachers and family members serving on the school's family engagement team to take a leadership role in establishing structures and spaces to support adult learning about issues of race, racism, justice, and power. Drake invited a different group, the school climate team, to take responsibility for helping teachers access the time, support, and resources necessary to integrate heritage months into their curriculum units.

The school climate team at Roberts Elementary, made up of teacher representatives from each grade level, focuses on initiatives related to fostering a healthy and positive school climate for students and staff members. Participation is not mandatory, but most teachers are excited to contribute to the school being a good place to work and learn. Many also appreciate the opportunity to play a substantive role in shared leadership of the school. Although not the case at Roberts, at other schools we have worked with, leaders also invite students to join the committee to ensure their perspectives, voices, and needs are considered as the group works to create and maintain a positive school environment.

At the start of each school year, the Roberts school climate team identifies which heritage months the school community will honor and celebrate in the year ahead. The team's goal is for every student in the school to feel like the curriculum offers mirrors that reflect their own family's experiences and windows into other families' experiences. In other words, the selection of heritage months is influenced by the demographics of the school community as well as by events in the local community and the wider world.

For the past school year, the climate team identified six heritage months for the school to honor (see Figure 6.3). They further supported their colleagues by curating a set of resources for each month related to the honored group's history, contributions, genius, and lived experiences. Curated resources can give teachers a starting place to strengthen their knowledge and pedagogy, allowing them to efficiently devote their limited time to determining how best to share their learning with students.

In preparation for honoring Asian American, Native Hawaiian, and Pacific Islanders Heritage Month (AAPI Month) in May, the school climate team pulled together a range of resources in the form of teacher's guides, online articles, biographies of notable

FIGURE 6.3

**Heritage Months Observed by Roberts Elementary School**

| Month | Recognized Group |
|---|---|
| September–October | National Hispanic Heritage Month |
| November | National Native American Heritage Month |
| February | National Black History Month |
| March | Women's History Month |
| May | Asian American, Native Hawaiian, and Pacific Islanders Heritage Month |
| June | Lesbian, Gay, Bisexual, Transgender, Queer, and Intersex Pride Month |

AAPI community members and activists, age-appropriate read-alouds, and videos (see Figure 6.4). These resources, which were housed in a shared Google Drive, include a short explanation that May was chosen as AAPI month to honor the first wave of Japanese immigrants to the United States in May 1843 as part of the California Gold Rush, as well as the efforts 26 years later by Chinese immigrants to finish building the Transcontinental Railroad in May 1869. Importantly, these curated resources include materials celebrating the genius, history, and contributions of AAPI communities as well as materials that deepen knowledge about the injustices that members of this group have faced historically and in the present day.

The school climate team curated a similar set of resources for each of the heritage months celebrated by the school. They also identified two to three core texts for each month for the entire school community to read and discuss and purchased enough copies to distribute the texts to every classroom. (Some texts were chosen to span grade bands, e.g., K–3, 3–5.) Although it is important for teachers in different grade levels and classrooms to share resources that resonate with their particular group of students, asking a school community to read core texts creates shared understandings among the entire community. For each selected core text, the climate team developed a brief teacher's guide including sample questions to engage students before, during, and after their reading.

These illustrations of shared leadership and resource curation highlight how an intentional focus on *building adult capacity* supports teachers in centering justice in their curriculum during heritage months. As a result of these efforts, Roberts teachers felt more confident and prepared as they transitioned into justice-related lesson and unit planning.

FIGURE 6.4

## Example of Resources Curated by Roberts School Climate Team

| | Resources for Asian American, Native Hawaiian, and Pacific Islanders Heritage Month (AAPI Month) |
|---|---|
| **First week of May—Background resources related to AAPI Month and community** | Common slides (optional)<br>Principal Drake video launch<br>• Origins of AAPI Month<br>• Where are Asia, Hawaii, and the Pacific Islands?<br>• Who are we celebrating?<br>• How do communities celebrate?<br><br>Upper grades are welcome to explore multitudes of identity, stereotypes, and racial injustice:<br>• "What Is the Model Minority Myth?" (www.learningforjustice.org/magazine/what-is-the-model-minority-myth)<br>• *We Are Not a Stereotype* video series—Videos produced by the Smithsonian that break down Asian Pacific American bias (https://apa.si.edu/learn/not-a-stereotype/) |
| **Read-alouds** | Core texts:<br>• *I Am Golden* by Eva Chen<br>• *Priya Dreams of Marigolds and Masala* by Meenal Patel<br><br>Supplemental texts:<br>• "12 Books to Celebrate Asian American, Native Hawaiian, and Pacific Islander Heritage Month" from PBS (www.pbs.org/parents/thrive/books-to-celebrate-asian-american-and-pacific-islander-heritage-month)<br>• "Themed Booklist: Celebrating Asian Pacific American History and Culture" from Reading Rockets (www.readingrockets.org/books-and-authors/booklists/asian-asian-american-and-pacific-islander-history-and-culture-0)<br>• "24 Books That Feature Asian American Heroes and Leads" from Tinybeans (https://tinybeans.com/kids-books-with-asian-american-characters/)<br>• *A Kids Book About Anti-Asian Hate* by Kim Pham (https://drive.google.com/file/d/15eeY2CK1zsiRrATnZpsBKv_AjkOBW2jE/view)<br>• "10 Great Books to Read for Asian American Pacific Islander (AAPI) Heritage Month" from the Anti-Defamation League (www.adl.org/resources/blog/10-great-books-read-asian-american-pacific-islander-aapi-heritage-month) |

| | Resources for Asian American, Native Hawaiian, and Pacific Islanders Heritage Month (AAPI Month) |
|---|---|
| Background information | - *AAPI Data* (https://aapidata.com)<br>- Website for Asian American Resource Workshop, a pan-Asian grassroots activist organization (www.aarw.org/)<br>- *How to Pronounce the Top Ten Chinese Family Names? (Part 3-2)* (www.youtube.com/watch?v=b9LPTxCG-38)<br>- "'We Are Always Waiting Our Turn to Be Important.' A Love Letter to Asian Americans" (https://time.com/5947724/a-love-letter-to-asian-americans/)<br>- *Teacher's Guide: Asian American and Pacific Islander Heritage and History in the U.S.* from the National Endowment for the Humanities (https://edsitement.org/teachers-guides/asian-american-and-pacific-islander-heritage-and-history-us)<br>- "Asian American Pacific Islander (AAPI) Heritage Month Resources" from the Anti-Defamation League (www.adl.org/education/resources/tools-and-strategies/asian-american-pacific-islander-aapi-heritage-month)<br>- AAPI materials search from the Southern Poverty Law Center's Learning for Justice project (www.learningforjustice.org/search?query=AAPI)<br>- "Asian American Pacific Islander Heritage Month Resource Collection for Educators" hosted by Wakelet (https://wke.lt/w/s/VZAFz9) |
| AAPI activists and community members to highlight | Individuals:<br>- Kumu Hina—Hawaiian transgender teacher who works against colonization erasure efforts to keep Native Hawaiian culture alive through gender expression and Native Hawaiian arts. (Note: In Native Hawaiian culture there is a third gender that sits between female and male.) (www.yesmagazine.org/issue/make-right/2015/07/27/what-native-hawaiian-culture-can-teach-us-about-gender-identity)<br>- Yuri Kochiyama—Japanese American civil rights activist inspired by her 1943 incarceration at an American internment camp for people of Japanese descent. (https://instituteforpr.org/pioneer-yuri-kochiyama/)<br>- Ai-jen Poo—Asian American labor activist and co-founder and executive director of the National Domestic Workers Alliance. (www.domesticworkers.org/ai-jen-poo) |

*(continued)*

FIGURE 6.4

## Example of Resources Curated by Roberts School Climate Team
*(continued)*

| | Resources for Asian American, Native Hawaiian, and Pacific Islanders Heritage Month (AAPI Month) |
|---|---|
| **AAPI activists and community members to highlight** *(continued)* | Individuals *(continued)*:<br>• Ashlyn So—13-year-old Asian American activist and designer who was named "People's Hero" at the E! People's Choice Awards. Organized a Stand for Asians rally after recent violence against the AAPI community. (www.teenvogue.com/story/ashlyn-so-aapi-hate-activist)<br>• Constance Wu—Actress who spoke out about representation in media and whitewashing of Asian roles and characters. (www.teenvogue.com/story/constance-wu-activism-speaking-up-whats-right-big-hundred-mirys-list)<br>• Malala Yousafzai—Pakistani activist for girls' education, winner of Nobel Peace Prize. (https://malala.org/malalas-story)<br><br>Lists:<br>• "30 Revolutionary Asians and Pacific Islanders to Celebrate for AAPI Heritage Month" from Negra Bohemian (www.negrabohemian.com/blog/aapi-heritage-month)<br>• "Asian American Activists to Watch" from PBS SoCal (www.pbssocal.org/shows/asian-americans/asian-american-activists-watch)<br>• "23 Asian American Heroes Our Kids Need to Know About" from Tinybeans (https://tinybeans.com/asian-american-historical-figures/)<br>• "20 Asian American and Pacific Islander Women to Know" from YWCA Minneapolis (www.ywcampls.org/blog-content/all-our-voices-blog/20-asian-american-and-pacific-islander-women-to-know)<br>• "Five Wāhine Māori Protestors (Who Other Māori Thought Were a Pain in the Ass)" (https://thespinoff.co.nz/atea/02-08-2019/five-wahine-maori-protestors-who-other-maori-thought-were-a-pain-in-the-ass/) |
| **Classroom ready** | • Newsela collection of texts about AAPI communities sorted by grade and Lexile level<br>• Article to read (for grades 3–5) about the term 'Asian American' |

# Center Justice in Curriculum and Pedagogy: Collaborative Planning Time

As should be clear from everything we've written so far, the work of nurturing students' critical consciousness goes far beyond using an isolated resource. Instead, it demands the thoughtful, intentional incorporation of sociopolitical topics and excluded and marginalized histories and communities into the existing curriculum. Such efforts take dedicated time for both planning and implementation. To bolster their work toward building adult capacity, including providing teachers with resources for their own education each heritage month, the leadership at Roberts Elementary created spaces and structures for teachers to work together to ensure that their daily activities, lessons, and assignments during heritage months were robust, meaningful opportunities for students to learn and develop their critical consciousness.

Collaborative structures allow teachers to use the resources, time, support, and professional learning they have received to develop action plans for incorporating texts and learning activities about a particular identity group into their curriculum units. Research suggests that teachers benefit from clear timelines for producing action plans, and there is great value in asking teachers to share plans across classrooms and teams so they can learn from each other and adapt or borrow from their colleagues' efforts (Gutierez, 2021; Parker, 2024).

## Collaborative Planning Time in Action

At the start of the school year, members of the school climate team led a whole-staff professional learning session focused on kicking off the school's preparations for heritage months. During the session, the team shared which heritage months had been selected and reminded colleagues about the school's "both/and" approach—introducing students to the genius of marginalized and minoritized groups *both* during particular heritage months *and* throughout the school year.

The session included designated time for grade-level teams to consider a series of guided questions about how they might shine the light on recognized identity groups during heritage months *and* the school year:

- Where in your curriculum units can you naturally infuse relevant texts?
- What materials (e.g., books, research) do you need to implement this?
- What, if anything, do you need to guard against in creating these lessons?
- How are these texts/lessons aligned with our justice framework?

Importantly, grade-level teams also had opportunities to continue these discussions during the 90 minutes of common planning time contractually built into their weekly schedule and during their two planning days each semester (described in Chapter 2). This concentrated time to intentionally think about how to center justice in the curriculum helped hold teachers accountable for creating meaningful learning opportunities for students that nurtured their critical consciousness and created internal coherence across the school.

At Roberts, the school climate team houses curated resources for each heritage month in a shared Google Drive. The drive also contains a chart for each heritage month, to which each grade-level team is expected to add their plans for honoring and celebrating the month. Figure 6.5 displays the chart for AAPI Heritage Month.

## FIGURE 6.5
## AAPI Heritage Month Action Plan

| Whole school/ administration | • Principal launches month of study during morning announcements<br>• Bulletin boards to spotlight work<br>  • Capture student work from classrooms<br>  • Rotate depending on heritage month<br>  • Reinforce the idea that celebration does not live in a single month but must be woven in all year long<br>• Heritage month morning announcements:<br>  • Teams share a blurb and sample student work during morning announcements.<br>• Updates in emails to Roberts community |
|---|---|
| Kindergarten | Kindergartners will read several books to discuss the different experiences of AAPI characters. Students will also learn about the history of bao and dumplings, rice, and noodles, which are all staple foods of Asian cuisine. We will also learn about the work that goes into harvesting rice, making dumplings and noodles, and creating the components of each dish. |
| 1st grade | First graders will read many books that showcase different parts of AAPI culture and connect these texts with discussions about the things that make us different and unique. |
| 2nd grade | Second graders will explore the geography of Asia and immigration trends in the United States. We will learn more about the experiences of Chinese, Indian, Filipino, and Korean immigrants to the United States. |
| 3rd grade | Third graders will read books by AAPI authors and about AAPI characters that demonstrate that the wealth of cultures, religions, customs, traditions, and beliefs of the AAPI community cannot be put under one label. |
| 4th grade | Fourth graders will learn about the history of discrimination faced by Asian communities in the United States, such as the Chinese Exclusion Act and bigoted stereotypes. |
| 5th grade | Fifth graders will deepen their research skills by selecting one Asian country to become an expert on, finding trustworthy sources about that country, organizing their learning in a note-catcher, crafting slides to share with the class, and adding their own creative touches to their presentation. |

*(continued)*

## FIGURE 6.5
**AAPI Heritage Month Action Plan** *(continued)*

| Art | K—Body art form known as henna or mehndi |
|---|---|
| | G1/G2—Japanese art form of origami |
| | G3—Super-flat art style of Takashi Murakami |
| | G4—Paper sculptures of Lexy Ho-Tai |
| | G5—Ceramic food sculptures of Reniel del Rosario |
| Science | Students in different grade levels will learn about contributions of AAPI scientists. |
| | K—Physicist Chien-Shiung Wu |
| | G1— Physicist Narinder Singh Kapany |
| | G2—Marine botanist Isabella Aiona Abbott |
| | G3—Inventor Soichiro Honda |
| | G4—Computer scientist Reshma Saujani |
| | G5—Meteorologist Tetsuya (Ted) Fujita |

As always, teachers draw on the school's justice framework—Muhammad's culturally and historically responsive literacy framework—to guide their thinking about how their heritage month plans will nurture students' skills, intellect, identity, critical consciousness, and joy. For example, even in the brief descriptions reproduced in Figure 6.5, we can see how the 4th grade team's plan to focus on anti-Asian discrimination and the Chinese Exclusion Act raises awareness of the history of racism against Asian Americans in the United States. And the 1st grade team's plan to introduce students to books that illuminate different parts of AAPI culture serves as a springboard for discussions about students' identities and what aspects of their own lives and cultures make them unique. Combining *centering justice in curriculum and pedagogy* with *fostering powerful partnerships*, grade-level teams are also encouraged to reach out to the school's justice partner, Little Uprisings, for additional support in developing their plans.

# Foster Powerful Partnerships: Communicate Objectives to Families

As with any school initiative focused on developing students' critical consciousness, it is important to coordinate, communicate, and engage with families and caretakers. Launching a heritage month should always include communications with students and their families and caretakers about the purpose and intention of honoring the identity group as well as the school community's learning goals and objectives for the month. This communication can be designed and carried out by the school principal, school climate team, equity committee, or another stakeholder group within the school community, but time, thought, and resources need to be invested in this effort.

## *Communicating Objectives to Families in Action*

At Roberts, the launch of each heritage month begins with a letter to families co-authored by Principal Drake and the school climate team that articulates the school's goals for the upcoming month. Figure 6.6 contains the letter sent to Roberts families a week ahead of AAPI Heritage Month.

These letters home play an important role in keeping families and caretakers updated on what their students are learning about in school and planting the seeds for conversations to continue at home. The letters also reinforce the overarching goals and principles that guide the school's approach to this work. The letter in Figure 6.6 reminds families and caretakers about the school's "both/and" approach to honoring the history, ideas, and contributions of groups that have been marginalized in the United States, and stresses that the school's dedication

FIGURE 6.6

**Letter to Families to Launch AAPI Heritage Month**

---

Dear Roberts families and caregivers,

The month of May is Asian American, Native Hawaiian, and Pacific Islanders (AAPI) Heritage month. As a school community committed to antiracism and racial equity, we recognize the importance of shining the light on the strength and beauty of all diverse, intersectional identities, including people of Asia, Hawaii, and the Pacific Islands. Asia, Hawaii, and the Pacific Islands are a vast geographical area, home to many different ethnic groups and multitudes of identities. Therefore, this month we will devote time and space to highlighting the rich racial, cultural, and linguistic diversity within AAPI communities past and present through curriculum, instruction, and cultural celebrations.

To support shared learning in our community, we have invested in two core texts: *I Am Golden* by Eva Chen and *Priya Dreams of Marigolds and Masala* by Meenal Patel. Both texts present strengths-based narratives of diverse Asian identities and cultures. Additionally, teachers will connect students' learning about the AAPI community to the content studied in the classroom. We will culminate our learning with a schoolwide showcase during morning announcements the week of June 6 to allow students across grade levels to learn from and with each other. We will also share student artifacts with families in a future email.

While heritage months are valuable, they are not sufficient or exhaustive in building respect for human differences. We recognize that to truly cultivate an inclusive, affirming, antiracist learning community, we must be intentional about celebrating diverse, intersectional human identities all year long. Thank you, as always, for your support and commitment to our shared vision and values of inclusivity, excellence, and agency. We look forward to working with you and welcome your feedback.

Sincerely,

Bethany Drake, Principal, and the School Climate Team

---

to nurturing students' critical consciousness of these groups' genius and systemic challenges will not wane once a particular heritage month has passed.

The next step in launching a heritage month is to frame the month's learning goals for students (who, of course, are also essential partners in this work). School leaders and teacher leaders can choose from multiple approaches to do so. At Roberts, Principal Drake prepares a short video in which she speaks directly to students about the upcoming heritage month and some of the things they can expect to learn. These videos also remind students of some of the overarching goals for embarking on this learning. Specifically, Drake reminds students that they attend a school committed to learning about and celebrating a wide range of groups and identities, and that engaging in this work benefits us all. She prefers for students to watch the videos in their classroom, so that they can follow up by asking questions and sharing initial thoughts with their classmates and teachers. Principal Drake also shares links with interested family members so they can view the videos. Both letters home and launch videos *foster powerful partnerships* with students and families/caretakers to support learning.

## Engage Students in Social Action: Transform Learning into Action

It is essential that school leaders and teacher leaders put in place structures and practices that create opportunities for students to transform their heritage month learning into social action. As we discussed in Chapter 4, social action can take many different forms, including spreading knowledge, debunking false statements, and pushing others to reconsider what they know. People rarely intervene in injustices they don't see or understand, so it's important that students have the opportunity to put their newly expanded consciousness to work by spreading their learning across the school and to the broader community.

### *Transforming Learning into Action in Action*

At the end of every heritage month, Roberts students and teachers at each grade level put together short presentations on what they learned and take turns sharing their presentations with the larger school community during morning meetings. This practice embodies a meaningful form of consciousness-raising and social action within the Roberts community. Each grade level expands the critical consciousness of the other grades and hold one another accountable to heightened critical reflection.

> Leaders must put in place structures and practices to transform heritage month learning into social action.

For example, after AAPI Heritage Month, Roberts 4th graders shared with their schoolmates what they had learned about Queen Liliʻuokalani of Hawaii and her efforts in the late 1800s to maintain Hawaii's independence and resist annexation by the United States. This learning resonated with the curriculum unit on the American Revolution they were concurrently studying. Specifically, the 4th graders learned—and grappled with the fact—that the United States sought to colonize Hawaii just a hundred years after fighting for its own independence from England. Engaging in this learning nurtured students' critical consciousness of the United States as a country that has participated in both revolutionary *and* imperialistic actions. In their AAPI Heritage Month presentation, the students shared this nuanced understanding with the school community.

Roberts 4th graders also shared what they learned in art class about British-Asian artist Lexy Ho-Tai, who creates sculptures out of fabric. The art teacher explained, "Ho-Tai's work is centered around the importance of play and imagination, so when we learned about her work in class, we discussed radical imagination. We talked about how imagination is an essential skill to nurture because it allows us to imagine a different world than the one we currently live in." This ability is a key element of young people's critical consciousness development because it allows them to envision a future that they can play a role in building.

Educators and school leaders can also help students share their heritage month learning with family members, caretakers, and community members. One way is through an electronic school newsletter with pictures of student work and links to videos of student presentations. At Roberts, Principal Drake links each grade-level presentation in the electronic newsletter that goes out to families and supporters at the end of the heritage month. Sharing these presentations in this way once again amplifies opportunities for students and their families to talk together at home about the experiences and contributions of identity groups in the United States that have been excluded, misrepresented, and underrepresented in school curriculum and textbooks for generations, thus spreading consciousness of the topics learned inside the classroom to the broader school community.

The examples of knowledge-raising described in this chapter are just two examples of integrating opportunities for social action during heritage months. Schools that we have worked with have also intentionally participated in campaigns supporting the identity group centered during a specific heritage month and taken direct action locally to challenge issues that deeply affect the centered communities. There are many possible avenues for engaging students in social action during heritage months.

## Fitting It All Together

Combining and interweaving the four principles we've identified is an important component of educating for justice. Imagine preparing a package containing precious contents for mailing. After you tape it up, you might step back and decide it isn't secure enough for the journey. So you reinforce the package with another layer of tape, and then another. With each additional layer, your package becomes sturdier and better able to weather the trip. Similarly, by layering or binding together the four principles identified in this book, you strengthen your efforts to support students in learning how to advance justice and push for social change. Fitting all these pieces together is a critical lever for initiating, maximizing, and sustaining any effort at schoolwide critical consciousness building.

> Layering the four principles will strengthen your efforts to support students in learning how to advance justice and push for social change.

For heritage months to be truly powerful learning opportunities that disrupt existing injustices and nurture students' critical consciousness, school communities must invest significant time and resources in connecting all four principles. At Roberts, the community worked to *build adult capacity* (the school climate team curated resources for the entire staff for each heritage month); *center justice in curriculum and pedagogy* (grade-level teams spent planning and professional learning time integrating these resources into their curriculum); *foster powerful partnerships* (Principal Drake and the school climate team communicated proactively with families about student learning during each heritage month); and *engage students in social action* (students at each grade level shared their learning with peers, family, and community members).

School communities that have invested in tightly connecting these four principles can lean into them even in unplanned moments, as we illustrate in the next chapter.

## Questions for Reflection

1. How would you assess your own school community's approach to heritage months as an opportunity to nurture students' critical consciousness (critical reflection and critical action)?
2. Is your school community more (or less) prepared to take up some heritage months and identity recognitions than others?
3. Which of the four principles—building adult capacity, centering justice in curriculum and pedagogy, fostering powerful partnerships with families and community partners, and engaging students in social action—is/are contributing powerfully to this work?
4. Which of these four principles could be leveraged more meaningfully in your school community to support the uptake of learning opportunities such as heritage months?

## Additional Resources

Chiariello, E. (2015, February 2). Heritage months: Hard to handle? *Learning for Justice.* https://www.learningforjustice.org/magazine/heritage-months-hard-to-handle

Menkart, D. J. (1999). Deepening the meaning of heritage months. *Educational Leadership, 56*(7), 19–20.

The New School Libraries Research Guides. *Heritage months and recognition days.* https://guides.library.newschool.edu/recognition

Nichols, H. (2024, February 21). When Black history meets women's history. *Edutopia.* https://www.edutopia.org/article/black-history-womens-history-months/

U.S. Department of State. (n.d.). *State Department celebrates heritage and history months.* https://www.state.gov/state-department-celebrates-heritage-and-history-months/

# Respond to Local, National, and Global Tragedies

Heritage months are annual occurrences that educators and schools can plan and prepare for. But sometimes tragic, traumatic, and unjust events locally, nationally, or internationally arise quickly, leaving little or no time to plan (Dunn, 2022). Examples include police violence, school shootings, natural disasters, political uprisings, the outbreak of war, and more. When events like these occur, there is often little time for educators to develop, communicate, and execute a plan for engaging students in reflection and learning about what is happening and supporting the students most affected. This chapter will explore how the four principles for cultivating students' critical consciousness schoolwide—building adult capacity, centering justice in curriculum and pedagogy, fostering powerful family and community partnerships, and engaging students in social action—can be applied in concert to make space for students to articulate and process their pain, learn more about the root causes of continued violence and harm against communities, and plan together how they might actively respond.

When tragic and unjust events occur, some schools and districts explicitly prohibit teachers from talking about them with their students, as if such prohibitions will protect youth from having to contemplate or experience the world around them. Unfortunately, as numerous studies highlight, *not* talking about injustices leaves young people on their own to try to make sense of the information flooding their social media feeds and dominating the news and adult conversations (Gewirtz, 2020). To be silent in the wake of horrific events also implicitly teaches students that silence during moments of injustice is justified, that emotional responses to such events are not appropriate for school, and that there is little value in reflecting upon or taking action in response (Jones & Hagopian, 2020).

Students need and deserve opportunities to discuss, process, reflect on, learn from, and respond to tragic and unjust events (Delpit, 2021). Although educators and school leaders cannot plan precisely for all the injustices and tragedies that may arise in our lives and communities, they can establish structures and practices that support the critical work of talking about and responding to these events with students. School communities that have invested in—and proactively connected—the four principles are far better positioned to engage their students in critical reflection and action when these events occur. This chapter outlines several key steps that a school community can take to engage students in processing, learning from, and responding to tragic and unjust events, illustrated by descriptions of how staff and students at Roberts Elementary School responded to the 2020 police killing of George Floyd in Minneapolis, Minnesota, and the 2022 invasion of Ukraine by Russia.

To be clear, the three of us are not trained as trauma specialists. Our goal in this chapter is to help school leaders and teacher leaders consider how the structures, practices, and processes introduced in the previous chapters can help members of a school community—both students and adults—process, learn from, and respond to local, national, and global tragedies. That said, school leaders and teacher leaders also need to consult with mental health specialists and trauma-informed experts to support school communities during these times. Some districts have intentional protocols and resources for responding to a tragedy that ensure safe, developmentally appropriate, and differentiated supports for students and staff. Some districts also curate talking points and processes for student circles and share educational resources and supportive strategies with families and caretakers in their home languages. In sum, the guidance we offer in this chapter is just one component of a comprehensive strategy for guiding your school community through unexpected local, national, and global tragedies.

## Foster Powerful Partnerships: Seek Out Wisdom from Community Partners

On May 25, 2020, in Minneapolis, police officer Derek Chauvin murdered George Floyd by kneeling on Floyd's neck for nearly 10 minutes while Floyd was handcuffed and lying face down in the street. When cell phone video footage of this gruesome murder became public, protests and demonstrations erupted across the country. At Roberts, Principal Drake knew that her students were seeing footage of Floyd's death on the news and social media, listening to their parents and family members express rage and despair, and experiencing their own tumult of emotions. Children as young as 6 and 7 years old were aware that something awful had happened. Drake also knew that she and her staff needed to be ready to support their students in processing, understanding, and reflecting on the brutal murder and resulting protests, but she wasn't exactly sure how to proceed.

Chapter 2 described the role community partners can play in supporting a school's justice efforts and defined *justice partner* as an external partner whose core expertise is in equity and justice, and whose work and training can inform, deepen, and challenge educators' teaching about these topics. The educators facilitating affinity groups at the school (described in Chapter 5) are examples of justice partners, as are the Little Uprisings coaches (described in Chapter 2) who consult with Roberts teachers during curriculum planning days. A justice partner may also be able to offer counsel to teachers and school leaders about how to respond to tragic and unjust events.

## *Seeking Out Wisdom from Community Partners in Action*

Principal Drake decided to turn to the school's justice partners after footage of George Floyd's murder was released. She drafted a letter to Roberts staff and families, then reached out to the educator who had been facilitating the affinity group for teachers of color for feedback. This justice partner encouraged her to consider how both the critical reflection and critical action components of critical consciousness might be important in this moment. She advised Drake to frame the conversations with

Roberts students first with a deep acknowledgment of the violent, horrible act that occurred and a genuine acknowledgment of their pain and the ways in which structural racism contributed to this inhumane crime. She also suggested that Drake remind students of activist efforts to curb police brutality and persistent anti-Black violence in the current moment and historically.

The justice partner also advised the principal to call an emergency staff meeting to brief them on this approach to responding to George Floyd's murder and worked with her ahead of the meeting to pull together resources to share with staff to support their upcoming conversations with students about the event. Together, Principal Drake and her justice partner also identified different resources for teachers working with the early grades versus the upper elementary grades.

In short, in the wake of an unexpected traumatic event, both the school leader and the school community benefited deeply from the guidance and counsel of a justice partnership that had been established and strengthened over many years. Powerful partnerships are key to almost all work in a school, and they can be invaluable when navigating the complex realities of daily experiences with systems of marginalization. As we see from this example, a justice partner was able to remind Drake that, in this case, students would benefit from opportunities for healing, time to process the depths of the injustice, and connections to activist efforts.

# Build Adult Capacity and Center Justice: Hold Space

Each year, during beginning-of-the-year training, school leaders should share or co-construct with teachers schoolwide commitments and protocols for responding to local or national tragedies. For example, teachers should understand the school's priorities related to offering students (and themselves) space to process, learn, and act. Proactive protocols can also outline who in the school community will offer teaching resources as well as timelines for when teachers can expect guidance from school leaders. Proactively and intentionally defining the school's commitments and process helps ensure that adults are on the same page about how the school will respond in these moments and can help mitigate some of the immediate anxiety teachers and leaders feel when tragic sociopolitical events occur.

> Each year, school leaders should share or co-construct with teachers schoolwide commitments and protocols for responding to tragedies.

It is often valuable to gather school staff immediately after an unexpected tragedy or act of injustice, even if this involves meeting outside school hours. One goal of this gathering is to help staff coordinate how to approach the event with students and to share guidance and resources for doing so. An equally important goal is to give teachers a space to process their own thoughts and emotions before asking them to stand in front of a classroom and facilitate conversations with students. Often, school leaders overlook the practice of responding to teachers in the aftermath of a tragedy as we would want them to respond to their students. Yet as leaders, we want to keep in mind that teachers are human beings who deserve care and consideration.

### *Holding Space in Action*

Following George Floyd's murder, Principal Drake reached out to staff via email and called an emergency Sunday afternoon meeting. Part of her message was explicitly addressed to the school's teachers of color:

> I want to acknowledge that, as a White woman, I will never know how this feels on the ground for you, and you are facing the double challenge of experiencing racialized violence as a person of color who navigates this every day, and also knowing that you have the responsibility of kids coming in who are reeling from it too. You are welcome to join [this Sunday meeting]. Your voices are valued. But if you are not in a place right now where you want to lean into this conversation, that is OK.

Several teachers of color took up Drake's invitation not to attend the emergency meeting but instead spend the weekend focusing on their and their family's well-being and participating in social action in their communities. Other teachers of color chose to join the Sunday meeting.

In the same email, Principal Drake spoke directly to the school's White teachers:

> White educators, I am now speaking directly to you. You need to show up to this planning meeting. White person to White person, we are not living through this the same way. Most of the students that are coming through the doors on Monday identify as people of color, and a lot of our colleagues are in a tremendous amount of pain right now. So we need to do our homework to make sure that we enter into this as supportive, aspiring allies.

Principal Drake's explicit acknowledgment of the different positionalities of White teachers and teachers of color was only possible because of all the work and conversations that Roberts staff had already engaged in about racial and systemic inequities. As we described in Chapter 5, adults in the school community had facilitated cross-racial dialogues for several years, and many had participated in racial affinity spaces. As described in Chapter 1, teachers had also already worked to build a justice framework into their curriculum planning processes. Because of this foundational work, Principal Drake's acknowledgment of the differential impact of this tragedy on different members of the staff was neither surprising nor divisive. Leaders in school communities that have not done this foundational work might not feel able to communicate with staff in such straightforward terms.

George Floyd's murder led Principal Drake to take the unprecedented step of an emergency weekend staff meeting because his death was one of the most visceral and visible contemporary examples of the extrajudicial violence that Black Americans suffer at the hands of police, and because his murder inspired the biggest racial justice protests seen in the United States since the 1960s. Additionally, the violent crime affected many of the school's students and families.

There have been other events and circumstances that led Principal Drake to communicate and connect with staff to facilitate a schoolwide response. When Russia invaded Ukraine in February 2022, the school was closed for winter break, so Drake reached out to faculty during the break to help them prepare to support students when they returned to school the following Monday (see Figure 7.1).

In her note, Drake sought to accomplish many of the same goals that led her to bring her staff together following the murder of George Floyd. She urged her staff to be mindful of their own well-being and invited them to reach out to her or other members of her administrative team to process their own thoughts and emotions about the Russian invasion. She shared resources that teachers could use to engage students in discussion, and she encouraged teachers, particularly those in the upper grades, to do so. Finally, she reminded her staff that they had worked hard throughout the school year to engage their students in reflection on topics of power, injustice, and resistance to injustice, and they could draw upon students' knowledge of these topics to help them process and analyze the events in Ukraine. This last point, in particular, serves as a powerful reminder that the

FIGURE 7.1
## Letter to Faculty in Response to Russia's 2022 Invasion of Ukraine

Good evening, Roberts faculty,

I hope everyone had a warm, restful, and rejuvenating school vacation week.

I'm saddened to welcome you back with a letter about the devastating events transpiring in Ukraine. Whether this war touches our community directly or indirectly, this is a senseless, baseless, and inhumane invasion motivated by power, with costs that are all too familiar to the Ukrainian people. It's also heartbreaking to see that even amid this humanitarian crisis, racism is rearing its ugly face as refugees experience disparate treatment based on race. As I said in a family letter due to go out tomorrow before school, as a school community committed to antiracism we can *both* stand with the people of the Ukraine *and* advocate for more inclusive and equitable treatment of *all* people. One injustice does not justify another.

As you prepare to greet students tomorrow morning, I wanted to provide you with some resources. Given that we don't know how aware students are of the events, I'm not expecting you to lead formal content circles. However, I do recommend that circle/community spaces are used to provide space for questions, concerns, or feelings should they be necessary, particularly in the upper grades. This is also an opportunity to connect current events to some of the themes students have learned about this year, including structural inequities, power, forms of resistance, and avenues for advocacy. This not only helps students better understand the structural and societal forces that contribute to what is happening but also shines a light on the way people are resisting and how people outside of Ukraine are mobilizing to support Ukrainians. To support both formal and less formal discussions, you may want to explore the following resources:

- **"How to Talk to Kids About the Ukraine Invasion"** from PBS SoCal (https://www.pbssocal.org/education/how-to-talk-to-kids-about-the-ukraine-invasion)

    This article has wonderful ideas on how to talk to elementary-aged children about the context specifically and generally. I used some of these resources with my own children when they had questions about something they heard on the news.

- **"Head, Heart, Conscience" teaching strategy from Facing History & Ourselves** (https://www.facinghistory.org/resource-library/head-heart-conscience)

    This activity can be used with students in the upper grades.

*(continued)*

FIGURE 7.1
**Letter to Faculty in Response to Russia's 2022 Invasion of Ukraine**
(continued)

> - **"Ukraine–Russia Conflict 2022 Media Literacy Choice Board from professors at University of Amherst Massachusetts** (https://docs.google.com/document/u/0/d/1YoqsH0T3xfheEWbdsA1LY8OqZJo_jCCPZo7d1jm6Ixg)
>
>   This choice board has good information about Ukraine and the media contexts related to the invasion.
>
> Our support team will be available throughout the day to assist with circles, check-ins, or crisis response with students. Please reach out to us via WhatsApp. Some staff have asked for an opportunity to do some planning together. I will open my office at 8:30 for staff members who would like to connect or process their approach with their students.
>
> Finally, please take care of yourself. If you are having difficulty supporting a student or are experiencing your own feelings in response to the events in the Ukraine, please do not hesitate to reach out to a member of the support team or the administration.
>
> In solidarity,
>
> Bethany Drake, Principal

foundational work that schools and educators do to help students recognize, analyze, and challenge injustice can facilitate their ability to support students' well-being when tragic and unjust events arise in local communities, the national context, or across the globe.

 ## Engage Students in Social Action and Foster Powerful Partnerships: Communicate Learning Goals

In the wake of tragedy and injustice, many family members and caretakers want to know whether and how their children's teachers are planning to address the events in school. Some families have strong opinions on it, and others will simply want to know what the school's plan is so that they can engage with their children at home accordingly. Given that there is never a singular correct way to respond to tragedy or injustice, there is also no way that the set of actions a school community elects to carry out will meet the approval of every student's family. As a reminder, school leaders should anticipate and expect some resistance to critical consciousness and justice work, including from some members of students' families (see Chapter 3 for more information on responding to this resistance). What we have found in numerous cases, however, is that even parents and caretakers who hold divergent perspectives on how to respond to tragic events appreciate clear communication from the school about what types of discussions and learning will (or will not) take place in school and why those educational decisions have been made.

Family members who disagree strongly with the school's approach will often reach out to their children's teachers and administrators to voice their disagreement, and these family members deserve earnest engagement with their viewpoints. They may express worries about teachers' ability to facilitate conversations on these topics or have questions about how differing viewpoints will be handled. One of the most common perspectives voiced by parents and caretakers in these circumstances is that their children are too young to learn about the events that have unfolded. We have been explicit about our own belief that children and adolescents

> Even families who hold divergent perspectives on how to respond to tragic events appreciate clear communication from the school about educational decisions.

need and deserve opportunities to discuss, process, reflect upon, learn from, and respond to tragic and unjust events, but we recognize that this parental concern is reasonable and understandable. Remember, in the wake of tragic events, all but the youngest of our children hear *something* and see *something* about the events preoccupying the adults in their lives, and they naturally start trying to figure out what is going on. Accordingly, we urge concerned family members and caretakers to shift their question from whether their children are developmentally ready to handle discussions about the tragedy to whether they want their children to have these conversations on their own, without guidance from caring adults in their lives.

### *Communicating Learning Goals in Action*

After Principal Drake convened the school's staff for an emergency meeting in response to George Floyd's murder, she reached out to students' families to apprise them of her plans (see Figure 7.2). In her letter, she worked hard to explain as specifically as possible *how* families could expect their children's teachers to approach George Floyd's murder with their children. She explained her plan to raise the issue in a developmentally appropriate way during the morning message for the whole school community, that upper grade teachers would use resources from a trusted organization to hold discussions with their classes, and that early childhood teachers would focus on positive narratives of people of color in trauma-sensitive ways. She sought to convey that the goal was not to focus on the grotesque details of George Floyd's murder with students but rather to acknowledge that some students—particularly those in the upper elementary grades—would want to talk about and process what happened with teachers and classmates they know

FIGURE 7.2
**Letter to Families in Response to the Murder of George Floyd**

---

Good afternoon, Roberts families,

I hope you all found the opportunity to get outside and enjoy the beautiful weather today.

I'm saddened to write another letter in response to the continued senseless and inhumane acts of violence occurring against people of color in our country. The pain and anger of Black and Brown communities in our city and across the country are palpable, justified, and real. Ahmaud Arbery, Breonna Taylor, George Floyd—we speak their names because their lives matter. We speak their names because we are a caring community. We honor their lives and those of their families and friends left mourning. We speak their names because this country can, and must, do better.

As we watch, groups of people across the country are taking action to resist racial violence and injustice. We are aware that these images are jarring and bring up feelings of fear, anger, and confusion for our children and for us. As a school leader, I can't bring back the lives that have been lost. I can't erase the images on the television screen or social media. What I can and will do is to center our school community in the history of oppression and the responses to it. For centuries, people of color and their White allies have strategized, mobilized, and fought for racial justice. Some are invisible in our history books, and others are prominently featured. Still, each has had a reason for their chosen path and has left blueprints for us to study. Today, more than ever, we need students to understand forms of resistance past and present so that they can make sense of what is happening and begin to identify opportunities to take agency for a better, healthier, and more inclusive future—a future that celebrates, honors, and protects Black and Brown lives.

Today, racial justice organization Wee the People is providing an opportunity for students and families to take agency by using their voices, bodies, and imagination to act and resist. We encourage Roberts staff and families to participate in Wee Chalk the Walk: A Day of Action for Black Lives and share with our community pictures, words, and videos.

Monday, I will acknowledge the current events in a developmentally appropriate manner during the morning message. Our students of color must know that we love them, see them, value them, and stand with them. This week, our upper grade teachers are preparing to lead discussions with students focusing on the concept of resistance past and present adapted from Facing History & Ourselves (www.facinghistory.org). They will do this with a developmentally appropriate trauma-sensitive lens. Early childhood teachers will continue to

*(continued)*

### FIGURE 7.2

**Letter to Families in Response to the Murder of George Floyd**
*(continued)*

> shine the light on the positive narratives of people of color. These narratives are all too often diluted and whitewashed throughout mainstream curricula.
>
> We have so very far to go as a nation. The physical violence we bear witness to today is a manifestation of the insidiousness of systemic oppression. It has always been here, but now it is painfully visible. It cannot be ignored. People of color deserve justice, love, and support. White people deserve to live in a world that is just for everyone. We all must resist our unjust systems. So, together, we will continue to academically examine the strength, courage, and resiliency of people. Our children are powerful and are empowered to change the world. Ahmaud Arbery, Breonna Taylor, and George Floyd's lives matter. We will not rest until Black lives matter!
>
> Sincerely,
>
> Bethany Drake, Principal

and trust. She communicated that teachers would be prepared to offer students safe, developmentally appropriate structures for having those conversations. Drawing on guidance from her justice partner, Principal Drake also assured parents that these discussions would also emphasize the rich history of Black people's resistance to horrific injustices like this one.

Principal Drake also explained *why* she and her staff had chosen to respond in these ways. She wrote that the school's children of color need to know that the entire community loves them, sees them, values them, and stands with them. She noted that shutting down students' questions and trying to proceed with business as usual sends the opposite message to students, and that students deserve time and space to process what happened in developmentally appropriate ways. She wrote that the entire student body needs to understand forms of resistance to these types of injustices past and present so that they can play a role now and in the future in building a society that honors and protects Black and Brown lives. She wrote that the school community needs to speak George Floyd's name because his and other Black lives matter, and because he deserves to be mourned. And she explained that teachers would address these events with students because nurturing students' critical consciousness of injustice is a key dimension of the education the school seeks to offer its students every day in every curriculum unit.

Principal Drake also encouraged family members and caretakers to engage their children in social action challenging racism and, in particular, extrajudicial violence against Black Americans. She pointed families toward a specific social action activity in their city that was designed for children and their families, and she encouraged families who participated in this event to share their experiences with the rest of the school community. As Principal Drake wrote, it is important to give students opportunities to learn about, process, and discuss injustices against Black Americans, but it is also essential to offer them opportunities to engage in action and resistance that contribute to dismantling these injustices.

There were certainly parents and family members who disagreed with these plans—or aspects of these plans—for engaging students in processing and reflecting upon the murder of George Floyd. One teacher acknowledged that a few of her students' parents reached out to her to express concern that 3rd grade is too young for these types of conversations. But many other families appreciated Principal Drake's clarity and leadership in this moment, and Drake hoped that all parents, whether they agreed or not, felt clarity about what their students would be learning in school and why they would be learning it.

Unfortunately, the murder of George Floyd was just one of many injustices that Principal Drake and Roberts staff needed to process with students. When a Black young adult named Daunte Wright was killed during a traffic stop by a Minnesota police officer just 11 months after the murder of George Floyd, Drake again coordinated with staff to make a proactive plan for supporting students and reached out to families to communicate that plan. In her letter to families, she wrote:

> In Minneapolis and across the country, the BIPOC [Black, Indigenous, People of Color] community is reeling with feelings of anger, frustration, and deep, deep pain because incidents like these are far too familiar to people of color and, more often than not, completely unchecked. As a White woman, I will never know this pain directly, but as a mother, sister, daughter, friend, colleague, and human being, it is absolutely devastating to witness. My heart goes out to the families of Daunte, George, and countless others who have been lost through racialized violence. I also want to acknowledge that it is the responsibility of the White community at Roberts and beyond, to listen, learn, support, and stand with communities of color. We must extend love, patience, and compassion to all students, families, and staff but in particular those of the BIPOC community directly affected by recent and ongoing events. We must also continually seek to hear, center, and empower the voices of our BIPOC community members as valued partners in our collective journey toward a more inclusive and equitable future. Racism is a problem created by White people, but it is only by working together that we can disrupt and dismantle it.

She then detailed how she and staff members planned to address Daunte Wright's killing with students and the reasoning underlying these decisions. Some parents and educators may ask whether expending instructional time and resources on these tragedies takes away from students' academic learning, but Roberts Elementary School's vision of powerful teaching and learning—represented by its culturally and historically responsive literacy justice framework—positions nurturing students' positive identities and critical consciousness of injustice as central goals for student learning that are intertwined with and inextricable from students' development of skills and knowledge.

## Put All the Pieces Together

The first five chapters of this book described structures, practices, and professional learning that can help a school community put in place principles to nurture students' critical consciousness schoolwide. Establishing these structures, practices, and professional learning is time-intensive work that, truthfully, requires multiple years of sustained investment on the part of school leaders and teacher leaders in collaboration with students, their families, and community partners. What we have worked to demonstrate in Chapters 6 and 7 is that putting these pieces into place by activating a school community's commitment to *build adult capacity, center justice in curriculum and pedagogy, foster powerful partnerships with families and community members,* and *engage students in social action* will amplify the school's capacity to implement learning opportunities for students in robust and meaningful ways.

Many schools abstain from engaging their students in processing national tragedies because school leaders fear that these topics are too fraught to take on and because, frankly, they doubt staff members and students will be able to consider these topics in nuanced and meaningful ways. Scott was a second-year teacher when the World Trade Center buildings were attacked on September 11, 2001, and he can still remember being directed by his school district's central office not to discuss the attacks with his students (a directive that he and many other teachers ignored). In reality, the problem in many schools is not the staff or the students but the absence of structures, practices, and professional learning to provide the scaffolding and trust needed for educators, students, and families to work together to reflect on and respond to these important events and circumstances. School communities that have done the work to put these pieces in place are poised to help their students interrogate the world we live in on both inspiring and harrowing days.

 ## Questions for Reflection

1. How would you assess your own school community's capacity and willingness to engage students in processing, learning, and acting in response to local, national, and global tragedies?
2. Are there particular types of injustices that your school community is more or less prepared to process, learn from, and respond to?
3. Which of the four principles—build adult capacity, center justice in curriculum and pedagogy, foster powerful partnerships with families and community members, engage students in social action—is contributing powerfully to this capacity and readiness?
4. Which of these four principles could be leveraged more meaningfully in your school community to support your school's capacity and motivation to respond to national tragedies?

# Additional Resources

Anderson, J. (2023, November 16). Talking to kids when the world feels scary [Podcast]. *EdCast*. Harvard Graduate School of Education. https://www.gse.harvard.edu/ideas/edcast/23/11/talking-kids-when-world-feels-scary

Boudreau, E. (2021, January 7). Making space for difficult conversations. *Usable Knowledge*. Harvard Graduate School of Education. https://www.gse.harvard.edu/ideas/usable-knowledge/21/01/making-space-difficult-discussions

Dunn, A. H. (2022). *Teaching on days after: Educating for equity in the wake of injustice*. Teachers College Press.

Facing History & Ourselves. (2021, August 31). Head, heart, conscience. https://www.facinghistory.org/resource-library/head-heart-conscience

Facing History & Ourselves. (2022, May 22). Current events in the classroom. https://www.facinghistory.org/resource-library/current-events-classroom

Kris, D. F. (2022, February 25). How to talk to kids about the Ukraine invasion. *PBS SoCal*. https://www.pbssocal.org/education/how-to-talk-to-kids-about-the-ukraine-invasion

Shafer, L. (2017, February 21). Talking race, controversy, and trauma: How to open space for reflection and conversation amid difficult events. *Usable Knowledge*. Harvard Graduate School of Education. https://www.gse.harvard.edu/ideas/usable-knowledge/17/02/talking-race-controversy-and-trauma

# Conclusion: Justice Is a Verb

In 1963, writer and cultural critic James Baldwin gave a speech to K–12 teachers in New York City in which he observed that societies are afraid of changemakers. He explained, "What societies really, ideally, want is a citizenry which will simply obey the rules of society" (as cited in Zinn Education Project, n.d., para. 2). The problem, he added, is that societies that succeed in quelling their changemakers will surely perish.

Accordingly, Baldwin issued a challenge to the teachers, individuals whom he believed possessed both the power and the opportunity to prevent social stagnation and turn the tide toward transformative change. He called on teachers to teach every child that they have "the right and the necessity to examine everything" (para. 19) and insisted that it is up to teachers to "change these standards [of society] for the sake of the life and the health of the country" (para. 19). In these words, Baldwin emphasizes that a central purpose of education *has* to be preparing youth to engage in critical reflection and critical action—the two key elements of critical consciousness.

Watching just five minutes of local or national news reveals that much work remains to ensure the life and health of our country and the thriving of our children. The call to nurture a new generation of changemakers is more urgent than ever. However, with astounding power and force, groups and institutions in our country are actively trying to keep young people from learning about the roots and consequences of injustice. Courses on African American history have been shelved (Pendharkar, 2023); teachers are prohibited from discussing sexual orientation or gender identity with their students (Burga, 2023); spending on equity, diversity, and inclusion has been outlawed (McGee, 2023); and more than 800 books that feature LGBTQ+ characters, address issues of race and racism, and focus on themes of human rights and activism have been banned from school and public libraries (Restrepo, 2023). All these laws, prohibitions, curriculum mandates, teacher sanctions, and book bans explicitly and unabashedly seek to prevent young people from learning, in Baldwin's words, how to "examine everything" so that the status quo remains intact.

We wrote this book because we know James Baldwin was right. Educators are the difference between a society producing informed, capable, and proactive agents of social change and a society having none. And each day that we don't leverage the tools we have at our disposal to undo the harm we see around us and participate in creating more just conditions, we are complicit.

> Educators are the difference between a society producing informed, capable, prepared, and proactive agents of social change and a society having none.

We know that many educators want to work with students to advance justice yet lack the tools or time to do so effectively.

Therefore, the best way that we know to support our vision of a more just society is to offer in this book as many concrete ideas as possible to school leaders and teacher leaders for creating the structures, processes, and conditions for embedding this commitment in their own schools. In the preceding chapters, we have offered specific examples and guidance for how to do the following:

- Establish structures that enable adult learning about injustice and resistance to injustice
- Build an arc of professional learning to help educators integrate their own learning about injustice and strategies for action into their curriculum, and, in so doing, build their students' critical consciousness
- Leverage the expertise of community experts or justice partners to support educators and schools in their justice-focused work
- Partner with students' families and caretakers to amplify and strengthen students' critical consciousness and equip them to transform the world
- Put structures in place to help teachers and students respond together to injustices in their communities and the wider world
- Design school-based structures for educators and students to work together to challenge injustice through social action

Offering specific structures, practices, and professional learning in support of critical consciousness development schoolwide is a balancing act because, of course, there is no single pathway to operationalize a schoolwide commitment to justice work. Every school community is unique, and one size never fits all. We anticipate that you might need to adjust, reimagine, or even set aside some of the approaches we've discussed to make them fit your own school community. We want you to think of *Educating for Justice* as more of a guide than a blueprint. However, we firmly believe you will be able to adapt many of the structures, practices, and professional learning experiences you have encountered in this book to meaningfully foster students' critical consciousness in your own school context.

## Committing to Critical Consciousness Work

In his "Talk to Teachers," Baldwin also offered an important reminder to teachers who take up their responsibility to nurture students' critical consciousness:

> Any citizen of this country who figures himself as responsible—and particularly those of you who deal with the minds and hearts of young people—must be prepared to "go for broke." Or to put it another way, you must understand that in the attempt to correct so many generations of bad faith and cruelty, when it is operating not only in the classroom but in society, you will meet the most fantastic, the most brutal, and the most determined resistance. There is no point in pretending that this won't happen. (as cited in Zinn Education Project, n.d., para. 1)

As educators and scholars who have tried hard to take on the responsibility of this work, we know from firsthand experience that the determined resistance Baldwin speaks of is inevitable. The work is hard, and it comes with risks. But so too does living in an unjust world.

If we care about our students, our students' families, and our communities, we must be willing to do the hard work necessary to nurture students' critical consciousness, even if that work entails facing resistance from those who wish to preserve the status quo. If the world before us—a world where genocide and war still happen, mass shootings are commonplace, and life opportunities are shaped by class, race, gender, language, and ability—is not the one we want our students to inherit, we have to be willing to step forward and accept Baldwin's call to action; we have to be willing to "go for broke." As we embark on this work individually and collectively, we offer a few last reminders:

> We must be willing to do the hard work necessary, even if that work entails facing resistance from those who wish to preserve the status quo.

1. **Challenging injustice is a verb.** Activist Stacey Abrams reminds us that challenging injustice is a verb, a daily commitment, a choice we must make collectively over and over again (Helm, 2019). One initiative, one policy change, one engagement strategy, one tool, one curricular adaptation alone will not radically transform our schools into living and breathing organizations that advance justice. There are simply no shortcuts in this work. The structures, practices, and professional learning we have presented cannot all be launched or carried out in a single school year. Becoming a school community that nurtures students' critical consciousness development schoolwide is a deep, steady, long-term commitment.

2. **Academic excellence and critical consciousness building are not separate goals.** All critical consciousness work requires both content knowledge and skills. We don't need to choose between meeting state standards and supporting students to create and sustain a better world. Put another way, excellent teaching and learning *definitionally* include opportunities for students

to explore their own and others' identities, learn about injustices in our society based on those identities, and participate in challenging those injustices.

3. **Seeing, affirming, and leveraging our students' and their families' funds of knowledge is our job.** Many will say that a parent or caregiver is a child's first and most important educator. However, saying that, and even believing that, does not automatically translate into actions that truly honor and affirm every family's knowledge and insight into their child's strengths and needs. In our own development as educators, we have found ourselves unlearning and re-envisioning our understanding of authentic engagement and school–home partnerships that are culturally and linguistically affirming and truly inclusive of our diverse family communities. We have also had to learn how to create more authentic spaces to listen to and learn from the voices that we as educators and school leaders are least likely to hear. Sometimes those voices have told us things that were hard to hear, and we had to learn to be grateful for that candor and feedback. We have also learned that to be truly inclusive, we sometimes have to stop using practices that engage a privileged minority to provide more equitable access for others. Overall, just as a tree's health and strength are deeply dependent on its roots, our students' educational journey and growth are significantly influenced by their school's connection and involvement with their families.

4. **This work is a commitment to collective learning and unlearning.** Beverly Daniel Tatum (2017) famously and powerfully compared racism and other oppressive forces to smog in the air that we are constantly breathing

in, consciously or unconsciously. For this reason, there is never an endpoint or finish line for our own adult learning about injustice and resistance to injustice. We must continually engage in reflection and analysis about how our own ideas and perspectives are shaped by the pernicious ideas, images, and ideologies steeped in the air we breathe. And we must do so in ways that do not burden those who live and endure the consequences of injustice every single day. This type of self-work and learning is not easy, but it is necessary and must be done with intentionality, partnership, and care.

> There is never an endpoint or finish line for our own adult learning about injustice and resistance to injustice.

5. **Critical consciousness work benefits all students.** All children deserve to see accurate, affirming, strengths-based narratives of themselves in the curriculum they study. All students have a right to learn about and celebrate their identities and those of their peers. All students must be equipped and empowered with the knowledge and skills to recognize, question, and challenge injustices around them. These learning experiences build students' capacity for active citizenship and meaningful civic engagement (Bañales et al., 2021; Hope & Jagers, 2014). They position students to deepen their relationships with themselves and their communities (Burson & Godfrey, 2020; Pinedo et al., 2024). And they prepare students to thrive in and transform the world (Rapa et al., 2018; Seider et al., 2023). We do not believe there are schools or student bodies for whom critical consciousness work is not relevant or important. *All* students benefit from

learning to recognize, analyze, and challenge injustice, as do the various communities in which they live, learn, and lead.

6. **Our students are ready.** When Julia's son's 3rd grade teacher introduced the class to counternarratives of Thanksgiving from the perspective of Indigenous peoples, he came home motivated to share his learning with his younger sister: "Mila, it's important that you know the whole story!" He was more than ready to continue the conversation. After Aaliyah's 6-year-old niece learned about climate change and its differential impact on economically marginalized communities from her kindergarten teacher, she came home eager to hold her family accountable for doing their part in preserving the planet for everyone. She talked to her parents and siblings about the importance of recycling and was ready to jump into action. When Scott's 4-year-old son had a religious school teacher who identified as nonbinary, he came home from the first day of class and explained matter-of-factly that some people don't see themselves as exclusively a boy or a girl, and so they use "they" instead of "he" or "she." His new understanding of gender nudged him to start questioning friends at preschool who talked about boy colors and girl colors, or boy toys and girl toys. Even our youngest students enter our classrooms with ideas, opinions, and perspectives they want to share. They are eager to question, challenge, and contribute to their classrooms and school communities, and they will leverage whatever platform is made available for them to do so. When we avoid challenging topics in the classroom or fracture the story to avoid the discomfort of sharing the complete and

ugly truth, every learner is affected, every child misses out, and our children respond to our avoidance by losing trust, disengaging, or revolting.

If there is one thing we have learned in our collective 60 years in K–12 education, it is this: *Trust young people.* They are capable of doing hard things if we offer them the conditions to do so. We have seen elementary schoolers thoughtfully consider charged topics like book bans in schools, middle schoolers demand counternarratives be included in their curriculum, and high schoolers suss out injustice and take meaningful action to advance social justice in their own neighborhoods. Our students are ready. The question is, are we?

James Baldwin infused his 1963 "A Talk to Teachers" with a call to action: "The obligation of anyone who thinks of himself as responsible is to examine society and try to change it and to fight it—at no matter what risk. This is the only hope society has. This is the only way societies change" (as cited in Zinn Education Project, n.d., para. 2). For educators contemplating taking up this call to action—or already doing so—we hope that these pages can contribute to your vital efforts to transform society and build a better, more just world.

## Questions for Reflection

1. What steps toward centering justice in your school community are you ready to take now?
2. What steps will come next?
3. What steps will you hold off on until later, and why?
4. What questions or concerns do you have about moving this work forward?

## Additional Resources

Duncan-Andrade, J. M. R. (2022). *Equality or equity: Toward a model of community-responsive education.* Harvard Education Press.

Zinn Education Project. (n.d.). A talk to teachers. https://www.zinnedproject.org/materials/baldwin-talk-to-teachers

# Acknowledgments

First and foremost, we are grateful to the staff, students, and family members at the Sarah C. Roberts Elementary School and all the other K–12 schools featured in this book who welcomed us into their classrooms and made the time to speak with us for this project. Maintaining your confidentiality means we cannot thank you by name, but please know how truly grateful we are to each of you for sharing your experiences, perspectives, and insights. It was a privilege to spend time in your classrooms, committee meetings, planning days, and consultations.

We are also greatly indebted to the members of our research team who helped us to collect field notes, transcribe interviews, and keep this project moving forward. Thank you in particular to Brianna Diaz and Kelly Ward for their hard work and for being such wonderful colleagues, collaborators, and scholars. Our sincere thanks as well to Tatisha McKay, Farida Mama Graham, and Meg Parquette for reading and offering valuable feedback to us on draft chapters, and to Ben Nosek for helping design the graphic of our four principles.

We are deeply grateful to ASCD editors Stephanie Bize and Jennifer Morgan for championing and supporting this project from the very beginning.

## From Scott

I am also grateful to my co-authors, Aaliyah and Julia, for the brilliance they brought to this project. I am grateful to my colleagues and students at Boston College, my community of critical consciousness scholars, and Christina Dobbs and Daren Graves, my close collaborators of many years.

Every one of my projects over the last decade has been inspired in part by my investment in doing work that my wife, Amanda Seider, will believe is worthwhile and important. I am grateful for the high bar that Amanda models for me every day about what it means to do work and live a life that contributes to building a better, more just world.

After spending the past two decades teaching and researching adolescents, my interest in learning more about how to nurture younger children's critical consciousness was sparked by the immense privilege and joy of parenting two elementary schoolers, Naomi and Isaac. I wrote my last book *for* Naomi, and Isaac knows that this one is *for* him, even if we ultimately decided not to take his advice to put a soccer ball on the cover! I am also grateful to be part of a loving extended family that includes my mother Bonnie; sister Wendy; sisters-in-law Beth, Brittany, Domonique, Elizabeth, and Gloria; brothers-in-law Brad, Drian, and Fletcher; parents-in-law Fletcher Jr. and Trayce; and grandmother-in-law Barbara. Finally, my father, Ross Seider, tragically passed away while we were finishing this book. The person I am today has everything to do with having been Ross Seider's son, and not getting to celebrate this book's publication with him is just one of the countless reminders of how much I miss him.

## From Aaliyah

I am deeply grateful for my family—particularly my parents, who instilled in me from an early age the importance of viewing the world through a critical lens and taught me never to let racial injustice go unchallenged. From watching them notice, analyze, and act against racial injustice, even at significant risk to themselves, I learned that I could and should do the same. It is perhaps because of their example that my siblings put up with my endless rants about systems of oppression, even during TV shows, movies, and quiet time, and I am grateful to them for this supportive space to stand firmly in my purpose. I am also truly indebted to all the beautiful little humans whom I had the opportunity to meet, love, and be loved by as an elementary school teacher, particularly my 4th and 5th grade students at Paul L. Dunbar Elementary School. It is with them that I came to firmly believe that schools have immense power to move us from observers to actors, as well as the tremendous responsibility to do this work. I am held accountable to this conviction by my three amazing nieces, Zahra, Amina, and Raya, whose sense of possibility and commitment to joy continually remind me that the next generations need and deserve a better world than the one they inherited.

And lastly, I am grateful to so many members of my Boston community who helped me feel confident enough to work on this project, especially Scott Seider, who has single-handedly guided my publication journey in this book and much of my other work, and Julia Bott, whose wisdom about leading and creating the conditions in schools for critical consciousness development consistently inspires and pushes me. I am also grateful to all the members of my teaching team for my course on critical pedagogy, whose collaboration, camaraderie, and insights helped me work through some of my early thinking about ideas in this book and who became close friends along the way. Finally, thanks go to all my friends and loved ones who offered advice, meals, compassion when I was late on *so* many things, a listening ear, and emotional support during the writing journey, with special thanks to Gretchen Brion-Meisels and Daren Graves.

## From Julia

I am grateful to the students, families, educators, mentors, and colleagues I have worked with throughout my career as an elementary educator and school leader. In particular, I am a better leader, learner, and person because of the faculty I served with in my former school community. Their commitment to inclusion, excellence, and the cultivation of student agency was not just inspiring, it was truly transformative for everyone in our school community. The families were invaluable partners in our journey, elevating our shared work because of their deep knowledge and commitment to the collective good. Finally, the students proved to be the best teachers I have ever worked with. Their ability to see, affirm, and celebrate human differences; root out injustice; and demand accountability for a better, more inclusive future gives me hope for the world they will inherit. It was the gift of a lifetime to learn and lead in the company of their genius.

This is my first book, and it would not have been possible without the incredible collaboration of my esteemed colleagues and co-authors, Scott and Aaliyah. I am truly humbled by the opportunity to learn alongside them and benefit from their scholarly expertise on this project.

Finally, I would not have been able to do this without the love, patience, and support of my husband, Ben, and my two children, Maddox and Mila. As the children and spouse of a school leader, they know what it is to make sacrifices, yet throughout this project they held me accountable to the most challenging, inspiring, and important title I will ever hold, being their mother—and I am eternally grateful. I dedicate this book to my beautiful children and my former school community, both of whom continue to inspire me to do and be better, and both of whom will always hold a piece of my heart.

As two White children in our public school system, I am hopeful that they, too, will have opportunities to recognize structural and systemic injustices, explore meaningful counternarratives as part of the everyday curriculum, identify productive pathways to disrupt and challenge inequities, and take meaningful social action. I believe education for civic engagement is the promise and potential of public education, and I want my children, and all children, to be equipped and empowered to do their part and contribute to a better, more just world.

# Appendix: Organizational Structures Referenced in *Educating for Justice*

# Chapter 1: Adopt a Justice Framework

| | Description | Contribution to Educating for Justice |
|---|---|---|
| Instructional Leadership Team (ILT) | A group that typically includes the principal, instructional coaches, grade-level team leaders, and content-area department heads that works collaboratively to strengthen teaching and learning across the school | The ILT establishes and drives the instructional vision of the school. They ensure that there is a coherent vision of excellent teaching and learning that centers equity, justice, and the cultivation of critical consciousness. They inform the development and implementation of the arc of adult learning to build this knowledge and capacity in educators and monitor its impact on student learning, engagement, and sense of belonging. |
| Grade-Level Teams | Educators who teach at the same grade level within their school and have sustained and regular opportunities for collaboration with one another | Grade-level teams engage in cycles of learning involving unit and lesson/task consumption and interrogation, student work analysis, and action planning. This is where the overarching vision of a justice-centered curriculum takes root— through intentional planning to ensure the curriculum both aligns with standards and nurtures students' critical consciousness. |

# Chapter 2: Collaborate with Justice Partners

|  | Description | Contribution to Educating for Justice |
|---|---|---|
| Justice Partner | An external partner whose core expertise is in equity and social justice, and whose work and training can inform, deepen, and challenge educators' teaching about these topics | Educators need to develop the knowledge and skill to interrogate curriculum and infuse it with meaningful standards- and content-aligned opportunities for students to deepen their understanding of identity, explore inequities, and engage in relevant real-world activism. Justice partners can build content knowledge related to topics of equity and justice to help inform educators planning and teaching around these topics. |

## Chapter 3: Elevate the Wisdom of Families and Caretakers

| | Description | Contribution to Educating for Justice |
|---|---|---|
| Family Engagement Team | A diverse group of family members and educators who seek to bring a wider range of family voices into the life of the school community | Engaging, affirming, and empowering the voices, ideas, and vast funds of knowledge of families is essential to truly committing to justice-centered schooling. A family engagement team can contribute to the design of the vision, strategy, and implementation of practices related to school–home communication, parent/caregiver education, schoolwide family engagement events, and so on. |
| Justice Roundtable | A diverse group of parents, teachers, and community members charged with ensuring that students of color, students with disabilities, multilingual learners, unhoused students, and other groups of systemically marginalized students receive equitable access to learning experiences, resources, and support | This team serves as an advisory to school leadership and helps ensure that a social justice lens both informs and evaluates practices and policies across the school, including but not limited to school discipline policy, curriculum selection and implementation, budget decision making, student governance, and so on. |

# Chapter 4: Empower Students to Take Action

|  | Description | Contribution to Educating for Justice |
|---|---|---|
| Youth Participatory Action Research (YPAR) | A structure and process for working collaboratively with young people to identify problems affecting their lives, collect and explore data about these problems, and generate ideas for actions that can effect change (Brion-Meisels & Alter, 2018) | YPAR can bring the ideas, insights, voices, and brilliance of young people into the work of addressing important issues and challenges within the school community. YPAR can also strengthen young people's feelings of agency and self-efficacy, increasing their likelihood of taking active roles in other communities now and in the future. |
| Community Improvement Project | A school-based group consisting of students and one or more educators that meets weekly for a sustained period of time to learn about and address a local community issue | Similar to YPAR, a community improvement project engages young people in addressing issues relevant to their own communities and strengthens their belief that they can have a meaningful impact on community issues. |

# Chapter 5: Let Teachers Be Learners

| | Description | Contribution to Educating for Justice |
|---|---|---|
| Cross-Identity Dialogues | Facilitated discussions among individuals from two or more identity groups that seek to help members of these groups build trust and connection by learning from and with each other about key concepts related to identity groups, identity differences, and commonalities in people's lived experiences across identities (Zúñiga, 2003) | Cross-identity dialogues can be powerful opportunities for members of diverse identity groups to gain greater awareness and valuing of identity (both individual and collective), strengthen relationships, and build shared ownership for collective problem solving directly related to matters of diversity, inclusivity, equity, and justice. |
| Affinity Spaces | Spaces for individuals who share an identity to come together, compare experiences, and consider the unique affordances or challenges they experience within an organization (Hirsch, 2021) | Affinity spaces can be leveraged to provide safe spaces for families and/or staff to connect, reflect, identify unique challenges related to their lived experiences, and generate recommendations to disrupt inequities and advance the work of cultivating a more just community for all. These spaces can be used flexibly within other learning spaces as needed or woven into the structure of the school intentionally. |
| Justice Groups | A small group of staff members who meet on a regular basis to talk about issues or questions related to justice or equity that are relevant to their work with students | A justice group provides educators with time, space, and trusted colleagues who work together to recognize, analyze, and address real-life situations and dilemmas related to justice work in their shared school community. |
| Professional Learning Communities (PLCs) | Collaborative spaces for educators to engage in proactive and planful learning about a justice-related topic that affects their classroom practice | PLCs offer educators an opportunity to work with colleagues over a sustained period of time to learn about a justice-related topic or practice relevant to their school community and strengthen their capacity to nurture students' critical consciousness. |

# Chapter 6: Amplify the Impact of Heritage Months

|  | Description | Contribution to Educating for Justice |
|---|---|---|
| School Climate Team | A collection of teachers from each grade level or content area within a school community that focuses on initiatives related to fostering a healthy and positive school climate for students and staff members | Injustices live in all facets of a school, especially its climate and culture. It is essential that a team focused on supporting and maintaining the systems, structures, and supports necessary for a strong, positive, and inclusive school climate and culture do so through a justice lens. The team may regularly review discipline referral data to identify and disrupt patterns of disproportionality, monitor the implementation of routines and practices to ensure fidelity and identify opportunities for growth, plan and implement professional development to build educator capacity to implement culturally and linguistically affirming practices that cultivate a sense of belonging, facilitate restorative justice practices, and so on. |

# References

Abt Associates & Philadelphia Youth Network. (2016, October). *Successful school-based partnerships: What does it take?* https://www.abtglobal.com/insights/publications/report/final-report-successful-school-based-partnerships-what-does-it-take

Agarwal-Rangnath, R. (Ed.). (2020). *Planting the seeds of equity: Ethnic studies and social justice in the K–2 classroom.* Teachers College Press.

Alfonseca, K. (2023, October 2). School culture wars push students to form banned book clubs, anti-censorship groups. *ABC News.* https://abcnews.go.com/US/school-culture-wars-push-students-form-banned-book/story?id=103377259

American Psychological Association, Presidential Task Force on Preventing Discrimination and Promoting Diversity. (2012). *Dual pathways to a better America: Preventing discrimination and promoting diversity.* American Psychological Association. https://www.apa.org/pubs/reports/dual-pathways-report.pdf

Arao, B., & Clemens, K. (2013). From safe spaces to brave spaces. In L. M. Landreman (Ed.), *The art of effective facilitation: Reflections from social justice educators* (pp. 135–150). Stylus Publishing.

Bañales, J., Hope, E. C., Rowley, S. J., & Cryer-Coupet, Q. R. (2021). Raising justice-minded youth: Parental ethnic-racial and political socialization and Black youth's critical consciousness. *Journal of Social Issues, 77*(4), 964–986. https://doi.org/10.1111/josi.12486

Bañales, J., Mathews, C., Hayat, N., Anyiwo, N., & Diemer, M. A. (2020). Latinx and Black young adults' pathways to civic/political engagement. *Cultural Diversity and Ethnic Minority Psychology, 26*(2), 176–188. https://psycnet.apa.org/doi/10.1037/cdp0000271

Bandura, A. (2006). Adolescent development from an agentic perspective. In F. Pajares & T. Urdan (Eds.), *Self-efficacy beliefs of adolescents* (pp. 1–44). Information Age Publishing.

Barnes, D. (2017). *Crown: An ode to the fresh cut.* Agate Bolden.

Bell, L. A. (2010). *Storytelling for social justice: Connecting narrative and the arts in antiracist teaching.* Routledge.

Benson, T. A., & Fiarman, S. E. (2019). *Unconscious bias in schools: A developmental approach to exploring race and racism.* Harvard Education Press.

Bishop, R. S. (1990a). Mirrors, windows, and sliding glass doors. *Perspectives: Choosing and Using Books for the Classroom, 6*(3).

Bishop, R. S. (1990b, March). Windows and mirrors: Children's books and parallel cultures. In M. Atwell & A. Klein (Eds.), *California State University, San Bernadino Reading Conference: 14th annual conference proceedings* (pp. 3–12). CSUSB Reading Conference. https://files.eric.ed.gov/fulltext/ED337744.pdf

Borko, H. (2004). Professional development and teacher learning: Mapping the terrain. *Educational Researcher, 33*(8), 3–15. https://doi.org/10.3102/0013189X033008003

Branje, S. (2018). Development of parent–adolescent relationships: Conflict interactions as a mechanism of change. *Child Development Perspectives, 12*(3), 171–176. https://doi.org/10.1111/cdep.12278

Brion-Meisels, G., & Alter, Z. (2018). The quandary of youth participatory action research in school settings: A framework for reflecting on the factors that influence purpose and process. *Harvard Educational Review, 88*(4), 429–454. https://doi.org/10.17763/1943-5045-88.4.429

Brisk, M. E. (2015). *Engaging students in academic literacies: Genre-based pedagogy for K–5 classrooms.* Routledge.

Bullard, J. (2019). *Creating curriculum in early childhood: Enhanced learning through backward design.* Routledge.

Burga, S. (2023, April 20). What to know about Florida's new "Don't Say Gay" rule that bans discussion of gender for all students. *Time.* https://time.com/6273364/florida-dont-say-gay-expansion/

Burson, E., & Godfrey, E. B. (2020). Intraminority solidarity: The role of critical consciousness. *European Journal of Social Psychology, 50*(6), 1362–1377. https://doi.org/10.1002/ejsp.2679

Burtka, A. T. (2018, April 24). Native American mascots—Honoring culture or symbol of disrespect? *Global Sport Matters.* https://globalsportmatters.com/culture/2018/04/24/native-american-mascots-honoring-culture-symbol-disrespect/

Cammarota, J. (2007). A social justice approach to achievement: Guiding Latina/o students toward educational attainment with a challenging, socially relevant curriculum. *Equity & Excellence in Education, 40*(1), 87–96. https://doi.org/10.1080/10665680601015153

Cammarota, J., & Fine, M. (Eds.). (2008). *Revolutionizing education: Youth participatory action research in motion.* Routledge.

Cardichon, J., Darling-Hammond, L., Yang, M., Scott, C., Shields, P. M., & Burns, D. (2020). *Inequitable opportunity to learn: Student access to certified and experienced teachers.* Learning Policy Institute. https://learningpolicyinstitute.org/media/392/download?inline&file=CRDC_Teacher_Access_REPORT.pdf

Carnes, M., Devine, P. G., Isaac, C., Manwell, L. B., Ford, C. E., Byars-Winston, A., Fine, E., & Sheridan, J. (2012). Promoting institutional change through bias literacy. *Journal of Diversity in Higher Education, 5*(2), 63–77.

Carter, D. J. (2008). On spotlighting and ignoring racial group members in the classroom. In M. Pollock (Ed.), *Everyday antiracism: Getting real about race in school* (pp. 230–234). New Press.

Chatterji, R., Campbell, N., & Quirk, A. (2021). *Closing advanced coursework equity gaps for all students.* Center for American Progress. https://www.americanprogress.org/wp-content/uploads/sites/2/2021/07/AdvancedCoursework-report1.pdf

Chen, E. (2022). *I am golden.* Feiwel and Friends.

Cherry, M. A. (2019). *Hair love.* Kokila.

Cruz, R. A., Manchanda, S., Firestone, A. R., & Rodl, J. E. (2020). An examination of teachers' culturally responsive teaching self-efficacy. *Teacher Education and Special Education, 43*(3), 197–214. https://doi.org/10.1177/0888406419875194

Davis-Delano, L. R., Gone, J. P., & Fryberg, S. A. (2020). The psychosocial effects of Native American mascots: A comprehensive review of empirical research. *Race Ethnicity and Education, 23*(5), 613–633. https://doi.org/10.1080/13613324.2020.1772221

Davison, M., Penner, A. M., Penner, E. K., Pharris-Ciurej, N., Porter, S. R., Rose, E. K., Shem-Tov, Y., & Yoo, P. (2022). School discipline and racial disparities in early adulthood. *Educational Researcher, 51*(3), 231–234. https://doi.org/10.3102/0013189X211061732

Dee, T. S., & Penner, E. K. (2017). The causal effects of cultural relevance: Evidence from an ethnic studies curriculum. *American Educational Research Journal, 54*(1), 127–166. https://doi.org/10.3102/0002831216677002

Delpit, L. (2021). *Teaching when the world is on fire: Authentic classroom advice, from climate justice to Black Lives Matter.* New Press.

Diamond, J. B., & Gomez, K. (2004). African American parents' educational orientations: The importance of social class and parents' perceptions of schools. *Education and Urban Society, 36*(4), 383–427. https://doi.org/10.1177/0013124504266827

Dobbs, C. L., Ippolito, J., & Charner-Laird, M. (2017). Scaling up professional learning: Technical expectations and adaptive challenges. *Professional Development in Education, 43*(5), 729–748. https://doi.org/10.1080/19415257.2016.1238834

Duncan-Andrade, J. M. R. (2022). *Equality or equity: Toward a model of community-responsive education.* Harvard Education Press.

Duncan-Andrade, J. M. R., & Morrell, E. (2008). *The art of critical pedagogy: Possibilities for moving from theory to practice in urban schools.* Peter Lang.

Dunn, A. H. (2022). *Teaching on days after: Educating for equity in the wake of injustice.* Teachers College Press.

Dynarski, S. (2015, June 2). For the poor, the graduation gap is even wider than the enrollment gap. *The New York Times,* A3. https://www.nytimes.com/2015/06/02/upshot/for-the-poor-the-graduation-gap-is-even-wider-than-the-enrollment-gap.html

Dys, S. P., Peplak, J., Colasante, T., & Malti, T. (2019). Children's sympathy and sensitivity to excluding economically disadvantaged peers. *Developmental Psychology, 55*(3), 482–487. https://doi.org/10.1037/dev0000549

Edelman, M. W. (2014, May 10). *Commencement address, Lewis & Clark College.* https://college.lclark.edu/live/files/17133-edelman-commencement-speechlewis-clark

Edutopia. (2019, August 26). Thabiti Brown on empowering students. *YouTube.* https://www.youtube.com/watch?v=yOkO1Pl9opc

El-Amin, A., Seider, S., Graves, D., Tamerat, J., Clark, S., Soutter, M., Johannsen, J., & Malhotra, S. (2017). Critical consciousness: A key to student achievement. *Phi Delta Kappan, 98*(5), 18–23. https://doi.org/10.1177/0031721717690360

Elenbaas, L. (2019). Perceptions of economic inequality are related to children's judgments about access to opportunities. *Developmental Psychology, 55*(3), 471–481. https://doi.org/10.1037/dev0000550

Elenbaas, L., Rizzo, M. T., & Killen, M. (2020). A developmental-science perspective on social inequality. *Current Directions in Psychological Science, 29*(6), 610–616. https://doi.org/10.1177/0963721420964147

Elliott, Z. (2016). *Milo's museum.* CreateSpace Independent Publishing.

Emdin, C. (2016). *For White folks who teach in the hood... and the rest of y'all too: Reality pedagogy and urban education.* Beacon Press.

Epstein, M. H., Munk, D. D., Bursuck, W. D., Polloway, E. A., & Jayanthi, M. (1999). Strategies for improving home–school communication about homework for students with disabilities. *The Journal of Special Education, 33*(3), 166–176. https://doi.org/10.1177/002246699903300304

Ewing, E. L. (2020, July 2). I'm a Black scholar who studies race. Here's why I capitalize "White." *Medium.* https://zora.medium.com/im-a-black-scholar-who-studies-race-here-s-why-i-capitalize-white-f94883aa2dd3

Fenton, P., Ocasio-Stoutenburg, L., & Harry, B. (2017). The power of parent engagement: Sociocultural considerations in the quest for equity. *Theory into Practice, 56*(3), 214–225. https://doi.org/10.1080/00405841.2017.1355686

Figueroa, A. (2022, April 8). York, Pa. students who fought ban tell their story to U.S. House panel. *Pennsylvania Capital-Star*. https://penncapital-star.com/arts-culture/york-pa-students-who-fought-book-ban-tell-their-story-to-u-s-house-panel/

Frantell, K. A., Miles, J. R., & Ruwe, A. M. (2019). Intergroup dialogue: A review of recent empirical research and its implications for research and practice. *Small Group Research, 50*(5), 654–695. https://doi.org/10.1177/1046496419835923

Freire, P. (1970). *Pedagogy of the oppressed* (M. B. Ramos, Trans.). Herder and Herder.

Gewirtz, A. (2020). *When the world feels like a scary place: Essential conversations for anxious parents and worried kids*. Workman Publishing.

Ginwright, S. A. (2010). *Black youth rising: Activism and radical healing in urban America*. Teachers College Press.

Ginwright, S., Noguera, P., & Cammarota, J. (Eds.). (2006). *Beyond resistance! Youth activism and community change: New democratic possibilities for practice and policy for America's youth*. Routledge.

Godfrey, E. B., Burson, E. L., Yanisch, T. M., Hughes, D., & Way, N. (2019). A bitter pill to swallow? Patterns of critical consciousness and socioemotional and academic well-being in early adolescence. *Developmental Psychology, 55*(3), 525–537. https://doi.org/10.1037/dev0000558

Gonser, S. (2021, September 20). Ron Berger on the power of "beautiful work." *Edutopia*. https://www.edutopia.org/article/ron-berger-power-beautiful-work/

Gutierez, S. B. (2021). Collaborative lesson planning as a positive "dissonance" to the teachers' individual planning practices: Characterizing the features through reflections-on-action. *Teacher Development, 25*(1), 37–52. https://doi.org/10.1080/13664530.2020.1856177

Hammond, Z. (2015). *Culturally responsive teaching and the brain: Promoting authentic engagement and rigor among culturally and linguistically diverse students*. Corwin.

Heberle, A. E., Rapa, L. J., & Farago, F. (2020). Critical consciousness in children and adolescents: A systematic review, critical assessment, and recommendations for future research. *Psychological Bulletin, 146*(6), 525–551. https://doi.org/10.1037/bul0000230

Helm, A. (2019, October 28). "They'll erase us from the future": Stacey Abrams understands why we fear the census but says we must participate anyway. *The Root.* https://www.theroot.com/they-ll-erase-us-from-the-future-stacey-abrams-under-1839423881

Helms, J. E. (2019). *A race is a nice thing to have: A guide to being a White person or understanding the White persons in your life* (3rd ed.). Cognella.

Hernández-Linares, L. (2021). *Alejandria fights back!* The Feminist Press.

Hipolito-Delgado, C. P., & Zion, S. (2017). Igniting the fire within marginalized youth: The role of critical civic inquiry in fostering ethnic identity and civic self-efficacy. *Urban Education, 52*(6), 699–717. https://doi.org/10.1177/0042085915574524

Hirsch, A. (2021, September 20). An inside look at workplace racial affinity groups [Blog post]. https://arlenehirsch.com/an-inside-look-at-workplace-racial-affinity-groups/

Hodge, E. M., López, F. A., & Rosenberg, J. M. (2022). How to respond to community concerns about critical race theory. *Phi Delta Kappan, 104*(3), 48–53. https://doi.org/10.1177/00317217221136599

Hope, E. C., & Jagers, R. J. (2014). The role of sociopolitical attitudes and civic education in the civic engagement of Black youth. *Journal of Research on Adolescence, 24*(3), 460–470. https://doi.org/10.1111/jora.12117

Huguley, J. P., Cleveland, K. C., Davis, C. D., Haynik, R. H., & Wang, M. T. (2023). Parenting while Black: Promising results from a strengths-based parent intervention supporting African American families. *Children & Schools, 45*(4), 251–254. https://doi.org/10.1093/cs/cdad021

Huguley, J. P., Wang, M.-T., Vasquez, A. C., & Guo, J. (2019). Parental ethnic–racial socialization practices and the construction of children of color's ethnic–racial identity: A research synthesis and meta-analysis. *Psychological Bulletin, 145*(5), 437–458. https://doi.org/10.1037/bul0000187

Individual Freedom Act, 48 Fla. Stat. § 1000.05 (2022).

Irby, D. J. (2021). *Stuck improving: Racial equity and school leadership.* Harvard Education Press.

Irwin, J. (2012). *Paulo Freire's philosophy of education: Origins, developments, impacts and legacies*. Continuum.

Jones, A., II. (2022, March 28). Teachers speak out against Florida's "Parental Rights in Education" bill. *CBS News*. https://www.cbsnews.com/news/teachers-florida-parental-rights-in-education-dont-say-gay-bill/

Jones, C. (2018, May 22). Latino, African-Americans have less access to math, science classes, new data show. *EdSource*. https://edsource.org/2018/latino-african-americans-have-less-access-to-math-science-classes-new-data-show/598083

Jones, D., & Hagopian, J. (Eds.). (2020). *Black Lives Matter at school: An uprising for educational justice*. Haymarket Books.

Jones, J. K. (2023). *Dismantling anti-Blackness in teacher education: Centering Black epistemologies to (re)construct elementary language arts education for linguistic and racial justice* (Unpublished doctoral dissertation). Old Dominion University, Norfolk, VA.

King, H. T. (2021). *Saving American Beach: The biography of African American environmentalist MaVynee Betsch*. G. P. Putnam's Sons Books for Young Readers.

Kirshner, B. (2015). *Youth activism in an era of education inequality*. New York University Press.

Ladson-Billings, G. (1995). Toward a theory of culturally relevant pedagogy. *American Educational Research Journal, 32*(3), 465–491. https://doi.org/10.3102/00028312032003465

Ladson-Billings, G. (2014). Culturally relevant pedagogy 2.0: a.k.a. the remix. *Harvard Educational Review, 84*(1), 74–84. https://doi.org/10.17763/haer.84.1.p2rj131485484751

Lamb, L. M., Bigler, R. S., Liben, L. S., & Green, V. A. (2009). Teaching children to confront peers' sexist remarks: Implications for theories of gender development and educational practice. *Sex Roles, 61*, 361–382. https://doi.org/10.1007/s11199-009-9634-4

Legal Defense Fund. (n.d.). *The CROWN Act: Creating a respectful and open world for natural hair*. https://www.naacpldf.org/crown-act/

Leung, J. (2019). *Paper son: The inspiring story of Tyrus Wong, immigrant and artist*. Schwartz & Wade Books.

Levinson, M. (2012). *No citizen left behind.* Harvard University Press.

Lorde, A. (1984). *Sister outsider: Essays and speeches.* Crossing Press.

Love, B. L. (2019). *We want to do more than survive: Abolitionist teaching and the pursuit of educational freedom.* Beacon Press.

Maker Castro, E., Wray-Lake, L., & Cohen, A. K. (2022). Critical consciousness and wellbeing in adolescents and young adults: A systematic review. *Adolescent Research Review, 7,* 499–522. https://doi.org/10.1007/s40894-022-00188-3

Maloney, T., Larkin, D. B., & Hoque, N. (2023). The role of teacher education programs in developing teacher candidates' antiracist stance on teaching. *Equity & Excellence in Education,* 1–13. https://doi.org/10.1080/10665684.2023.2248468

Mapp, K., Carver, I., & Lander, J. (2017). *Powerful partnerships: A teacher's guide to engaging families for student success.* Scholastic Professional.

Massachusetts Department of Elementary and Secondary Education & Department of Health. (2019). *Health and risk behaviors of Massachusetts youth: Spring 2019 student survey results highlights.* https://www.mass.gov/doc/health-and-risk-behaviors-of-massachusetts-youth-2019/download

Mathews, C. J., Medina, M. A., Bañales, J., Pinetta, B. J., Marchand, A. D., Agi, A. C., Miller, S. M., Hoffman, A. J., Diemer, M. A., & Rivas-Drake, D. (2020). Mapping the intersections of adolescents' ethnic–racial identity and critical consciousness. *Adolescent Research Review, 5,* 363–379. https://doi.org/10.1007/s40894-019-00122-0

Maye, A., & Sherer, J. (2023, June 28). How state policies that censor race and gender discussions in classrooms maintain economic inequality [Blog post]. *Working Economics Blog, Economic Policy Institute.* https://www.epi.org/blog/how-state-policies-that-censor-race-and-gender-discussions-in-classrooms-maintain-economic-inequality-florida-has-adopted-particularly-dangerous-laws-to-limit-academic-freedom/

Mays, B. E. (1942). The role of the Negro liberal arts college in post-war reconstruction. *The Journal of Negro Education, 11*(3), 400–411. https://doi.org/10.2307/2292678

McClellan, B. E. (1999). *Moral education in America: Schools and the shaping of character from colonial times to the present*. Teachers College Press.

McConnell, T. J., Parker, J. M., Eberhardt, J., Koehler, M. J., & Lundeberg, M. A. (2013). Virtual professional learning communities: Teachers' perceptions of virtual versus face-to-face professional development. *Journal of Science Education and Technology, 22*, 267–277. https://doi.org/10.1007/s10956-012-9391-y

McGee, K. (2023, May 27). Texas lawmakers find consensus on bill banning diversity, equity and inclusion offices in public universities. *The Texas Tribune*. https://www.texastribune.org/2023/05/27/texas-university-diversity-equity-inclusion-dei-bill-conference/

McGhee, H. (2021). *The sum of us: What racism costs everyone and how we can prosper together*. One World.

Miller, D. I., Nolla, K. M., Eagly, A. H., & Uttal, D. H. (2018). The development of children's gender-science stereotypes: A meta-analysis of 5 decades of U.S. Draw-A-Scientist studies. *Child Development, 89*(6), 1943–1955. https://doi.org/10.1111/cdev.13039

Milner, H. R., IV. (2013). Why are students of color (still) punished more severely and frequently than White students? *Urban Education, 48*(4), 483–489. https://doi.org/10.1177/0042085913493040

Morales, A. (2021). *Areli is a Dreamer: A true story by Areli Morales, a DACA recipient*. Random House Studio.

Morgan, I. (2022). *Equal is not good enough: An analysis of school funding equity across the U.S. and within each state*. The Education Trust. https://edtrust.org/wp-content/uploads/2014/09/Equal-Is-Not-Good-Enough-December-2022.pdf

Moulton, C. (2020, July 25). Native mascots called out. *Telegram & Gazette (Worcester, MA)*. https://www.telegram.com/story/news/regional/2020/07/25/national-controversy-over-native-american-mascots-reaches-central-mass/42484593/

Muhammad, G. E. (2012). The literacy development and practices within African American literary societies. *Black History Bulletin, 75*(1), 6–13. https://www.jstor.org/stable/24759714

Muhammad, G. E. (2018). A plea for identity and criticality: Reframing literacy learning standards through a four-layered equity model.

*Journal of Adolescent & Adult Literacy, 62*(2), 137–142. https://doi.org/10.1002/jaal.869

Muhammad, G. (2020). *Cultivating genius: An equity framework for culturally and historically responsive literacy.* Scholastic.

Muhammad, G. E. (2022). Cultivating genius and joy in education through historically responsive literacy. *Language Arts, 99*(3), 195–204. https://doi.org/10.58680/la202231623

Muhammad, G. E. (2023). *Unearthing joy: A guide to culturally and historically responsive teaching and learning.* Scholastic.

Murray, B., Domina, T., Petts, A., Renzulli, L., & Boylan, R. (2020). "We're in this together": Bridging and bonding social capital in elementary school PTOs. *American Educational Research Journal, 57*(5), 2210–2244. https://doi.org/10.3102/0002831220908848

National Congress of American Indians. (2013). *Ending the legacy of racism in sports & the era of harmful "Indian" sports mascots* [Policy paper]. https://archive.ncai.org/attachments/PolicyPaper_mijApMoUWDbjqFtjAYzQWlqLdrwZvsYfakBwTHpMATcOroYolpN_NCAI_Harmful_Mascots_Report_Ending_the_Legacy_of_Racism_10_2013.pdf

National Education Association. (2021). *Racial justice in education resource guide.* https://www.nea.org/resource-library/racial-justice-education-resource-guide

National PTA. (n.d.). *Why join PTA?* https://www.pta.org/home/about-national-parent-teacher-association/why-join-pta

The Nelson Mandela Foundation Archive at the Centre of Memory. (2003, July 16). *Item 909—Lighting your way to a better future: Speech delivered by Mr N R Mandela at launch of Mindset Network.* https://archive.nelsonmandela.org/index.php/za-com-mr-s-909

Paris, D. (2012). Culturally sustaining pedagogy: A needed change in stance, terminology, and practice. *Educational Researcher, 41*(3), 93–97. https://doi.org/10.3102/0013189X12441244

Parker, W. S. (2024, January 22). Should teachers have to submit lesson plans? [Blog post]. *Educators Blog, Graduate Programs for Educators.* https://www.graduateprogram.org/2024/01/should-teachers-have-to-submit-lesson-plans/

Patel, M. (2019). *Priya dreams of marigolds & masala*. Beaver's Pond Press.

Paz, I. G., & Cramer, M. (2021, October 2). How students fought a book ban and won, for now. *The New York Times*. https://www.nytimes.com/2021/10/02/us/york-pennsylvania-school-books.html

Pendharkar, E. (2023, February 17). 5 things we learned from 2 teachers piloting AP African American Studies. *EducationWeek*. https://www.edweek.org/teaching-learning/5-things-we-learned-from-2-teachers-piloting-ap-african-american-studies/2023/02

Perry, T., Steele, C., & Hilliard, A. G., III. (2003). *Young, gifted, and Black: Promoting high achievement among African-American students*. Beacon Press.

Pickhardt, C. E. (2014, November 3). When adolescents start talking less to parents [Blog post]. *Psychology Today*. https://www.psychologytoday.com/us/blog/surviving-your-childs-adolescence/201411/when-adolescents-start-talking-less-parents

Pinedo, A., Frisby, M., Kubi, G., Vezaldenos, V., Diemer, M. A., McAlister, S., & Harris, E. (2024). Charting the longitudinal trajectories and interplay of critical consciousness among youth activists. *Child Development, 95*(1), 296–312. https://doi.org/10.1111/cdev.13977

Planas, A. (2023, July 20). New Florida standards teach students that some Black people benefited from slavery because it taught useful skills. *NBC News*. https://www.nbcnews.com/news/us-news/new-florida-standards-teach-black-people-benefited-slavery-taught-usef-rcna95418

The Plenary, Co. (n.d.). *I am a scientist* [Website]. https://www.iamascientist.info

Pollock, M. (2004). *Colormute: Race talk dilemmas in an American school*. Princeton University Press.

Popa, A. B. (2009). Form follows function: A backward design to develop leadership ethics curriculum. *Journal of Leadership Education, 8*(1), 59–71. https://doi.org/10.12806/V8/I1/AB1

Quinlan, C. (2016, July 13). How marginalized families are pushed out of PTAs. *The Atlantic*. https://www.theatlantic.com/education/archive/2016/07/how-marginalized-families-are-pushed-out-of-ptas/491036/

Rapa, L. J., Diemer, M. A., & Bañales, J. (2018). Critical action as a pathway to social mobility among marginalized youth. *Developmental Psychology, 54*(1), 127–137. https://doi.org/10.1037/dev0000414

Rappaport, D. (2007). *Martin's big words: The life of Dr. Martin Luther King, Jr.* Jump at the Sun/Hyperion Paperbacks for Children.

Restrepo, M. L. (2023, April 25). Book bans are getting everyone's attention—including Biden's. Here's why. *NPR.* https://www.npr.org/2023/04/25/1172024559/book-bans-spike-biden-culture-wars-lgbtq-gender-queer-libraries

Rinker, J. M. (2021). *Send a girl! The true story of how women joined the FDNY.* Bloomsbury Children's Books.

Rios, V. M. (2011). *Punished: Policing the lives of Black and Latino boys.* New York University Press.

Rogers, L. O., Moffitt, U., & Foo, C. (2021). "Martin Luther King fixed it": Children making sense of racial identity in a colorblind society. *Child Development, 92*(5), 1817–1835. https://doi.org/10.1111/cdev.13628

Rymond-Richmond, W. (2023). Children of war resisters: Intergenerational transmission of activism, political orientation, injustice frames, and law resistance. *Law & Social Inquiry, 48*(4), 1261–1280. https://doi.org/10.1017/lsi.2023.59

Saad, L. F. (2020). *Me and White supremacy: Combat racism, change the world, and become a good ancestor.* Sourcebooks.

Safir, S., & Dugan, J. (2021). *Street data: A next-generation model for equity, pedagogy, and school transformation.* Corwin.

Saklayen, N. (2016, June 2). I (don't) look like a physicist. *Medium.* https://medium.com/@nsaklayen/i-dont-look-like-a-physicist-edcf2549967e

Savitz-Romer, M., & Bouffard, S. M. (2012). *Ready, willing, and able: A developmental approach to college access and success.* Harvard Education Press.

Scanlan, M. (2023). *Navigating social justice: A schema for educational leadership.* Harvard Education Press.

Seider, S. (2011). The role of privilege as identity in adolescents' beliefs about homelessness, opportunity, and inequality. *Youth & Society, 43*(1), 333–364. https://doi.org/10.1177/0044118X10366673

Seider, S., Clark, S., & Graves, D. (2020). The development of critical consciousness and its relation to academic achievement in adolescents of color. *Child Development, 91*(2), 451–474. https://doi.org/10.1111/cdev.13262

Seider, S., & Graves, D. (2020). *Schooling for critical consciousness: Engaging Black and Latinx youth in analyzing, navigating, and challenging racial injustice.* Harvard Education Press.

Seider, S., Henry, D. A., Edwards, E. C., Huguley, J. P., Diaz, B., & Daza, K. (2023). Investigating the relation between critical consciousness and academic achievement for adolescents of color and White adolescents. *Cultural Diversity and Ethnic Minority Psychology, 29*(4), 516–529. https://doi.org/10.1037/cdp0000613

Shanahan, T. (2013). *A beginner's guide to text complexity.* Generation Ready: Partnering for School Success. https://www.generationready.com/wp-content/uploads/2021/04/Beginners-Guide-to-Text-Complexity.pdf

Shor, I. (Ed.). (1987). *Freire in the classroom: A sourcebook for liberatory teaching.* Heinemann.

Shores, K., Kim, H. E., & Still, M. (2020, February 21). Categorical inequalities between Black and White students are common in US schools—but they don't have to be. *Brookings.* https://www.brookings.edu/articles/categorical-inequalities-between-black-and-white-students-are-common-in-us-schools-but-they-dont-have-to-be/

Sleeter, C. E., & Zavala, M. (2020). *Transformative ethnic studies in schools: Curriculum, pedagogy, and research.* Teachers College Press.

Stoughton, C., Lynch, M. E., & Lee, M. (2022). Family engagement and conflict about teaching for social justice. *Phi Delta Kappan, 103*(7), 23–27. https://doi.org/10.1177/00317217221092230

Sullivan, J. N., Eberhardt, J. L., & Roberts, S. O. (2021). Conversations about race in Black and White U.S. families: Before and after George Floyd's death. *Proceedings of the National Academy of Sciences, 118*(38), e2106366118. https://doi.org/10.1073/pnas.2106366118

Tatum, A. W. (2014). Orienting African American male adolescents toward meaningful literacy exchanges with texts. *Journal of Education, 194*(1), 35–47. https://doi.org/10.1177/002205741419400106

Tatum, B. D. (2017). *Why are all the Black kids sitting together in the cafeteria? And other conversations about race* (20th anniv. ed.). Basic Books.

Umaña-Taylor, A. J., & AERID Lab. (2020). *You may be wondering . . . Should we address* all *racial jokes?* https://umana-taylorlab.gse.harvard.edu/files/gse-umana-taylorlab/files/02_ymbw_stereotype_jokes_final_04-12-21.pdf

Valli, L., Stefanski, A., & Jacobson, R. (2018). School–community partnership models: Implications for leadership. *International Journal of Leadership in Education, 21*(1), 31–49. https://doi.org/10.1080/13603124.2015.1124925

Warren, M. R., Mira, M., & Nikundiwe, T. (2008). Youth organizing: From youth development to school reform. *New Directions for Youth Development, 2008*(117), 27–42. https://doi.org/10.1002/yd.245

Watts, R. J., Diemer, M. A., & Voight, A. M. (2011). Critical consciousness: Current status and future directions. *New Directions for Child and Adolescent Development, 2011*(134), 43–57. https://doi.org/10.1002/cd.310

Watts, R. J., & Flanagan, C. (2007). Pushing the envelope on youth civic engagement: A developmental and liberation psychology perspective. *Journal of Community Psychology, 35*(6), 779–792. https://doi.org/10.1002/jcop.20178

Watts, R. J., & Hipolito-Delgado, C. P. (2015). Thinking ourselves to liberation? Advancing sociopolitical action in critical consciousness. *The Urban Review, 47*, 847–867. https://doi.org/10.1007/s11256-015-0341-x

Westheimer, J., & Kahne, J. (2004). Educating the "good" citizen: Political choices and pedagogical goals. *PS: Political Science & Politics, 37*(2), 241–247. https://doi.org/10.1017/S1049096504004160

The White House. (n.d.). *Presidential actions.* https://www.whitehouse.gov/briefing-room/presidential-actions

Wiggins, G. (2007, November 15). What is an essential question? *Authentic Education.* https://authenticeducation.org/what-is-an-essential-question/

Wiggins, G., & McTighe, J. (2005). *Understanding by design* (Expanded 2nd ed.). ASCD.

Wilhelm, T. (2013). How principals cultivate shared leadership. *Educational Leadership, 71*(2), 62–66. https://www.ascd.org/el/articles/how-principals-cultivate-shared-leadership

Wimberly, G. L. (Ed.). (2015). *LGBTQ issues in education: Advancing a research agenda.* American Educational Research Association.

Wray-Lake, L., & Abrams, L. S. (2020). Pathways to civic engagement among urban youth of color. *Monographs of the Society for Research in Child Development, 85*(2), 7–154. https://doi.org/10.1111/mono.12415

YWCA USA [@YWCAUSA]. (2018, April 23). *Tell us: Why do you #StandAgainstRacism? What are things you and other people can do in their daily lives to* [Tweet]. Twitter. https://twitter.com/YWCAUSA/status/988492870247165952

Zinn Education Project. (n.d.). A talk to teachers. https://www.zinnedproject.org/materials/baldwin-talk-to-teachers

Zúñiga, X. (2003). Bridging differences through dialogue. *About Campus, 7*(6), 8–16. https://doi.org/10.1177/108648220300700603

# Index

The letter *f* following a page locator denotes a figure.

action, critical, 11
activist models, introducing, 133–137
adult capacity, building
    combining with other principles, 212–213
    heritage months, 196–202
    local, national, and global tragedies, responding to, 219–222, 222–223*f*, 224
    within the principles, 18*f*
adult learning, key elements to support
    avoid spotlighting, 185
    listening, 163–165, 186–187
    shared leadership, 179–181, 182–183*f*, 183–184
    space to learn, 184–185
adult learning, laying the groundwork for, 161–165. *See also* professional development
adult learning structures
    affinity spaces, 168–173
    cross-identity dialogues, 165–168
    justice groups, 173–176
    professional learning communities, 176–179

affinity spaces, 168–173, 186, 250
anxiety, quelling teachers', 70–74

backward design, 31
Baldwin, James, 234–235, 237–238, 242
Black Lives Matter at School Week of Action, 97, 101–104, 105–106*f*, 107, 108*f*
Black Lives Matter movement, 1, 89, 105–106*f*, 150
book bans, 5, 136–137, 235
bullying, 8

celebrations
    genius of oppressed and marginalized groups, 82–83
    successes and failures, 45–46
censorship, 5, 235
changemakers, Baldwin on, 234
children, challenging injustice by younger, 131–132, 145–153, 241
classroom observation tool, 50*f*
coaching, to support justice framework implementation, 49, 50*f*, 51, 58–59, 70–71
Community Improvement Projects (CIPs), 143–145, 249

community partnerships
    community-responsive resources, sharing, 76-77
    seeking wisdom from, responding to tragedies, 217-219
    with students in local activism, 142-149
    supporting cross-identity dialogues, 166-167
counternarratives, unveiling, 86-89
critical consciousness
    goal of, 129
    history of, 10-11
critical consciousness, nurturing. *See also specific principles*
    academic excellence and, 238-239
    Baldwin on, 237
    benefits of, 13-16, 240-242
    committing to the work of, 237-242
    curricular justice framework for, 31
    families and caretakers for, 95-98
    by integrating the goal of, 133
    justice partners supporting, 66-67
    local, national, and global tragedies, talking about, 215-217
    math class, 55-58
    principles for, 18*f*
    school for, 12
    time required for, 133
    window books and mirror books for, 134-135
criticality, 12
cross-identity dialogues, 165-168, 250
cross-race dialogues, 166
CROWN Act, writing letters to legislators about the, 2, 13
culturally and historically responsive literacy (CHRL) justice framework, 33-34, 45, 48, 111-112

curricular justice framework, 111-112
    buy-in, building, 103-104, 105-106*f*, 106-107
    defined, 31
    families and caretakers to help shape, 100-103
curricular justice framework, implementation
    coaching and feedback to support, 49, 50*f*, 51
    differentiated professional development in, 59
    intentional mentorship and coaching in, 58-59
    mandated curriculum, working with, 51-58
    new teacher orientation and, 58
    reasons for, 27-30
curricular justice framework, implementation steps
    celebrate successes and failures, 45-46
    create a common planning template, 42, 43-44*f*
    establish planning days, 46-48
    identify a framework, 31-34
    introduce and integrate, 34-42
curriculum
    centering justice in, 18*f*, 203-204, 206, 212-213
    critically consuming, 52-55
    heritage months, 203-206
    legislation regulating, 5, 235
    mandated, working with, 51-58
    thought partnerships, 74-76
curriculum planning templates, 42, 43-44*f*

dialogues, cross-identity/cross-race, 165-168
discipline, systemic injustice in, 8-9
dropout rates, high school LGBTQ+ students, 8

education, purpose of, 234
education, systemic injustice in, 7-12
excellence, academic, 238-239

failures, celebrating, 45–46
families/caretakers, partnering with
    building trust and buy-in, 103–104, 105–106*f*, 106–107
    to deepen student learning at home, 107, 108*f*, 109
    essential nature of, 124–125
    to evaluate and improve justice work, 109–117
    family engagement structures, evaluating for, 98–100
    learning from, 239
    to nurture students' critical consciousness, 95–98
    power of, 94
    resistance from, responding to, 117–124
    to shape justice-related curriculum and instruction, 100–103
family engagement teams, 100–104, 105–106*f*, 107, 181, 182–183*f*, 183, 248
fear, quelling teacher's, 70–74
feedback
    justice partners, supporting teachers through, 77–81
    to support justice framework implementation, 49, 50*f*, 51
Floyd, George, 53–54, 217–220, 222, 226, 227–228*f*, 229–230
funding education, injustice in, 7

genius of oppressed and marginalized groups, celebrating, 82–83
grade-level teams, 246

heritage months
    both/and approach to, 194–196, 195*f*
    defining, 192–194, 193*f*
    school climate team, Roberts Elementary example, 197–199, 200–202*f*, 203–204, 251
heritage months, applying the principles to
    building adult capacity, 196–202

heritage months, applying the principles to (*continued*)
    center justice in curriculum and pedagogy, 203–206
    combining to educate for justice, 212–213
    engage students in social action, 209–211
    foster powerful partnerships, 207–209
holding space, 219–222, 222–223*f*, 224

identity, developing a healthy racial, 15–16
Individual Freedom Act (FL), 5
injustice
    challenging, is a verb, 238
    connecting study of the past to the present, 89–90
    learning about, endpoint for, 239–240
    legislation prohibiting teaching about, 5, 235
    motivation to change, critical consciousness in, 10–12
    pervasive nature and impacts of, 6–9
    student protests to learn about, 5–6
    systemic, in education, 7–12
instruction, families helping to shape justice-related, 100–103
instructional leadership team (ILT), 35–39, 49, 51, 246

joy, celebrating legacies of oppressed and marginalized groups, 82–83
just society, creating a, 235–236
justice, contributors to educating for
    affinity spaces, 250
    Community Improvement Projects, 249
    cross-identity dialogues, 250
    family engagement teams, 248
    grade-level teams, 246
    instructional leadership team, 246

justice, contributors to educating for (*continued*)
   justice groups, 250
   justice partners, 247
   justice roundtables, 248
   professional learning communities, 250
   school climate team, 251
   youth participatory action research, 249
justice, educating for, 1–3, 6–16, 212–213. *See also* critical consciousness, nurturing
justice framework. *See* curricular justice framework
justice groups, 173–176, 250
justice partners
   collaborating with, 65–69
   defined, 247
   heritage months, 207–209
   power of sustained partnership, 91–92
justice partners, key guidance from
   celebrate genius and joy, 82–83
   connect past injustice to the present, 89–90
   emphasize resistance, 83–86
   unveil counternarratives, 86–89
justice partners, supporting teachers through
   feedback, 77–81
   helping to quell fear and anxiety, 70–74
   providing thought partnership on curriculum, 74–76
   sharing community-responsive resources, 76–77
   ways to support teaching critical consciousness, 66–67
justice roundtables, 109–117, 248

leadership, shared
   school climate team, Roberts Elementary example, 197–199
   to support adult learning, 179–181, 182–183*f*, 183–184

learners, teachers as, 157–161
LGBTQ+ students, bullying, threats, injuries, 8
listening, 163–165, 186–187

marginalized groups
   critical consciousness's impacts on, 15
   genius of, 82–83
   resistance by, emphasizing, 83–86
math, critical consciousness plus, 55–58
mentorship, to support justice framework implementation, 58–59
mirror books, 134–135
model unit discussions, training to lead, 36–37

new teacher orientation, 58

oppressed groups
   critical consciousness's impacts on, 15
   genius of, 82–83
   resistance by, emphasizing, 83–86
oppression, formation of systems of, 7
oppressor groups, learning about and challenging injustice of, 15

parents. *See* families/caretakers
partnerships, fostering powerful. *See also* community partnerships; families/caretakers, partnering with; justice partners
   combining with other principles, 212–213
   local, national, and global tragedies, responding to, 217–219, 224–226, 227–228*f*, 228–231
   within the principles, 18*f*
   with students, 140–149
planning days, establishing, 46–48

privileged identity groups, learning about and challenging injustice of, 15
professional development. *See also* adult learning
   differentiated, 59
   to hold teaching simulations, 39–42
   justice frameworks, introducing, 34–36
   to lead model unit discussions, 36–37
   learning to talk about injustice, 157–161
   to participate in unit interrogations, 37–39
professional learning communities (PLCs), 176–179, 250

racial affinity spaces, 168–173, 186
racial identity, developing a healthy, 15–16
racial injustice in education, 7, 8–9
reflection, 11, 149–153
resistance by oppressed and marginalized groups, emphasizing, 83–86

safety at school, 8
school climate team, 197–199, 200–202f, 203–204, 251
schools
   engaging students in social action within, 140–142
   safety at, 8
service, social action vs., 130–131
social action, engaging students in
   activist models, introduce varied, 133–137
   combining with other principles, 212–213
   follow up with reflection, 149–153
   heritage months, 209–211
   introduce a variety of strategies, 137–140
   local, national, and global tragedies, responding to, 224–226, 227–228f, 228–231

social action, engaging students in (*continued*)
   local activism, partnering with for, 142–149
   within the principles, 18f
   school-based social action, partnering with, 140–142
   younger children, including, 131–132, 145–153
social change
   Baldwin on, 242
   examples of students' commitment to, 2, 5–6, 13, 129–130
   skills needed for, 11
   vignettes showing schools commitment to, 1–3
Social Justice Education Project (Tucson), 15
social justice leadership experiences, 1
space to learn, supporting adult learning, 184–185
spotlighting, avoiding, 185
successes, celebrating, 45–46

teachers
   just society, creating a, 235–236
   justice partners supporting, 66–67, 74–76
   as learners, 157–161
   new teacher orientation, 58
teaching simulations, training to hold, 39–42
thought partnerships, 74–76
tragedies, responding to local, national, and global
   adult capacity, building, 219–222, 222–223f, 224
   centering justice, 219–222, 224
   communicating learning goals, 226–231
   critical consciousness, nurturing, 215–217
   partnerships, fostering powerful, 217–219, 224–226, 227–228f, 228–231

tragedies, responding to local, national, and global (*continued*)
    principles, combining the, 231–232
    reasons for, 216–217
    social action, engaging students in, 224–226, 227–228*f*, 228–231
    why schools abstain from, 216, 231–232
trust
    building with families/caretakers, 103–104, 105–106*f*, 106–107
    young people, 242

Ukraine–Russia conflict, 222, 223–224*f*
unit interrogations, training to participate in, 37–39

well-being, critical consciousness's impacts on, 14–15
White identity, developing a healthy, 15–16
window books, 134–135

youth and younger children
    challenging injustice, 131–132, 145–153
    trusting, 242
youth participatory action research (YPAR), 141, 249

# About the Authors

**Scott Seider** is a professor of applied developmental and educational psychology at Boston College. His research focuses on the role that educators can play in fostering young people's civic development and critical consciousness. A former secondary teacher, Scott is the author of more than 75 academic publications, including *Schooling for Critical Consciousness: Engaging Black and Latinx Youth in Analyzing, Navigating, and Challenging Racial Injustice* (co-authored with Daren Graves). Scott also currently serves on advisory boards for a number of youth-serving organizations, including EL Education, the *Journal of Adolescent Research*, and the Center for Parent and Teen Communication.

**Aaliyah El-Amin** is a faculty member at Harvard Graduate School of Education, where her research and teaching focus on ensuring that educators have the knowledge and tools they need to disrupt systems of oppression. Her specific interest areas include liberatory education models, social justice schooling, critical pedagogy, and youth participatory action research. Aaliyah has also worked as an elementary classroom teacher and a school instructional facilitator in Atlanta, Georgia; executive director of Teach for America in Charlotte, North Carolina; and interim vice president of program and innovation for the Black Teacher Collaborative.

**Julia Bott** is the executive director of inclusive education for Boston Public Schools, where she supports leaders and educators to cultivate more equitable and inclusive learning opportunities for all students. Over the past two decades, Julia has also worked as an early childhood teacher, assistant principal, and principal, and she was named a 2021 National School Principal of the Year for her exemplary leadership and service. Additionally, she has planned and led professional development courses for school leaders and teacher leaders focused on instructional leadership for equity. Julia earned her doctorate in educational leadership at Boston College, where her research focused on how leaders leverage instructional leadership to build the pedagogical knowledge and skill of educators for social justice.

## Related ASCD Resources: Equity in Education

At the time of publication, the following resources were available (ASCD stock numbers in parentheses):

*The Antiracist Roadmap to Educational Equity: A Systemwide Approach for All Stakeholders* by Avis Williams and Brenda Elliott (#123023)

*The Consciously Unbiased Educator* by Huda Essa (#121014)

*Cultural Competence Now: 56 Exercises to Help Educators Understand and Challenge Bias, Racism, and Privilege* by Vernita Mayfield (#118043)

*The Equity and Social Justice Education 50: Critical Questions for Improving Opportunities and Outcomes for Black Students* by Baruti K. Kafele (#12060)

*Five Practices for Equity-Focused School Leadership* by Sharon I. Radd, Gretchen Givens Generett, Mark Anthony Gooden, and George Theoharis (#120008)

*Fix Injustice, Not Kids and Other Principles for Transformative Leadership* by Paul Gorski and Katy Swalwell (#120012)

*Leading Within Systems of Inequity in Education: A Liberation Guide for Leaders of Color* by Mary Rice-Boothe (#123014)

*Leading Your School Toward Equity: A Practical Framework for Walking the Talk* by Dwayne Chism (#123003)

*The Way to Inclusion: How Leaders Create Schools Where Every Student Belongs* by Julie Causton, Kate MacLeod, Kristie Pretti-Frontczak, Jenna Mancini Rufo, and Paul Gordon (#123001)

For up-to-date information about ASCD resources, go to www.ascd.org. You can search the complete archives of *Educational Leadership* at www.ascd.org/el. To contact us, send an email to member@ascd.org or call 1-800-933-2723 or 703-578-9600.

www.ingramcontent.com/pod-product-compliance
Lightning Source LLC
Chambersburg PA
CBHW070534010526
44118CB00012B/1135